The ABCs of Parenting

A Guide to Help Parents and Caretakers Handle Childrearing Problems

Joan Barbuto

R&E Publishers
Saratoga, California

Copyright © 1994 by Joan Barbuto

All rights reserved.

R & E Publishers
P.O. Box 2008, Saratoga, CA 95070
Tel: (408) 866-6303   Fax: (408) 866-0825

Book Design by Diane Parker

Cover by Kaye Quinn

Library of Congress Cataloging-in-Publication Data

Barbuto, Joan.
    The ABCs of Parenting: a guide to help parents and
    caretakers handle childrearing problems by Joan Barbuto.
        p.   cm.
    Includes bibliographical references.
    ISBN 1-56875-062-5: $14.95
    1. Parenting. 2. Child rearing. I. Title.
HQ755.8.8373 1993
649'.1--dc20   93-12860
                                                        CIP

Dedication

To my husband, Paul

READ THIS BEFORE
BEGINNING THIS BOOK

This book is written for Moms, Dads, Grandmas, Grandpas, single parents, aunts, uncles, daycare center workers—in short, for all present or potential caretakers of children.

Please glance at the Table of Contents. Most of the major problems you might encounter dealing with children are covered, in alphabetical order, and suggestions given about how to handle them. Each chapter relating to a specific problem is treated as a complete unit. Hence, the book can be used as a specific reference as well as read from cover to cover.

Obviously all problems could not be addressed, and neither could all the problems necessarily have foolproof solutions since all situations are different. The book should be referred to as a guide. Serious emotional and/or physical problems in your children should, of course, be referred to a doctor or an appropriate professional.

Here's to happy children—and happy caretakers!

Foreword

The more things change, the more they remain the same. This maxim applies to no area of endeavor more strongly than it does to raising children. In *The ABCs of Parenting*, Joan Barbuto demonstrates her understanding that the timeless issues faced by parents and those that are unique to the late 20th century are often one and the same.

Parents in the 1990s are faced with an overwhelming array of choices, not the least of these being a vast selection of books, magazines, and television programming to advise them on how to raise their children. The present volume, however, is distinctive in its approach. With her many years of sound experience both as one who has studied and written about children and families, and as a parent herself, Joan Barbuto offers a view of managing children's behavior that is at once reasoned, humane, humorous, and effective.

Barbuto offers parents insights into the reasons why children misbehave, and a workable selection of approaches to help parents cope with difficult behavior—both the everyday variety all parents are familiar with and more serious problems that may rise as children mature. In addition, she puts children's behavior into a context that takes into account their families, their communities and our culture as a whole.

Most important, in this book parents will find the simplest and soundest parenting advice of all: discipline is not a synonym for punishment. In an era in which parents are stressed and overburdened, in which generations of the same extended family are often separated by hundreds, if not thousands of miles, in which child abuse is escalating at an alarming rate, the understanding and support that Barbuto offers parents is more important than ever. Her opposition to corporal punishment, and the realistic and workable alternatives to spanking that she offers to parents are grounded in a comprehensive, totally integrated *system* of bringing up children. In this system discipline takes its proper place as one of the cornerstones of a respectful, supportive, loving, predictable parent-child relationship.

-- Edward Zigler
Sterling Professor of Psychology, Yale University

Acknowledgments

My thanks to the many people who helped me during the five years I gathered material and did research for this book. Among them are some noted psychiatrists, psychologists, and pediatricians who were kind enough to grant me interviews and answer my questions about child management and mental health: Dr. Edward Zigler, Sterling professor of psychology at Yale University, director of the Bush Center in Child Development and Social Policy at Yale University and an originator of the Head Start program; Dr. Selby Jacobs, professor of psychiatry at Yale Medical School; Dr. Albert Solnit, Sterling Professor emeritus of pediatrics and psychiatry at Yale, former director of the Yale Child Study Center and now Commissioner of Mental Health in Connecticut; Dr. Joseph Woolston, associate clinical professor of psychiatry at the Yale Child Study Center and medical director of Yale New Haven Hospital's children's psychiatric in-patient service; Dr. Bruce Wexler, associate professor of psychiatry at Yale; Dr. H. Stephen Glenn, South Carolina psychologist and internationally known speaker and author on parenting; Dr. Morris Wessel, associate clinical professor of pediatrics at Yale; Dr. Dorothy Noyes Sproul, public health expert whose work has helped alert people to health and mental health hazards to children; Dr. Donald Grinder, Dr. Scott Woods, associate professor of psychiatry and diagnostic radiology at Yale, Dr. Melvin Lewis, professor of psychiatry, Yale Child Study Center, and many others from whom I learned much while covering mental health issues for a large city newspaper. My thanks also to Dr. Earl Patterson of Meriden for telling me about the "stop his world" technique and for encouraging my writing.

I also appreciate the information that the following directors or teachers at Connecticut day care centers and nursery schools gave me about good methods of handling typical problems that arise with preschoolers: Dolores Andreucci, director of Cradles to Crayons Day Care Center, Guilford, Connecticut; Louise Miller, director, and teachers at Spring Glen Church Nursery School, Hamden, Connecticut; Sue Marcio, director of R&K Tiny Tots Nursery School, Hamden; Maureen Myers, director of The New School for Young Children, Hamden; Laura Spencer and teachers at The Stork Club, Inc., Meriden; Susan Hunter, director of the Child Development Center, Masonic Home and Hospital, Wallingford; and Josee Bancroft, a former day care center director.

I thank my husband for his encouragement and for being an innately good father who always, no matter how busy he was, had time and love to give to his children. And finally I thank my children for growing into such wonderful adults despite the mistakes I now know I made in raising them. Now I can even thank them for the typical problems they gave us as parents. From them I learned much, and without them this book would not have been written.

Permission to excerpt material from *A Guide to Discipline*, by Jeannette Stone has been granted by the publisher, the National Association for the Education of Young Children. Permission to use material in this book from the articles "Tell kids they're loved while there's time," by Darrel Sifford and "We can't be brothers' keepers, but must be brothers' brother" by Clyde Lewis of Knight-Ridder Newspapers is granted by the Knight-Ridder/Tribune News Service. Permission has been granted by Random House, Inc. to use material from *Positive Discipline*, by Jane Nelson, c. 1981. Ann Landers has granted permission to excerpt material from her column "Exceptional children need time to grow," April 11, 1986. Quotations from William Raspberry's article "A course in parenting would greatly help couples" have been reprinted with permission of The Washington Post Writers Group.

Permission to use material from *Your Child Step by Step Toward Maturity* by Dorothy Noyes Sproul is granted by Doubleday, a division of Bantam, Doubleday, Dell Publishing Group. Dr. Ken Magid has granted permission to use information on attachment breaks and Danny's story from his book *High Risk, Children without a Conscience.* Penguin USA has granted permission to excerpt material from *The Complete Dr. Salk: an A to Z Guide to Raising Your Child,* by the late Dr. Jonas Salk. Mrs. Salk has granted permission to use material from the Salk Letter, Inc., Vol. 1, No. 8, 1982. Mrs. Loyd Rowland and Family Publications Center have granted permission to use material contained in the *Pierre the Pelican* newsletters for new parents by the late Dr. Loyd Rowland. Carol Publishing Group has granted permission to use material from *Phobias: The Crippling Fears,* by Arthur Henley, c. 1987, published by arrangement with Carol Publishing Group, A Lyle Stuart book.

Dr. Foster W. Cline of Evergreen Consultants in Human Behavior has granted permission to use material from his books *Parent Education Text, Understanding and Treating the Difficult Child,* and *Understanding and Treating the Seriously Disturbed Child.* The Record-Journal Publishing Co. has granted permission to use material from an article, "Teasing natural but hurtful for children," Sept. 20, 1988. Georges Sorchardt, Inc. and The *Reader's Digest* have granted permission to use the example in my introduction that came from "Emotional Child Abuse: The Invisible Plague," by Susan Jacoby, in the *Reader's Digest,* Feb. 1985, and originally appeared in *Glamour,* Oct., 1984, in the article "Emotional Child Abuse" by Susan Jacoby, Father Daniel Lowry's comments on self-esteem from the newsletter *Advent and You* are reprinted with permission of Liguori Publications, Liguori, MO 63057-9999. No other reproduction of this material is permitted.

The *New Haven Register* has granted permission to reprint various articles by the author which appeared in that newspaper. Jossey-Bass, Inc., publishers have granted permission to excerpt material from *The Psychologically Battered Child,* by James Garbarino, Edna Guttman, and Janis Wilson Seeley. Dr. Louise Bates Ames has granted permission to use material from her newspaper columns and from her book *Questions Parents Ask.* Random House and Alfred A. Knopf, Inc. have granted permission to use material from the book *P.E.T.: Parent Effectiveness Training,* by Dr. Thomas Gordon. Dr. Lee N. Robins has granted permission to use a summary and brief quote from the article "The Influences of Childhood Disciplinary Experience on the Development of Alcoholism and Depression," by Holmes, S.J. and Robins, in *Journal of Child Psychology and Psychiatry,* 1987.

The American Academy of Pediatrics and *Pediatrics* magazine have granted permission to use material from an article on crying by Barr and Munziker in *Pediatrics,* May, 1986; from "The Pediatrician and Corporal Punishment" by Dr. Morris Wessel in *Pediatrics,* Oct. 1980; from "Spoiled Child Syndrome," by Dr. Bruce McIntosh, *Pediatrics,* 1989; from "School phobia; Finding cause key to getting child back in school" in "Young Health" bulletin, Fall, 1987; from a news release on an article on thumbsucking in *Pediatrics,* July, 1986. Information on the research of Dr. Paul Mandel was taken from the article "Criminality is linked to brain chemistry imbalances," by Jon Franklin, July 30, 1984 in *The Mind Fixers,* a supplement to *The Evening Sun,* and excerpted with permission of the Baltimore Sun Company.

Material from The Fairfield University Teachers' Center bulletin "Building Trust and Guiding Behavior," 1979, was excerpted with permission from June S. Gould, editor. Material from the article "Psychopathology and Development; I. Childhood Antecedents of Adult Psychiatric Disorder," by Dr. Michael Rutter, was used with permission of the *Australian and New Zealand*

Journal of Psychiatry. Jack Scovil has granted permission to excerpt some material from the article "We All Have a Place We Feel Locked Out Of," by Michael Ryan in *Parade* magazine, April 6, 1986. It is also used with permission of *Parade*, c. 1986. Meadowbrook Press has given permission to use material from *Practical Parenting Tips*, by Vicki Lansky, c. 1980, 1982, 1992. The Associated Press has granted permission to use material from the article "School bullies fail to make grade in life, study shows, " which ran in the *New Haven Register*, Feb. 24, 1987.

Jeffrey M. Gandolfo, president of The Stork Club, Inc. has granted permission to use information from its teachers and from its childrearing guides, "How to Show Approval and Acceptance to a Child" and "Some Words of Encouragement." United Press International has given permission to paraphrase its article "Many 'latchkey' teens found to be depressed," which ran in the *New Haven Register* in August, 1986. Dr. T. Berry Brazelton and Dell Publishing have granted permission to use material from his book *Toddlers and Parents*. Dr. Brazelton and *Newsweek* have given permission to use material from his *Newsweek*, Feb. 13, 1989, article "Working Parents." Prima Publishing has granted permission to use material from *Raising Children for Success*, retitled *Raising Self-Reliant Children in a Self-Indulgent World*, by H. Stephen Glenn and Jane Nelsen. New York University Medical Center has granted permission to use material from its article "Children need help coping with sibling rivalry" which appeared in the *New Haven Register,* August 11, 1987.

Newspaper Enterprise Association has granted permission to use some material from Dr. Peter Gott's column, "Our Health," which ran in the *New Haven Register*, Aug. 18, 1987. The National Committee for the prevention of Child Abuse has granted permission to reprint its "Twelve Alternatives to Lashing Out at Your Child." Laurie Scogland of *The Hartford Courant* has given permission to use material from four "Family Affairs" columns by Mary Jo Kochakian. Ballantine Books has granted permission to excerpt material from Barbara Brenner's book *Love and Discipline*. Oxford University Press has granted permission to use material from "On Being a Parent" by Dr. Edward Zigler and Rose Cascione in the book *Socialization and Personality Development*. Dr. W.K. Frankenberg has granted permission to adapt some material from the Denver II revision, Denver Developmental Screening Test, *Pediatrics*, Jan. 1992, vol. 89, p. 91.

CONTENTS

PART II: SPECIFIC PROBLEMS WITH CHILDREN AND HOW TO HANDLE THEM

PART I

THE BASICS OF CHILD DISCIPLINE

INTRODUCTION

Two young mothers were talking about their children in the dressing room of a local health salon after their exercise class one morning. One noticed a mark on the other's arm and asked her about it. "Oh, Johnny did that. He bit me," she said. "You can be sure I beat him good."

At the hairdresser's one day I asked a new beautician if she had any children. She said she had two girls, age nine months and four years, and she had been having a lot of trouble with the four-year-old ever since the new baby was born. "She's so jealous," she said. "If the baby takes her toy, she snatches it away, and the baby starts screaming. And when I have the baby on my lap, she wants to climb on too. I tell her she's a big girl now, she doesn't need to have a bottle or to be sitting on my lap all the time. But it doesn't do any good. And it doesn't do any good if I punish her either. She just gets worse. I don't know what to do any more. The two of them are driving me crazy."

Author Susan Jacoby tells of the time she was going for a swim at a local YMCA and met a mother coming out of a swimming class with her three-year-old daughter. The mother was ridiculing the little girl because she had been afraid to put her face in the water. "You're such a little coward," she said. "It's the same every week. You always make your daddy and me ashamed." The little girl was in tears.

Examples like this are legion, and they all illustrate one thing: there are a lot of parents who don't know how to raise children.

It's not surprising. No one ever teaches us how to handle the situation if our child has a temper tantrum in the middle of a supermarket, refuses to go to bed at night, hits a playmate, develops a sudden fear, or refuses to do what he is asked. We're supposed to know such things automatically when we become parents. But most of us find we're at loose ends when suddenly we are parents and our own children start doing these things. All we can do usually is react the way our parents reacted with us. If we had sensitive, patient parents, we'll probably stumble through all right instinctively, and our children will be in luck. But if our own parents were harsh and demanding, or negligent and uncaring, we'll handle a lot of things wrong, and our children will suffer for it, and maybe their children as well, as destructive patterns are passed down from generation to generation.

The young mother whose son bit her only taught him by beating him that it's acceptable to meet one kind of violence and aggression with another. The woman scolding her three-year-old daughter was emotionally abusing the child, making her feel guilty, inadequate and a disgrace to her parents just because she had a fear that was perfectly normal for a child her age. Such an attitude can leave lasting scars on a child's developing personality and lead to feelings of inferiority, withdrawal and depression later in life.

The hairdresser obviously had no idea that her four year old's behavior was a normal reaction to a new baby in the family, and she had no idea how to handle it. Consequently, the four-year-old's jealousy grew and continued longer and stronger than it normally would. Instead of punishment, the older child needed more attention, special times when her mother did things with her alone, times when she had her mother's attention all to herself again. Her mother also needed to acknowledge to her daughter that she knew she was feeling angry and jealous because the baby was taking so much of mother's time, and it was okay for her to feel that way, but she mustn't show her anger by hurting the baby or taking away her bottle. Instead, she should tell her mother when she needed some extra loving. And mother would try to recognize when she felt that way and give her a special hug and kiss, and spend some time alone with her as soon as she could, so she would realize her mother still loved her as much as ever.

But nowhere do parents learn how to handle such situations in a way that is emotionally healthy for the child unless they make a point of reading books on parenting or were fortunate enough to learn sensible and sensitive ways of raising children from their own parents. Schools don't teach parenting. They give instruction in everything from cooking to chemistry, but give no preparation for the most important job most of their graduates will have—the job of being a parent. And according to psychologist H. Stephen Glenn and educator Jane Nelson 94% of teachers and 98% of parents use negative and ineffective methods of managing their children, such as criticizing in detail what they do wrong, but giving just vague generalized praise for success.

Even writings by many child psychologists and psychiatrists, although they have a wealth of information about what children are expected to do at different ages, often don't get down to practical advice on how to handle the day-to-day problems with children. They talk about the *terrible twos* but don't tell you what to do about the terrible two-year-old whose only word seems to be "No." They tell you spanking is not a good way to discipline a child, but they don't tell you what else to do. And so parents who were disciplined by hitting or shouting or constant criticism go on disciplining their children the same way, with the same bad results.

Yet how parents interact with a child during the first five years of his life determines his future psychological development. It influences his sense of self-worth and determines whether he thinks he is an okay person as he matures or has a low sense of self-esteem. It sets the pattern for his interactions with other people and can lay the groundwork for a life of delinquency and crime or a life of tremendous achievement.

These early years are crucial for both the child and his parents. If parents don't establish control over their child during these years, they probably never will. If they establish that control by authoritarian methods, harsh discipline or abuse, the child may do what they say for a while, but rebel or run away as soon as he thinks he can make it on his own. If they establish control by using lots of criticism and little praise, it can have serious and damaging effects on the child's personality and even lead to psychological problems later in the child's life.

There are better methods and they work. I found this out with my third child. By the time he was four, I had lost control of him. He never napped, woke us up several times a night, had an unlimited supply of energy, climbed on anything climbable, and generally did what he wanted to do. Although I had had no trouble with his two older sisters, I couldn't manage this boy. The situation came to a head one day when I asked him to bring in his shoes, which he had left outside. He said no. I told him if he didn't do as I said by the time I counted five, I'd spank him. (Never use this method!) I counted to five, he didn't move, so I spanked him. He hit me back. I hit him harder. He hit me back harder. I stopped then, for I saw suddenly how easily child abuse could occur when there was a tired, inexperienced mother who felt she was losing control of a defiant child. I realized I needed help in finding better ways to discipline my son, and I went to see a psychiatrist who had a lot of experience with children. I told him about my son, and about the situation with the shoes, and asked how else I could handle it when spanking didn't work.

In a few minutes the psychiatrist told me the method I should use when my child wouldn't do as he was told. I tried it the next time my son said "No." It worked like a charm. I didn't have to hit him. I didn't have to raise my voice. I only said a few words. Yet within a few minutes my child had done what I asked. He wasn't mad. I wasn't angry. It was so easy. All it took was knowing the right words to say. And the same method even worked when he was a teenager and left his coat on a chair or his room in a mess. (See p. 128 for this method, which I call the "stop his world" technique.)

I thought to myself that there must be other simple ways to handle problem situations that typically come up with children. And I figured I had better start looking for them because the psychiatrist said if I did not change my methods of dealing with my son and get him under control soon, I would have a lot of problems with him when he got older. What started out as a way to solve my difficulties with my son has grown into a consuming interest.

To find the best methods of dealing with children, I have been reading material on parenting for 20 years and have consulted with noted pediatricians, psychologists, and child psychiatrists. I have also polled nursery school teachers, figuring that if anyone should know what methods work best in managing children, the women who deal with children daily should be an invaluable resource. What I have learned has helped me raise a fine, responsible son, and two wonderful daughters, of whom I am very proud. And from all I have learned comes this book. I hope it will be used in high schools to give young people some basic knowledge of how to treat children which will help them when they become parents. I hope that in some cases it may prevent child abuse. And I hope it will make parenthood easier for many of you and make your children less of a problem and more of a joy.

Test Your Parenting IQ

How would you handle the following situations that might arise with your child?

1. You and your husband are doing your grocery shopping with your three-year-old son. He sees a bag of candy on the shelf and wants it. When you say no, he throws himself on the floor, kicks and screams and has a full-fledged temper tantrum. Do you (1) spank him? (2) tell him if he doesn't stop you are just going to leave him in the store? (3) take him out of the store? (4) walk away from him and pretend he's not your child? (4) give him the candy?

2. You are trying to write a letter and your three-year-old keeps whining for you to come and play with her and trying to climb into your lap. What do you do? (1) Tell her to go away and stop being a pest. (2) Tell her Mommy is busy and can't play now. (3) Give her a hug. (4) Send her to her room. (5) Give her a toy to play with or a cookie.

3. You take your five-year-old child to the supermarket and you find her touching the things on the shelves even though you have told her a number of times not to do so. What do you do? (1) Spank her. (2) Slap her hands. (3) Say, "Don't you touch those things or you'll get punished." (4) Say, "Do you remember what I asked you to do when we went shopping?" (5) Put her in her room when you get home.

4. Your toddler discovers your African violet plant and starts to pick off the flowers. What should you do? (1) Put her in the playpen. (2) Slap her hands. (3) Say "No" and move her away. (4) Give her a spanking. (5) Put the plants somewhere where she can't reach them.

5. Your daughter gets angry because her little brother has grabbed a picture she was drawing and crumpled it up, so she hits him. What do you do? (1) Say, "You shouldn't get angry at your little brother." (2) Spank her. (3) Send her to her room. (4) Refuse to let her watch television. (5) Send them both to their rooms. (6) Other.

6. You are visiting Aunt Aggie, who has a lot of knick-knacks around, and your two-year-old reaches out and picks up one of her valuable Hummel figurines.

What do you do? (1) Grab it from her hand as fast as you can. (2) Say "Give that to me. You can't have that." (3) Say, "No," slap her hand and take away the statue. (4) Quickly take something interesting from your purse and say "Oh, look at this." (5) Put out your hand, palm up, and say "Thank you."

7. Your two-year-old starts to run into the street. What do you do? (1) Spank her. (2) Hold her and prevent her. (3) Send her to her room. (4) Yell at her. (5) Explain that she can get hurt very badly if she runs into the street.

8. Your high school friend Susie has dropped in for a visit, and the two of you get so busy talking and reminiscing that you're not paying any attention to your three-year-old daughter. Suddenly she says to Susie, "You stink. Go home." What do you do? Do you (1) send her to her room? (2) spank her? (3) tell her she is never to talk to anyone that way? (4) tell her to apologize to Susie? (5) remark that she is angry? (6) tell her good girls don't talk to guests that way?

9. Your six-year-old daughter comes in upset and says, "Elaine and Lucy won't play with me. They keep whispering about me and laughing at me." What do you say to her? (1) "Then find someone else to play with." (2) "Don't be such a crybaby. You're too sensitive." (3) "Maybe you should just ask them what they are whispering about." (4) "You're really angry and hurt that they were talking about you and wouldn't play with you." (5) "I'll go find out what's the matter and why they won't play with you."

10. You are trying to vacuum the living room and your three-year-old has his blocks all over the floor. What do you do? (1) Say nothing and try to vacuum around the debris. (2) Say, "Put those things away before I trip over them." (3) Say, "You are making a mess in my living room. Take your things and play in another room." (4) Say, "I can't vacuum with these things all over the floor. They are getting in my way." (5) Put away the blocks yourself. (6) Other.

Answers

1. (3) Specialists in child management say you should calmly take your child to the car or to a rest room, explaining that people don't behave that way in a store. Stay with him and let him finish his tantrum off away from other people. This is easier if you are shopping with your spouse, of course, but even if you are alone, it's best to just leave your shopping cart and take your child out of the store until he calms down. Giving in and letting him have the candy will reinforce this type of behavior and you will just be in for more tantrums when he doesn't get his way. Spanking him will just make him yell more and teach him that when you are annoyed with people, you hit them.

Leaving him or threatening to leave him will just make him frightened as well as angry and even more out of control because a child's greatest fear is the fear of abandonment by his parents. (See p. 208 for further information on handling tantrums.)

2. (3) If your child is whining and trying to get on your lap, she obviously has a need for you to give her love and attention. So give her a hug, and tell her that you love her very much. That may be enough to make her content enough to go play on her own. If not, go play with her a while. Don't tell her she is being a pest. That is name-calling and makes her feel inferior and unloved just when she has shown she has a need for love. Such comments can damage your child's self esteem and give her feelings of inferiority. After all, how would you like it if someone you loved called you a pest? Just telling her to go away, that you will play with her later, will not satisfy her immediate need for some evidence of your affection, nor will giving her a toy or a cookie. Also, giving food to a child when she is unhappy or upset sends the message that when you are unhappy, you eat, a habit which can lead to obesity. And sending her to her room for trying to get close to you is just punishing her for wanting love.

3. (4) This answer, of course, presumes that you have explained to the child before going to the supermarket that she is not to touch things on the shelves. You also should have explained that the reason is that the items belong not to us, but to the person who owns the store. We can only take them if we are going to buy them. Reminding her is a way of showing you believe she can behave well if she knows what you expect her to do. She will most likely remember that you told her not to touch things on the shelves. Then ask her why to make sure she understands. You might also tell her ahead of time that she can point out one thing she would like to eat on the shopping trip, and you will get it. If you want to narrow the choice, tell her she can pick out the cereal or the snack she wants. Spanking or slapping her will just make her angry and resentful, and she may just touch something else and perhaps drop it out of spite when your back is turned. It will also embarrass her to be disciplined in front of other people. And answer (3) will also embarrass her and it may make her do the opposite, which is how children sometimes respond to a threat. Sending her to her room when you get home does nothing to solve the problem in the store.

4. (1) or (5) Toddlers need to explore their environment, and as a parent you probably have been encouraging your toddler to walk around, look at things and touch them and learn their names. If you spank or slap her now, you are sending a contradictory message, and a toddler isn't likely to understand

why a parent who encouraged her to crawl and walk around and explore before is now hurting her when she is trying to do this. Spanking and slapping a child also gives her the idea that it's okay to hit people if you don't like what they are doing. Saying "No" can lose its effectiveness if it is used too often, and child specialists advise saving "No" for really important things. Your best move is to prevent her from touching things you don't want by childproofing your environment and moving "untouchables" out of her reach. But if she touches something she shouldn't which can't be moved, put her in the playpen immediately. If you do this a few times, she should get the idea that her activity is going to be limited if she touches certain things.

5. (6) Say something like "I can understand that you got angry at your brother for what he did. But I can't let you hit him." Then suggest that she go hit one of her stuffed animals or a pillow if she needs to express how mad she is, and when she feels better you will talk about this more with her. After she has calmed down bring them both together and talk about what happened and why it happened. Explain that one of the rules in your family is that people are not to take things that don't belong to them without their permission. Another rule is that you don't hit people when you get angry. Decide with them what will happen if either of these events happens again. This is where you might set up a punishment such as sending them to their rooms or prohibiting television. Then if hitting or taking someone else's possession occurs again, stick to the punishment you have all agreed upon. Telling a child she "shouldn't" be angry or afraid is one of the worst things you can do because it teaches the child to suppress normal emotions and feel guilty about them. By naming and acknowledging a child's unpleasant emotions and their validity, you help to dissipate them and show the child you understand her feelings. And spanking, of course, would just send the message that you can't hit when you are little, but it's okay when you get bigger.

6. (4) and (5). Grabbing something from a child just teaches impolite behavior, and she may copy your action with others. Answer (2) is directing and ordering the child, and too much of this is likely to make a child rebel and do just the opposite. Slapping will just cause pain and tears and sends the message that hitting is okay. It also squelches the natural curiosity of a toddler to explore her environment, which is important for development at this time. The best thing to do is to distract her by showing her something more interesting, and then politely request the statue.

7. (2) and (5). Hold her and explain that cars go in the street and they go very fast and can hit you and hurt you if you are there. Then holding her by the

hand, lead her away from the street. You may have to repeat this a number of times, but you should be with your child and able to do this if she is ever near a street. Spanking her only causes her pain and anger, and she isn't likely to understand why you are hurting her for walking somewhere. Yelling at her can make her both frightened and angry. And an obstinate toddler may just do the opposite of what you want if she gets angry. Sending her to her room is not likely to teach her that she needs to stay out of the street for her own safety. However, if you can't break this dangerous habit, you may have to take her inside when she does it.

8. (5) Realize that your child is angry because the person she loves most, her mother, has been ignoring her, and acknowledge those angry feelings. Say something like, "You're kind of mad, aren't you, because we have been so busy talking we haven't paid any attention to you?" Then give her some attention. Ask her to tell Susie about your trip to the zoo yesterday, show her a favorite toy, or some such thing. Take her on your lap or have her sit next to you and give her a hug, and let her be part of your conversation for a while and talk about things in her life. Then you can suggest that she go play for a while, and promise you will do something specific with her when you are finished talking. Sending her to her room would emphasize even more than your ignoring her that you don't think she's very important, and it will damage her self esteem even more. Spanking sends two wrong messages— she and her feelings are not acceptable, and it's all right to hit people if you don't like what they say. And at three she is really too young to understand about apologizing to people. However, you can begin explaining to her after your friend leaves that people should talk nicely to guests in their house. If something is bothering her when you have guests, she should tell you she needs to talk to you alone about it.

9. (4) When your child has some problem that is bothering her a lot, say a problem at school or with friends, it's important that you listen, take it seriously and get her to talk about it and express her feelings. One good way to do this is by a technique called active listening, repeating what the child has said in different words and naming the emotion she is experiencing. When children can get negative feelings like fear, anger, hurt and resentment out and can talk about them, it helps to get rid of these feelings. It also sometimes helps them see that they can cope with such feelings, and may aid them in finding ways to deal with them or prevent them. Active listening also promotes good communication and a warm relationship between children and their parents because the children learn that they parents have time to listen to their concerns and understand their feelings. And it has often been shown that children who have a good relationship with their parents

and feel they can talk openly with them are much less apt to turn to alcohol and drug abuse, delinquency or promiscuous behavior as teenagers. Answer (1) is poor because it ignores the seriousness of the problem to the child and her feelings. Answer (2) is name-calling and a put-down and damages the child's self-esteem. Answer (3) offers advice or solutions, which are just likely to annoy your child and turn off conversation. And Answer (5) is just rescuing your child instead of having her work through her own problems. It would also probably annoy and embarrass your child.

10. (4) When a child's behavior is directly affecting you, a good way to handle it is to send what psychologist Thomas Gordon calls "I" messages. Tell the child clearly and politely how you feel about what is happening and how it is affecting you. Answer (4) does this and leaves it up to the child to remedy the situation on his own. It gives clear feedback and helps build consideration for others' wants and feelings and responsibility for one's behavior. Answer (1) obviously does nothing to solve the problem. Answers (2) and (3) are directing and blaming your child, and are likely to not get much of a response. In fact, if you have been directing and blaming too much, your child is likely to do the opposite of what you want just to show his independence. Answer (5) gives him the idea that Mommy will pick up after him. It's not his responsibility.

What is Discipline?

To grow into a mature, responsible and well-adjusted adult a child needs discipline. He must be taught he cannot do certain things because they are not safe, they infringe on the rights of others, or are unacceptable behaviors. The preschooler, for example, must be taught that he must not touch a hot stove, punch another person when he's angry, spill his food on the floor if he doesn't like it, or take something from a neighbor's yard. Older children must be taught to be polite and respectful to others, to study and do their homework, to do their chores, to be truthful and responsible.

Discipline, however, is not the same as punishment. Webster's Dictionary gives as a definition of discipline "training which corrects, molds, strengthens, or perfects." This is what is meant by the word discipline in this book. Punishment is one form of discipline, and although it frequently is used in raising children, it often is not very helpful, particularly if it is physical punishment. It may stop the child from doing something the parent doesn't want him to do, but it can build resentment and doesn't really get to the root of what is causing the problem. In fact, some kinds of punishment, such as corporal punishment, are the worst forms of discipline to use, claim many psychologists and psychiatrists. Before we discuss why, let's think about what we want to accomplish in disciplining a child.

All of us undoubtedly want to raise a child who is happy, responsible, and likes himself, who gets along well with others, has self control and self respect as well as respect for others. We want our child to grow into a person who will be able to make the most of his talents and abilities, set worthwhile goals for himself, and have the self-discipline to do the work and get the training and education needed to achieve them. A day-care center director, Josee M. Bancroft, states the purpose of discipline very clearly: "to help children gain self control, to learn to respect the rights of others, and learn the rules by which the adults' world operates." Good discipline isn't just forbidding and directing. "It incorporates teaching respect and caring for other people, reasons for limits, and especially for the very young child, helping to provide the controls or willpower which the child lacks," says Bancroft.

But how do we do this?

Good discipline doesn't just happen. You have to work at it. And often many parents have to learn the techniques because if they just raise their children the way they were raised, they may find they don't get very good results, especially if they were raised by very authoritarian or very permissive parents. In fact, by using such methods they may even harm their child psychologically. From the evidence in our country today many parents do not know how to deal with their children. There were more than 2.7 million reports of child abuse in 1992, according to the National Center for the Prevention of Child Abuse. Alcoholism and drug abuse are widespread among teenagers, teenage pregnancy is a major problem, and mental illness is increasing in children. The International Congress of Pediatrics predicted several years ago that the main health problems children will have in the future will be emotional, not physical. Even today one of of seven children suffers from mental illness, and four out of five children with mental illness receive no care or inadequate care, according to a National Mental Health Association Study. It is estimated that 1.8 percent of children seven to 12 suffer from depression. Although some children may have a genetic vulnerability to depression, environmental stress generally triggers it, according to child specialists.

Some children are disturbed or get into trouble because they have parents who don't care about them, who are mentally ill, or are cruel and abusive. But many troubled children have parents who love them, yet don't know how to manage them and who show their love and concern in the wrong ways, for instance by overly strict or overly permissive discipline. And because of the way they manage their children, their offspring grow up rebellious, irresponsible or emotionally disturbed.

But it's no wonder many parents go about disciplining their children in ways that get bad results because no one teaches us how to parent. Psychologists and psychiatrists know from countless studies what are good methods for raising responsible, self-controlled, and mentally healthy youngsters, but this knowledge is not getting to the general public. Some parents are trying on their own to learn the best ways to manage their children. In 1988, about 8,000 people took courses or joined support groups for parents conducted by the Connecticut Department of Children and Youth Services. Some agencies, such as Catholic Family Services and adult education programs are also offering parenting courses, and psychologist H. Stephen Glenn has been traveling throughout the country setting up courses in methods of raising responsible, well-adjusted children. But often the people who need the most help in parenting don't realize they need help and don't seek it out.

Psychiatrist Foster Cline believes it is important for parenting education courses to be offered to parents of young children because, he says, the sooner correct principles of discipline are put into practice, the better the results. He says that as a general rule if parents have been handling things incorrectly, once they start practicing good child management techniques, it will take one month for every year of the child's age for the child's behavior to change.

THE FOUNDATIONS OF GOOD DISCIPLINE

The best way to achieve the goals of discipline, say many experts, is to set a good example and reward children for doing what is right, instead of focusing on punishing them for what they do wrong. The rewards, however, should not be material things like toys or candy, but simple things like approval, attention, a smile and kind words. These are the rewards children really want and need. "They want you to like them so that they can feel good about themselves," says Bancroft.

In fact, psychologist Thomas Gordon says that parents can raise responsible, capable, and cooperative children without using punishment if they know the right methods to use and the right ways to talk to their children. Gordon developed Parent Effectiveness Training, a program which taught parents to use some of the skills and methods of communication with their children which are employed by professional therapists. He taught it to a quarter of a million parents through books and courses and says many of the parents using his methods "have proven that punishment can be discarded forever in disciplining children." Parents who used the methods found that their children often did not go through the rebellion considered typical of teenage years. "I am now convinced that adolescents do not rebel against parents. They only rebel against certain destructive methods of discipline almost universally employed by parents," says Gordon.

But good discipline does require setting limits. Adults must tell children what behavior is expected of them and what will not be tolerated. A child isn't born with a conscience. It has to be developed by telling children "in each kind of activity and in each kind of setting what they may and may not do," says Bancroft. And they must be told over and over again. And although physical punishment does not need to be used, and should not be used with children, in my opinion it's a rare parent who will not have to use some kind of punishment at times, such as a time out or withdrawal of a privilege, to make his words stick.

Parents also need to let children know that what they do and how they act are important to them. If children know it is important to their parents that they get along with others, act respectfully, do their chores or schoolwork, these things will become important to the child also, according to the National Association for the Care of Young Children. Good discipline, says the association, includes "affectionate care, reasonable order, security, and an interesting day...not punishment, not fear, not tension, not silence, not softness, not pity."

DISCIPLINE REQUIRES GIVING

Discipline requires giving as well as prohibiting, and the giving is more important. To be able to manage a child effectively without rebellion and tantrums on the part of the child or anger and frustration in the parents, the parents must give the child certain things, not just require certain behavior from him. If these essentials are not given, good discipline is impossible. If they are not given, the healthy social, mental and emotional development of the child is impossible. If you as a parent do no want to make the commitment to give your child these things, you won't have much success no matter what methods of discipline you use.

Four essential things parents must give to their children are LOVE, ACCEPTANCE, ATTENTION, and SECURITY.

The Child's Need for Love, Acceptance, Attention & Security

LOVE

Children of all ages need love to grow as much as a flower needs water. And that love must be unconditional. In other words, a child needs to feel his parents still love him even if he is behaving badly, or he doesn't get A's, or he can't hit a baseball. If a child doesn't feel loved by his parents or guardians, he doesn't feel lovable and doesn't develop a sense of his self worth. A sense of self worth is the foundation on which a child develops into a mature, well-adjusted and responsible adult, mental health experts say. And many studies have shown that children who grow up lacking in self esteem are likely candidates for drug and alcohol problems, teenage pregnancy, depression and other mental illnesses later in life.

A national PTA report on self esteem several years ago found that parents who hugged, praised and encouraged their children were able to guard against drug addiction and teenage pregnancy. "Psychologists tell us that problems such as drug and alcohol abuse and adolescent pregnancy are rooted in a lack of self-esteem," said Elaine Stienkemeyer, PTA president at the time. Parents who are interested in their children's ideas and feelings, who encourage them, praise their successes, and give them physical signs of affection, such as hugs, show their children they are loved and valued and build their self esteem.

It isn't enough just to tell a child you love him or show it by buying him things. Parents need to show their children they love them in different ways during the various stages they go through from infancy to adulthood. A minority of parents may be so selfish, mentally disturbed, or immature they are incapable of giving their children love. But some parents, I believe, just don't know how to show their children they love them.

HOW TO COMMUNICATE LOVE TO A BABY
AND WHY IT IS ESSENTIAL

In his infancy, the parent shows love to her child by providing milk, cuddling, smiles, eye-contact and movement (such as rocking him), and by responding to his needs when he cries. Such love in infancy is crucial to the individual's development. If the parent does not faithfully provide these things, the foundation on which the child builds a stable personality is weak, says psychiatrist Foster Cline. There is a repeated cycle of need and satisfaction of need set up between the infant and the caregiver in the early months of life, which Cline calls the "soul cycle." It is the foundation for the development for the human personality because it establishes a sense of basic trust and security in the child and the ability to love and emotionally empathize with others. The cycle is repeated about every four hours. First, the infant feels a need, usually the need for food, but sometimes also the need to be made comfortable, changed, picked up, or relieved of a gas pain. Because of his discomfort, he becomes angry and has what Cline calls a "rage reaction," which he expresses by crying. If the mother responds adequately to his need, by feeding him, holding him, changing him, etc., he then returns to a state of calm. This cycle is repeated hundreds of times in the first six months of the infant's life, and if the baby's needs are adequately satisfied, certain associational patterns are locked into the infant's subconscious mind. He develops a sense that the world is an okay place, that there are people who care about him and will take care of him, and he develops a trust, a closeness, a bonding with his mother or primary caretaker.

"The importance of this cycle cannot be overestimated," says Cline. "At any step, if things go wrong, lasting and severe psychopathology may result." Children separated from their parents in their first year of life often will have trouble forming attachments to adults and may have severe personality disorders, he claims. Even a break in the mother/child relationship in the child's first two years can have damaging effects on the child's personality.

Other child specialists also believe it is very important for the infant to have one primary caregiver who deeply loves the infant and who is there to respond to his needs most of the time during the first year of his life. Noted pediatrician T. Berry Brazelton believes it is crucial for the mother or primary caretaker to be with the infant steadily for at least the first four months of its life. During this time, he says, a pattern of nonverbal communication develops between mother and infant as she senses his needs for food, love, attention, and responds appropriately to them. The establishment of this pattern of communication forms the groundwork for later communication and for security and trust in the child.

Many things can cause a break in the bonding cycle. Children born to teenage mothers who aren't mature enough to respond to their infant's needs properly may become unbonded children. So may children who are abused or whose mothers just don't know or care enough about proper mothering. Separation or divorce of parents, depression in the mother, a mother returning to work too soon, the death of the mother, pain in an infant that parents can't relieve, and delayed adoptions may also result in unbonded children, according to Cline and psychologist Kenneth Magid.

Cline knows the psychological damage that such children suffer because he has been treating unbonded children for 20 years. These are children who cannot love and who seem to have no conscience because they never internalized a good parent, and so never developed basic trust in others, in themselves, or in society. As a baby who never developed a strong parental attachment grows into childhood, he is likely to develop such pathological symptoms as self-destructive behavior, cruelty to others, uncontrollable behavior, stealing, lying, gorging on food, speech problems, or preoccupation with fire and blood. These are the children who, if not helped, will become the psychopaths and sociopaths of tomorrow. But help must be given early, before age seven, Cline believes, or it is unlikely that professional help can change the ingrained psychological patterns in the child.

Danny is an extreme example of what can happen to an unbonded child. His case is described by Magid in his recent book *High Risk: Children without a Conscience*. Abandoned by his parents during the Vietnamese War, Danny was raised in a Vietnamese orphanage until he was five, when he was adopted by an American soldier. The orphanage was overcrowded with a small staff, and babies were often left unattended much of the day in their small cots. Although Danny seemed superficially friendly and lovable when the soldier met him, the way unbonded children often will act toward strangers, once he got Danny to this country and adopted him into his family, problems started. Within a few years Danny had done thousands of dollars worth of vandalism to a neighbor's house, terrorized his adopted sisters and brothers, tried to drown a visiting 12-year-old girl, threatened to set the house on fire and threatened to kill the members of the family. He had to be removed from the home and sent for institutional treatment for the family's safety.

However, not every child who is deprived in the first year or two of his life is doomed to become mentally ill or psychopathic. Children are very resilient, and studies by Dr. Jerome Kagan have shown that such children, if placed in healthy, nurturing environments, can straighten out. Early environment is very important, he acknowledges, but says "by changing environmental circumstances for infants and children who show pathology, the children can be helped."

HOW TO COMMUNICATE LOVE
TO A CHILD OF ANY AGE

You can communicate love to a child by physical contact, by the words you use, by spending time with the child, and by your actions.

• **BY PHYSICAL CONTACT:** Some parents don't realize that physical contact—touching, holding and hugging—are as necessary in communicating love to a child as they are in a romantic relationship. Showing love by touch and physical contact is vital to children of all ages. In infancy, physical contact is vital to the baby's survival. An infant needs to be held and cuddled just as much as he needs food and drink. Dr. Rene Spitz proved this in studies of infants in orphanages in New York in the 1940s, a period in which there was a great emphasis on everything being sterile for infants in their first months of life. The babies were kept in sterile cubicles, and their bottles were propped for feeding. They were seldom if ever picked up and held. Despite their clean surroundings and adequate nutrition the babies did not grow. Some even died for no reason except lack of physical contact and cuddling.

You can't spoil a baby by picking him up and cuddling him when he cries. A baby gets his ideas about life from the way he is treated, and if you hold and cuddle him when he is upset and take care of his needs, he will think life is pretty good and develop a sense of security. Yelling, hitting, and neglect, on the other hand, can do psychological damage to an infant.

Researchers at Stamford and McGill Universities in an experiment with rats found a startling way in which cuddling and holding in infancy affects the brain and brain chemistry. They discovered that rats handled in infancy had brain changes that made them less sensitive to stress and slower to age. The rats developed more brain receptors for substances called glucocorticoids which are secreted in response to stress than did rats who were not handled as infants. The additional receptors through a feedback mechanism resulted in less of the damaging glucocorticoids being secreted, and as a result, the rats handled in infancy were less stressed and had less mental impairment with age than the rats who had not been handled as infants.

For a child past infancy and through adolescence, it is also important to show love by holding, by hugs, an arm around the shoulder, a kiss. Such physical contact is crucial in making a child feel loved and wanted. Small children need to be held on their mother's and also their father's lap to help them feel wanted and secure. For an older child, an arm around the shoulder, a pat on the back, a hug and kiss can lift his spirits and make the disappointments, mistakes, rebuffs in his life bearable.

• **BY THE WORDS YOU USE:** Parents need to communicate with their children in ways that make the children feel good about themselves and build their self confidence. Not enough parents do this. Children need much more praise than criticism. They need to feel they are appreciated and loved by their parents, but too often this message doesn't come across to them. A husband and wife psychology team, Donald and Eleanor Laird, did a study years ago in which they found one third of the school children they questioned felt unloved by their parents. If the study were done today, with the rise in single parent families, the percentage would probably be even greater.

But many parents probably don't realize they are not communicating their love to their children. They are preoccupied with the activities and problems of everyday life, and most of their conversation with their children probably involves telling them what to do or criticizing them for doing or not doing something. They didn't pick up their clothes or do their chores. Their marks weren't good. They watch too much television. Even though parents may need to point out such things, they should spend much more time commending the child for what he does well. And accompanying criticism, when it is necessary, with a hug or an "I love you," may get more results than a disapproving tone.

Children need a lot of encouragement. It is important for parents to praise the good qualities of their children, their efforts and the contributions they make to the family. Tell your child you are proud of him when he has done a good job with something. Praise his efforts in front of others. If he doesn't do a good job or fails at something, don't scold or criticize. Instead let him know that everyone makes mistakes and we learn from our mistakes. See how you can help him improve. If parents are overly critical, children get discouraged and don't want to bother trying. Also, children soon stop wanting to communicate with a parent who is too critical. Don't expect too much of a child or set standards that are too high. Be sensitive to your child's feelings and ask what's wrong if he seems angry or upset. Then take the time to listen. Let him know you had problems like that when you were a child too. All these are ways parents can show love through the words they use.

Of course, there are times when parents will get angry with their child, but even anger can be handled with love. Child care experts suggest if you are angry with a child, don't yell and scream and give him a tongue lashing. Tell him you are angry at what he has done, but allow yourself to calm down and then explain calmly why what he did was wrong and specify the punishment that will happen if he does it again. Then stick to what you've said.

Above all, avoid ridiculing or belittling a child. This communicates the opposite of love and respect, and it can be emotionally devastating.

• **BY SPENDING TIME WITH YOUR CHILDREN:** This doesn't mean just being in the same house with them. It means doing things with them, being there to help them with problems, paying attention to them, talking to them, playing with them. It is vitally important for parents to talk to their children at all ages. It is by hearing talk that an infant learns to talk. It is by hearing parents talk about their ideas, work, values, proper behavior, etc., that a child internalizes the values and standards of their world. And it's important too for parents to play with their children, for play is a child's work. By playing with your children, you help them learn and develop, you build good parent-child communication, and you enjoy your children more.

Today, with both parents often working, it becomes very difficult for many parents to spend much time with their children, but the time spent should be quality time. Child behavior specialists say parents should try to set aside a period every day, even if it is only 15 minutes, when they can give their child undivided attention—just reading a story to him, playing with him or just talking with him. Parents who spend even 30 minutes a week in a regular structured activity with young children, and as little as 30 minutes a month in such activity with older children, are much less likely to have children who get in serious trouble than parents who don't spend time with their children, say psychologist H. Stephen Glenn and educator Jane Nelsen. Even if both parents work, they should make sure that someone who cares about their children is with them when they can't be home, even if the children are of school age. It may be difficult for parents to be home after school with their children in today's society when both parents often have to work to make ends meet, and when so many are single parents. But every effort should be made to have one parent or a relative or trusted friend at home most of the time when grammar school or high school age children are home.

This is important not just for their safety, but for their emotional health. Children who are left alone a lot can actually begin to suffer clinical depression, two researchers have found. Thomas Long, professor of education at Catholic University of America, and his wife, Lynette Long, an associate professor of education at American University, surveyed 400 children in grades 7 through 10 in Washington, D.C. and five surrounding counties to find out the emotional state of latchkey children. About one-third of the children were left alone after school one day a week, another third of the group for two or three days, and the remainder for four days or more. They found that the children left alone four or more days scored high on a test designed to measure depression. But those rarely or never left alone showed no evidence of depression on the test. They also found that children left alone the most were more apt to get involved with drinking and sexual activity.

• **BY YOUR ACTIONS:** Show a child you love him and think he is important by attending school activities, such as plays, concerts or sports events in which he is involved. Tape his good school papers or drawings to the refrigerator. Allow him to have friends in to play. Have a party for his birthday. Do things with your child you can both enjoy, such as planting flowers, baking cookies, or doing a jigsaw puzzle. And if there are several children in the family, make it a point to give each child some time alone with you. Take him on an outing or do something with him he enjoys. Be as respectful to your child as you would to an adult—don't interrupt him, make fun of him, or ignore him when he talks. Recognize the child's growing need for independence, and gradually give him more as he grows. Slowly widen his world, from the crib, to the playpen, to the house, the yard, the neighborhood as is appropriate. Gradually push back the limits of his world, but make sure you keep setting limits. He needs them.

THE IMPORTANCE OF LOVE

Baltimore news reporter Susan White-Bowden discovered in the winter of 1977 that her 17-year-old son Jody was smoking marijuana. He had been using it nine months, and she never knew it. She asked why he was doing it. He said it calmed him down and helped him do hours of homework. She was upset and disappointed in him. But Jody seemed to be able to keep up his grades, he wasn't getting in trouble, and she knew he was trying to cope with the loss of his father, who had killed himself three years before after he and Susan were divorced. She didn't tell him to stop, that drugs could be deadly. Instead she told him to try to cut back. She was busy with her career, not getting home until 8:30 at night. Jody came home at 4:30 to an empty house because his sisters were away at college. But she thought he could cope and that he knew how much she loved him. Later there would be more time for her to be with him.

In May of that year Jody shot and killed himself. Torn by guilt that she had failed him, she wrote a book called *Everything to Live For* about Jody's life and her anguish. "I loved my son more than I could ever put into words, and I was so sure he knew how much," she told Knight-Ridder Service reporter Darrell Sifford. "Now I'm not so sure. I don't think I showed him how important he was to me by being there whenever he needed me. Whenever he was lonely, all the talk and gifts and professions of love couldn't make up for the reality that I chose to be elsewhere. Never did I just sit with my son and say 'How are you feeling? What are your thoughts? Do you want to talk?'"

White-Bowden realized too late that it wasn't enough to love her son. What was more important was showing that love. In her case she should have shown it not only by taking the time to talk to him and find out what he was feeling, but by adjusting her work schedule to make sure she had that time to give him. "I needed to say to my boss, 'I'm a single parent, with a teenager at home. I need to be there.' I could have done it, worked from 8 to 4 or 9 to 5. But I didn't want to take a stand. I didn't want to ask for things that the men at the station didn't ask for." Also, she says she should have shown her love by insisting he had to stop using drugs. "He needed me to take a hard stand, to know that I cared enough about him to say 'no' to this. I think the message I left with him was that I loved him so little that I let him do what he wanted."

Although White-Bowden doesn't blame marijuana for causing her son's suicide, she says the drugs probably contributed to it in combination with a series of losses of love he had suffered. "His father had rejected him with suicide. His girlfriend had rejected him. I had rejected him with my career. His self-esteem fell. To him, it must have seemed he had nothing."

Columnist Claude Lewis wrote a column about a nine-year-old girl named Kizzy Jones who jumped to her death from the tenth floor window of her apartment in a housing project in Philadelphia. He said if Kizzy's mother failed her, the fault was not hers alone, but society's. "We assign a television set to babysit our young and, before long, we have lost contact with them," he wrote. "We see them but we no longer communicate; they become alienated from us, and home becomes a mere lodging place to a group of look-alike strangers. We are losing touch with one another."

Lack of parental love is at the root of many mental and emotional illnesses, many mental health experts believe. A study done by the University of Maryland's Institute for Child Study based on information from 20,000 teachers about children found that all the children who were emotionally troubled and insecure felt unvalued and unloved at home. In some cases it was because their parents had died or separated, but in the others it was because the parents either were unloved as youngsters themselves and never learned to give love, they were preoccupied with problems of their own, or they pressured the children to excel and be good, and disciplined by threatening withdrawal of love if the children didn't live up to their expectations.

It is very important for fathers as well as mothers to show love and affection to their children. Some men may think it isn't macho to show affection to a child, especially a son, but it is vital for a child's healthy psychological development. Fathers need to show their love, not just by providing material things, but by giving their child time, attention, appreciation and expressions of affection appropriate to the child's age—cuddling and kisses for a preschooler, a hug for a teenager.

ACCEPTANCE

Giving a child acceptance, attention, and security are all, in a sense, also ways of showing you love him, but they deserve some special mention. A child needs to be accepted by his parents for what he is, faults and all. There is tremendous danger to the child's developing personality if his parents are uninterested in him because of the way he looks or acts or because they see him only as an extension of themselves. The father who never made the football team, but is determined that his son will make it even if the boy dislikes sports, the "stage mother" who pushes her daughter through years of grueling practice to become an actress or performer—such parents are destructive.

Parents who seem to value their child for one thing, such as skill in sports, musical talent, or intellectual ability, send the message that they do not appreciate the child as an individual. If they push the child to excel in school, sports, music, etc., because this gives them prestige, but aren't interested in what he thinks, wants or feels, it can do significant psychological damage to the child, say child behavior specialists. For children can sense that they are valued not for what they are, but for how they perform for their parents. Such children may go along with what their parent wants and try to achieve their parents' goal with little complaint. But if the goal is not something the child herself really wants and enjoys, resentment will build. Mental illness, such as severe depression, may result in later years because the child of the "stage mother" type of parent never learns that she is of value herself as a person. She grows up seeing herself as valuable only for what she can accomplish, and when she cannot live up to parental goals, she not only suffers failure, but a loss of self-worth and identity as well. The result can be disastrous.

Parents also need to learn to stop talking in ways that show nonacceptance of their children. Criticizing a child, ridiculing or shaming him, threatening, moralizing, belittling, are all ways that show you are nonaccepting of the child. They turn the child off and stop communication. Acceptance is shown by talk that makes children feel good, appreciates their efforts, encourages expression of their feelings, builds their self esteem.

So parents, love and accept your children, warts and all. Even if your son is not as smart as his sister and not as good an athlete as his friend, don't mention it to him whatever you do. He knows it, and having his parents point it out to him will shatter his self esteem even more. Instead, recognize and value his good qualities and his accomplishments, even small ones, and praise him for them.

This doesn't mean, however, that you must always show acceptance toward your child no matter what he does. Certainly there will be times when he behaves in ways that are unacceptable and he must be clearly told his behavior is not acceptable. If you are not honest about this, and seem sweet and accepting toward him, but are seething underneath, you are doing him a disservice. A permissive parent who repeatedly gives a child such contradictory signals can harm her child psychologically, say mental health experts. The child generally knows he is doing something he shouldn't and senses that his parent really doesn't accept the way he is acting. But because she doesn't say anything about his offensive behavior, he becomes confused and anxious. He is likely to act out even more to try to get his parent to set limits on his behavior. If she doesn't, he will sense she doesn't love and care enough about him to make the effort to stop bad behavior that makes people dislike and avoid him. He is likely to become a spoiled, obnoxious adult who really feels he is inferior and unlovable.

ATTENTION

Parents must take the time to listen to their child, even if to an adult mind what the child is saying seems trivial, boring, or silly. Listen, sense what the child is feeling, try to put yourself in his place, and respond sympathetically to his feelings. Then, if he has a problem, help him solve it. If he needs to learn something, teach him. If he needs comfort, hug him. Many parents spend a lot of time telling their children what to do but don't bother listening to their children.

But how do you listen to a child? First, when your child comes in all enthusiastic or upset about something, don't be too busy to stop what you are doing, really listen, and respond sympathetically. Also, set aside some time each day, perhaps when you are putting your child to bed, to just sit and talk to your child about any problems he had that day, or anything especially good that happened to him.

It's even more important to "listen" to a child's behavior. Behavior, says public health expert Dorothy Noyes Sproul "is the unspoken language of children." You can "listen" to a baby by sensing his natural rhythm of sleeping, eating, waking, and by adjusting your schedule as much as possible to follow it. Older children can also indicate by their behavior, even more than by their words, that something is bothering them. A child who is unusually fearful or timid, or one who is withdrawn, or jealous, or destructive is showing by his behavior that somehow he has a problem he can't handle. The wise parent senses this and tries to find out what is bothering the child instead of shaming the child or punishing his misbehavior. A withdrawn or resistant child may have standards set that are too high for him, Sproul suggests, or may need more physical affection and cuddling. A timid child may need his parents' help in developing outside interests and making friends. A jealous child probably needs more attention from adults, not criticism, to help him build a better self-image. A destructive child may need more active or creative play, such as finger painting, hammering nails into a board, or throwing a ball against a wall, as an outlet for his energy and anger. But parents should also try to find out if he is being destructive because he is angry about something, and get the child to talk about what made him angry.

Parents need to learn to "listen" for the feelings behind their child's actions, then talk about the feelings and let the child know it's okay to have these feelings. If a seven-year-old comes home from school, for instance, slams the door, bangs his books down on the table, and throws his coat on the floor, a parent's immediate reaction is to scold and tell him what he should and shouldn't do—"Don't slam the door like that. Pick up your coat." But such behavior should be a sign to the parent who is "listening" that the child is angry about something, and the first thing to do is to deal with that anger. Ordering him around will only increase the anger and make him angry with you. A better approach is to say, "You really seem to be angry about something. What happened?" He may tell you that some child pushed him or the teacher made him feel dumb. A response such as "I can understand why you're mad. I'd be angry too if that happened to me" works well. It shows you are "listening" to his feelings and understanding them and it validates his emotions. Then you can talk about possible solutions, and later, when the child is calmed down, say you would appreciate it if he put away his coat.

One method many therapists use is active listening, which was mentioned in Chapter One. In this method, you repeat back what the child has said, but phrased in a different way. This encourages him to go on talking about his problem. However, just repeating the content of what he says is not enough. You also need to echo back what he is feeling or what he means, as in the paragraph above. Active listening helps children handle and get rid of negative feelings.

Another way to get children to talk so you can listen to what is on their minds is to ask open-ended questions. Instead of asking questions that call for a yes or no answer, like "Did you have a good day?" or "Did you have fun today?" ask "What did you learn today?" or "What things were fun for you today?" Glenn and Nelsen report that researchers found when they taught significant adults to talk this way to inner-city children ages four and five, the children's IQ rose an average of eight points, they were more confident and effective in school, and closer and more trusting with significant adults in their lives.

SECURITY

A child feels secure when he knows his parents love him, are there for him and won't leave him, and will provide the things he needs. A child needs a feeling of security from the time he is born. Parents who are kind and loving to an infant, who pick him up and respond quickly to his needs for food, changing, cuddling, etc., make the baby feel secure. Arguments and anger between parents can upset even a baby because he can sense his parents' moods and will feel a threat to his safety and security. If the strain of caring for a new baby is making the mother depressed or causing a lot of anger and strife between the parents, they should get professional help because this can affect the baby emotionally, mental health experts say. Throughout their childhood, and teen years also, children need the security of a mother and father who love them and love each other.

Strife between parents can cause emotional and psychological problems in their children. Discord between parents provokes a child's greatest fear—the fear of abandonment. If parents fight, the child becomes frightened that one or both will leave. Because the child is so completely dependent upon his parents for food, clothing, shelter and all his needs, the thought of losing them is terrifying. The effects of parental strife on children may be both immediate and long-term, and they can be devastating. In fact, mental health experts say one of the underlying causes of mental and emotional disorders in children and adults is strife between their parents.

Studies have shown that children who lose a parent by death or divorce are more likely to suffer from depression later in life. Greek pediatrician C.D. Papadatos, examining divorce in eight countries, said it has a great impact on children of all ages. Preschool children may revert to bedwetting, refuse to eat, have nightmares, or become aggressive. School age children have fears of abandonment, are sad, cry a lot, show resentment towards their parents, and their schoolwork may suffer. Adolescents may turn to premature sex, delinquency, and neglect their schoolwork. Other researchers have found younger children tend to become depressed and withdrawn when parents separate, and older children angry and aggressive. Children, in general, feel rejected by their parents and are both angry at their parents and frightened of being abandoned. They may have sleep difficulties, school problems, trouble getting along with their peers.

Even if the parents don't separate, if they are both often arguing, it can affect the child psychologically. Children who witness a lot of parental conflict often feel they are responsible for it, and it produces guilt and sometimes devastating fears in children. And if the marriage fails, the child gets the idea it's his fault, says Yale psychiatrist Selby Jacobs. "Parents are not only lost, but the incident is experienced as a rejection, and the child thinks he is unlovable, unsuccessful." Such family conflicts, says the psychiatrist, can lay the groundwork for a depression that surfaces later in life.

Much research has found that discord between parents harms the child's development, deprives the child of the nurturance he needs, and can cause aggressive behavior and other behavior problems in children. Studies have also found that parental arguing makes younger children frightened and older children feel guilty, and that children of parents who argue a lot are likely after a while to become overly fearful and withdrawn or have outbursts of anger. A study of children in battered women's shelters by Mindy Rosenberg found that children who repeatedly witness parental conflict develop feelings of worthlessness and mistrust, very passive or aggressive behavior and a possible slowdown in intellectual functioning. Psychologist Margaret Kovac found that children who witness one parent abusing another are also likely to have learning problems, be afraid to go to school, develop other fears, link affection with violence, and be torn by an inner conflict about which parent they should be loyal to, reports *Hartford Courant* Family Affairs columnist Mary Jo Kochakian. Kovac said the abuse doesn't have to be physical. Psychological abuse such as constant criticism, belittling, and lack of respect can have the same effects. If a child is not made to feel secure in his home and family, this childhood fear of abandonment can haunt his life and affect his behavior and adjustment not only as a child, but also an adult. Kovac noted that children who witness one parent physically or psychologically abusing the other may need therapy to help them express the hurt, fear, and guilt they feel, or some may develop serious psychological problems as adults.

A study by Barbara Long of about 200 women college students found that those with the lowest self-esteem were not the ones from broken homes, but the students having unhappily married parents who had stayed together. Laura Mellin found that even obesity can have its roots in a disturbed family relationship. In a study of obese teenagers, she discovered that a significant proportion came from chaotic families.

Divorce can have long-lasting devastating effects on children, psychologist Judith Wallerstein found. She conducted interviews for 15 years of 131 children from 60 families in which the parents had divorced when the children were between two and 18. She found that after five years a third of the children were very depressed and were having sleep problems or school or behavior problems. Ten years after the divorce almost half of the boys were unhappy and lonely and had few lasting relationships. Many of the girls had intense anxiety about being rejected by men. More than a third of the young men and women had little ambition and no definite goals and seemed to be living an aimless life. Presenting her findings in the book "Second Chances," with co-author Sandra Blakeslee, she reported that nearly half the children of divorced parents "entered adulthood as worried, under-achieving, self-deprecating and sometimes angry young men and women."

All of this doesn't mean that parents should never argue. Certainly occasions come up when one parent gets angry at the other, and this anger should be expressed verbally, but without belittling or insulting the other person. This shows children that it's okay to be angry at people you love sometimes, and it shows how this anger can be expressed with words. Parents who always suppress their own anger and never argue can do damage to their children because the children can get the idea that something terrible can happen if you express anger toward those you love. They may grow up suppressing their anger and later become depressed and have difficulty forming close relationships with people. It is a pattern of continuing anger and strife between parents that is harmful to children and makes them fear one or both parents will leave them.

One of our foremost experts in child rearing, Dr. Benjamin Spock, believes the large number of divorces in our country and the hostility between many parents are in part responsible for our high rates of delinquency, drug and alcohol abuse, mental illness, crime and suicide. If parents aren't committed to each other and to their children, he says it can impair the children's personality for life. Unfortunately half the marriages in our country today end in divorce. If more parents were aware of the devastating effects of divorce on their children, perhaps more would put their children's welfare first, work on their marriages and get therapy, if needed, to stay together.

If parents must divorce, however, mental health experts say it is vital that they explain to the children why they are getting the divorce and assure the children they are not to blame. It is also important that both parents continue to give their children nurturance and affection and see them regularly. They should not blame each other or keep fighting in front of the children after the divorce if they want to protect their children's mental health.

CONSISTENCY

Parents also need to be consistent in the behavior they expect from their children to make their children feel secure. Consistency in rules and expectations and what will happen if rules aren't obeyed help to give children a sense of stability in their home. It is very disturbing to a child when his parents say one thing one day and the opposite the next, or one day let him do something and the next day forbid him to do it or punish him for doing it. This makes the child unsure of how to behave and makes him feel he cannot rely on his parents for guidance.

It can also be harmful to the child's psychological development if one parent forbids things and the other lets him do these same things. If one parent is strict and the other easy, or if the parents are strict and the person who cares for your child during the day is permissive, your child is likely to grow up confused and disturbed. To prevent this, if you disagree with your spouse about how he is managing a child, disagree in private. Parents need to talk with one another and with regular sitters about household rules and expectations of behavior early, when the child is two, and keep talking and deciding what behavior will and will not be allowed as the child gets older.

4 When and How to Discipline

You have to make sure your child learns certain ways of behaving at certain ages if you want him to grow up self-controlled, well-adjusted and able to take care of himself. Discipline actually begins in infancy, certainly never through spankings or punishment, but as has been noted, by your responding to the child's cries and needs, setting up a routine and pattern of interaction with him so that he will know he can depend on you. This type of discipline builds love and trust in a child, which are the essential foundations for good discipline.

The ages of two and three are crucial times for discipline. This is when you need to set firm limits on the child's behavior. You must teach your child not to do dangerous things, like running into the road or touching the stove burner. You also need to stop harmful behavior, such as kicking and hitting, and out-of-control behavior like tantrums. The child needs to learn many things that he can and cannot do in these years. He also must learn how to control his angry feelings and needs help in dealing with his fears. Parents need to do all this while at the same time encouraging the child to explore his environment, learn new things, express his feelings and ideas, and gradually become more independent. It's a tall order indeed. But child behavior specialists warn that if you do not control your child in these early years, you may not be able to control him later.

Disciplining your child doesn't mean spanking or hitting him, however. Although an occasional whack on the bottom when your child reaches for something dangerous won't hurt him, it's not a good way to discipline because your child is likely to copy your hitting behavior if you hit him. It's better to discipline by removing him from the dangerous situation, saying "No" firmly, and distracting his attention to something else. Putting him in his room or taking him away from other children if he hits or bites, with a firm "That is not the way we behave" is a better way to rid him of this behavior than spanking him. What's important is to take action immediately at this age when unacceptable behavior appears, say child behavior specialists.

In preschool years, discipline may still be needed sometimes to control angry or aggressive behavior, but by four or five this isn't usually as much of a problem. Most children realize by then that hitting, biting or otherwise hurting a person are wrong and are beginning to develop a conscience. These are the years when discipline should emphasize social skills, such as politeness and showing respect for others. It's also a time when you can build a child's sense of morality, make him understand why things like lying, stealing and cheating are wrong. You can help him develop good learning habits by reading to him regularly, providing good books and educational toys, taking him to the library and museums and by generally encouraging learning. It's also a time when you can explain the reasons for the rules you have made and why certain behaviors are not permitted. At this age your child can communicate with you more if problems arise. Encourage this. Ask what happened if he gets into a fight with another child or comes in the door angry. Encourage him to talk about his feelings and help him find solutions to his problems. Most important, give a lot of encouragement and recognize and praise good behavior, accomplishment and effort.

By the time a child is in elementary school, punishment is often an ineffective way of disciplining, according to child development specialists. It often makes children angry and resentful, can damage their self esteem, and doesn't get to the cause behind the child's misbehavior. If the punishment is harsh, children may become timid and submissive, or may just learn to be sneakier when they misbehave, or they may become rebellious. But this doesn't mean you become permissive parents at this stage and let your children get away with everything because permissiveness can have disastrous results. Instead, sit down with your children and agree on household rules, explaining the reasons for them. Decide with them what will happen if someone breaks the rules, and make sure punishments are fair and not overly harsh. Treat your children with respect, listen to their ideas and opinions. Tell them how it makes you feel if they misbehave. And if they do, be sure to follow up with the punishments decided upon. Most important, don't use spanking and physical punishment at this age. Let children learn from the consequences of their behavior (for instance, if they leave their sneakers outside, they get wet and can't be worn), or use things like withholding of privileges, cuts in allowance, or grounding as punishments.

As your child grows, you gradually need to give him more and more control of his behavior and decision-making, as he develops more responsibility and self-control, yet you still set limits. In this way you keep control but allow him to develop independence.

TYPES OF DISCIPLINE

Authoritarian Discipline

Authoritarian parents are strict and demand immediate obedience from their children. They make all the rules and decisions in the household, order their children around, and punish them if they disobey. Authoritarian parents may spank children or use other physical punishment if children disobey them. They also tend to be very critical of their children's behavior. Some can be outright mean and will use harsh physical punishment, such as hitting a child with a belt, or ridicule or belittle the child who does not live up to the standards they have set. Even if they are not mean, authoritarian parents are very domineering and controlling, always telling their children what they should do, and how, when and where they should do it.

What kind of children do authoritarian parents produce? Child psychologists say the children of such parents often are hostile and resentful and tend to be more aggressive than normal. Because they are full of resentment over the way they have been treated, particularly if their parents were mean, they tend to take out on other children the anger they feel against their parents, but don't dare express. Such children may seem to conform when around their parents, but as soon as parental authority is removed, they are likely to kick over the traces and rebel. They may become behavior problems at school, develop emotional problems, and become delinquent.

Sometimes children of authoritarian parents turn out just the opposite. They become timid, overly good children and teenagers who are afraid of expressing their own ideas and feelings. They are so used to being directed that they have difficulty taking control of their own life and making their own decisions. Children of authoritarian parents who have had harsh discipline also get used to stifling negative feelings like anger out of fear of their authoritative parents. Then, when they are older, they may unconsciously turn this buried anger against themselves, feel inferior or worthless, and suffer from depression. Some of these children, even though meek through their childhood and youth, may echo their parents' attitudes as adults and become bossy and domineering when they become parents.

A number of studies have found that harsh, punitive discipline may make children conform initially, but builds buried anger and resentment, which eventually may take the form of antisocial or delinquent behavior, or depression or alcoholism, if the child turns his long-buried anger against himself. A 22-year study of about 400 people from age 8 through age 30 found that children whose parents were authoritarian, harsh or overly critical became self-centered, impulsive adults who were more likely to be violent and drug abusers than children raised by supporting, accepting parents. And another study has found that people who are disciplined harshly as children are more likely to suffer from depression or alcoholism later in life. (See pp. 55). Discipline that is very strict and prohibitive and makes children feel very guilty can also lead to their developing phobias, compulsions and obsessions later in life. So even though strict authoritarian discipline and punishment may work to stop a behavior for a time, it's not likely to make your child more cooperative, psychologically well-adjusted and responsible in the long run.

Don't get the idea from all this, however, that you should never be strict with your children. You do need to set limits on their behavior. Certainly there are times when parents must act in an authoritarian manner, particularly when a child is in danger. If a toddler starts running into the street or a teenager wants to go to a party where you know drugs are likely to be around, a firm, authoritarian "No" is needed, plus an explanation of why you said it. Also, there are degrees of authoritarian discipline. If parents are somewhat authoritarian, but respect their children, are sensitive to their feelings and are kind, fair and understanding, their children are likely to grow up to be responsible, well-adjusted adults.

The trick is to be firm and somewhat authoritarian, but be calm and relaxed about it, not angry and irritable. Control needs to be established by firm kindness, not by autocratic commands. For instance, if you send your child to his room because he has been misbehaving and he comes out, and you put him back, and he comes out again, you may have to put him back many times before he finally stays there. But do it in a calm manner that still shows you mean business. Eventually he will stay in his room for his time out.

Authoritarian discipline doesn't work today the way it did in past generations, it should be noted, because we no longer have the old-fashioned family with a mother who stays home and a dictatorial father who is the breadwinner and rules with an iron hand. With the women's lib movement and women in the workplace, housewives are no longer subservient to their husbands. Also, people and institutions that once had great authority, such as religion, government, teachers, policemen, are now often not looked on with respect or even listened to by a lot of people. And with the increasing violence in our cities, and violence and adultery shown daily on television, young people can get the idea that subservience to authority or a moral code is passé. Children see adults doing what they please rather than submitting to rules, authority, and other people, and naturally they copy that behavior.

Permissive Discipline

Some parents let their children do just about whatever they want. They may let their children leave their toys and clothes all over the house and then meekly pick up after them. They may permit them to be mean or selfish or rough with other children, to speak to others or their parents rudely and with disrespect, to watch whatever they want as late as they want on television. They don't require them to help around the house, get their homework done or insist on good manners, etc. Such parents may be afraid to discipline because they fear they will harm their children emotionally. Or they may just be too lazy or uncaring to make the effort, or too timid to take on a small child, or just have no idea of how to manage children. Whatever the reason, such permissive parents do significant psychological damage to their children.

All children need discipline. They need to know what behavior is acceptable in society and what is not, what activities are safe and which are dangerous. They also must learn to take responsibility for their actions, to be polite and helpful, to be kind and respectful to others, and much more. All this is the function of discipline.

Children who are not disciplined become anxious and insecure, say child behavior specialists. They sense that they are not getting the guidance and the limits on their behavior they must have at this stage of their life, and they soon begin to think that their parents don't care enough about them to show them how to behave. They are likely to become more and more unmanageable and obnoxious just to try and get their parents to pay attention to them and give them some direction. To others they seem spoiled, rude, out of control, but their behavior is really a cry for help. Such behavior is likely to make them disliked and shunned by both their peers and adults. This just increases their lack of self esteem, and a vicious cycle is set up. They are likely to grow up to become selfish, inconsiderate individuals with little sense of responsibility or moral sense. They may find it difficult to form relationships with people, have emotional problems, and get into all sorts of trouble. Parents who switch back and forth from between being permissive to authoritarian often have children who are the most disturbed, say mental health experts.

The type of parenting a child has and the strictness or permissiveness of his parents can often determine whether or not a young person will take drugs. It even influences the type of drug he will take, studies indicate. Glenn and Nelsen report that Fred Streit developed a test to measure how well parents are creating trust and closeness with their children based on the children's perceptions. The test, called EPAC (Expectations, Perceptions, Assessment and Change) measured 26 critical elements in personal relationships and then plotted the results to determine how much strictness or permissiveness and how much love versus hostility the parents exhibited.

Streit and his researchers gave the test to several thousand youngsters 11 to 18. Based on their responses they put them in one of three categories: high risk (for drugs, alcoholism, delinquency or other problems); low risk, or no marked tendency either way. They then compared the results with the teenagers' records and found that 90 percent of those shown at high risk by the test had high rates of involvement in drug and alcohol abuse, school problems, etc., and 85 percent of those at low risk were in the opposite situation. Those whose parents treated them with loving control to loving autonomy were considered low risk and were found least likely to use drugs, but those treated with permissiveness, strictness, and hostility were more likely to do so.

But the investigators didn't stop there. They divided the 11-year-olds into two groups and gave the parents and teachers of the children in one group guidance on how to communicate better with their children to build love and trust. Parents and teachers in the other group received no instruction. They retested the children when they were 16. They found that 90 percent of the adolescents in the control group were in the very high risk category, but only 15 percent of those whose parents and teachers had received guidance in parenting were at high risk. This shows that parenting education can help even when children are in their teens.

The researchers also found something else that was interesting. They gave the EPAC test to 4,000 drug-dependent people between 11 and 45. They then said they could predict the main drug the individuals used based on how they perceived their relationship with their parents, and were surprisingly accurate. They found those who were brought up by permissive parents tended to use marijuana, and if the permissive parents tended to be hostile, their offspring were more apt to use hallucinogens. Those brought up by very strict parents were more likely to use alcohol, cocaine or sedatives. And those whose parents were both very strict and very hostile became the heroin addicts.

Negative Discipline

Child behavior specialists sometimes talk about using negative and positive discipline in managing children. Negative discipline is doing something to stop a child from doing what he shouldn't do. It can include saying "No, stop that," physically removing a child from a place he shouldn't be, scolding the child, shaming him, slapping his hands, spanking him or punishing him in some way. Some types of negative discipline are poor ways to control a child. Slapping or spanking a child, for instance, may stop the child from doing something you don't like, but they build up anger and resentment in the child and just teach him that it's perfectly all right to hit people if you don't like what they are doing. Children under a year should never be hit or spanked because they are too young to make a connection between something they are doing and the pain inflicted, and it can be psychologically damaging to the child. However, many parents unfortunately do this. Belittling a child, shaming him, not talking to him or isolating him for a long time, frequently yelling and being irritable with him, or saying mean or sarcastic things to him are also poor forms of negative discipline that can be psychologically damaging to a child.

There are bound to be times when you have to use negative discipline, but you should use forms of negative control that don't hurt the child physically or mentally, says a pamphlet distributed by the Mental Health Association of

Connecticut. For example, if a child is about to touch a hot stove or some other dangerous object, you need to say "no" firmly and then either move the child away or move the object out of reach. You can show your disapproval when a child does something wrong and tell him he must not do certain things and explain why. And you can use such forms of punishment as sending the child to his room or withholding some privilege, such as watching television that day. But punishment in general, although it may stop a child from doing something you don't want, usually does not help him get to the root of why he has misbehaved so he can understand and change his behavior. For that, dialogue between parent and child is necessary. Parents need to explain why a certain behavior is unacceptable, and talk about why the child has done it and how he can gain better control of his behavior.

Positive Discipline

Positive control, said the late Dr. Loyd Rowland "is working with a child rather than against him." It is more difficult, but often more effective in the long run. It requires planning ahead and arranging situations so that the child will want to do the right thing, according to the psychologist. Putting things that are breakable or dangerous out of reach before the child gets into them is an example. Putting jar lids, dishcloths or other harmless things in lower kitchen drawers so a toddler can explore them without danger, and fencing a yard when a child isn't old enough to understand the danger of running into the street are some examples.

Positive discipline, as a child gets older, involves explaining clearly what rules you expect the child to follow and why, setting fair consequences that will occur if he chooses not to do so, shifting the responsibility for the choice to him, and then following up with the consequences if he chooses to break the rules. It is letting him have a say in making the household rules, if he is old enough, because he is more apt to follow them. It is using logical consequences as much as possible to guide him, rather than ordering and directing. Positive discipline stresses recognizing and praising good behavior. It is treating your child with respect. This means listening to what he has to say, even if you are busy or it seems unimportant to you. It means sympathizing with his feelings and treating him politely, saying "Please" and "Thank you" when you ask him for things, just as you would expect him to use these words with you. It is introducing him to people you meet and not ignoring him, listening to his ideas and letting him share in decisions about things affecting him when he gets old enough.

Positive discipline is more difficult and it may take a long time to get the knack of using it and to see results. But it is more likely to accomplish the main goal of discipline—getting the child to control his behavior himself and decide on his own what he should and should not do. This is how a child develops a conscience, and it begins earlier in life that most people think. The foundation is laid in the early years of life.

Authoritarian discipline provides order without freedom and no choice. Permissive discipline provides freedom without order and unlimited choices. Positive, democratic discipline provides freedom with order and limited choices, according to educator Jane Nelsen, who has written a book about the method entitled *Positive Discipline*. In an authoritarian household, if little Jimmy started to write on the wall with his crayon, the parent would say "Don't do that" and pull him away and spank him. In a permissive household, the parent would just let him enjoy himself and figure she would wash the wall later. In a household using positive discipline, the parent would use distraction and substitution. She would take a piece of paper and say, "Paper is for writing on, not walls," and show him how to draw on the paper, perhaps guiding his hand to make a picture of a tree or a house. Then she would reinforce his efforts by praising his picture and perhaps putting it up on the bulletin board.

The best kind of discipline, experts thus conclude, is discipline which provides love, acceptance, attention and security, and a reasonable amount of freedom for children, yet establishes certain rules of behavior which are expected to be followed.

One last word about discipline in general. There is no one right method for handling every problem that comes up with a child because children are all different. What works with one may not work with another. But whatever method you use, treat your child with firmness, but with kindness and respect. Psychologist H. Stephen Glenn says always remember the crucial three F's of discipline: be friendly, firm and fair.

How to Show Approval and Acceptance to a Child

The Stork Club Child Care and Development Centers in Connecticut give the following examples of things parents and other adults can do to encourage children and show approval and acceptance:

- Give a hug.
- Spend time with the child.
- Give children opportunities to try.
- Give a pat on the back.

- Share your feelings with the child.
- Laugh at your children's stories.
- Listen.
- Accept the child as he is.

- Allow children to make decisions and accept them.
- Tell children you need their help and show it.
- Involve children in family activities and a family council.
- Cuddle the child.
- Be interested, really interested, in what the child says and does.
- Surprise the child with treats at times.
- Give him challenging things to do to show him his abilities.
- Care about him.
- Refrain from criticism.
- Give him the idea he is a special, unique individual.
- Have a regular daily routine and regular naptime.
- Give him responsibility for things and for himself.
- Talk to your children.
- Use a happy, friendly tone of voice.
- Forget past problems.
- Smile.
- Wait for the child.
- Wink.
- Trust the child.
- Ask his opinion.
- Tell him he belongs.
- Touch your child.
- Mention small efforts.
- Share responsibilities with him.
- Review his accomplishments.
- Share with him.
- Build on his strengths.
- Repeat his questions, paraphrasing them, at times.

Words of Encouragement

Some words of encouragement the Stork Club suggests:

Yes	Wow!	Enjoy.
I like that.	I agree.	I feel good about that.
By yourself.	Looks nice.	How do you feel?
Fantastic!	Can I help?	I really enjoyed your company.
Let's talk about it.	Terrific!	That is a help.
I'm pleased.	Beautiful!	Let's do it.
Share.	I hear you.	Super!
You can do it.	Look at that!	Let's do it together.
That's great	I'm glad you're here.	We all make mistakes.
That's nice.	This is our time.	Fine.
Good job!	I need your help.	Attractive.
You really helped me.	I appreciate that.	What happens if we...?
I'm impressed.	Thank you.	Remember when...?

Twenty Basic PRINCIPLES of Good Discipline

Many parents have a problem managing their children, but they don't know what to about it or where to turn for help. If they seek help from the child's teacher or doctor, they may be told that their child is unruly, hyperactive, disruptive, aggressive, or overly shy and withdrawn, but may not be given any practical advice on how to solve the problem. As a result, the parents may ignore the problem, do things that make it worse, or finally seek help from a specialist in child behavior.

However, there are general principles of child management that will help parents manage children without yelling at them, spanking them, or punishing them repeatedly, principles that will help them raise children to become productive, capable, and responsible adults.

Here are 20 basic principles that psychologists, psychiatrists, and educators suggest parents follow in raising their children:

1. **Meet the psychological needs of infants and children because if you don't, they may continue into adolescence and adulthood and result in psychological problems.**

Psychologist Lee Salk has noted that there is a mistaken belief in our society that being kind and responsive to children makes them weak, while strictness and punishment build strong character. But the opposite is true. Children have basic needs: In infancy they need to have their crying responded to quickly by one main caretaker who answers their need for food, comfort, cuddling, stimulation, love. As children get older, they also need to be loved and important to at least one adult; to feel accepted despite their faults; to have some control over their lives. If these needs are not met, Salk says, the result is likely to be a disturbed adolescent and possibly a violent adult. (See Chapter 2)

2. **Praise your child and be specific in your praise.**

Praise good behavior, accomplishments and progress. If you praise and encourage good behavior you will have better results than if you make a habit of correcting and criticizing bad behavior.

Although parents of older generations often refrained from praising their children because they thought it would spoil them, psychologists today know that children need praise and encouragement to build their sense of self worth. Psychologist H. Stephen Glenn in his talks on parenting throughout the country says that encouraging children and adolescents is a much better way of helping them develop into capable and responsible adults than criticizing and correcting them. Encouragement can even prevent misbehavior.

Father Daniel R. Lowery notes that as a priest and counselor he has observed that many people have a poor self image and low self esteem. Some he has encountered, in fact, even seem to hate themselves. Why is this so? According to the looking glass self theory of social psychology, people get their self-image from the reflection by other people of what they are like, he says. "If important people in our lives, such as parents, teachers, pastors, peers, send us mostly negative feedback, we will naturally begin to see ourselves in this light. If 'significant others' imply that we are evil or ugly or worthless, we gradually begin to believe that we are so."

"Conversely, our self-image or self-love can become much more positive and healthy when we receive positive affirmation from those with whom we live and work." Affirmation means accepting people as important, showing them that they are appreciated and important, that we are happy they belong to our family or are our friends and are grateful for their good qualities. "We all need affirmation from those whose lives touch ours," says Lowery. Children, whose sense of self is in the process of being formed, especially need it. "Affirmation," he says, "is not a luxury, it's a necessity."

Josee Bancroft, a day care center director, says small children should be praised for desired behaviors, such as waiting, sharing, cooperating, showing self control. The praise should be specific, such as "Thank you for giving him the toy," rather than "You're a good girl."

Beware of unqualified praise, however, for it can cause problems, say specialists in child behavior. Too much of it (you're such a good girl), and a child may need to keep hearing it to assure himself he is worthwhile. Or it can come across as phony, especially if the child knows he has done some things that aren't very good. And if you tell a child she is a good girl only when she achieves something, such as good marks, it can make her feel her self worth only depends on how she performs for you.

Praise specific behaviors, accomplishments, actions, good traits. To be specific in your praise, tell your child what you liked about something they did and why. A useful way of communicating praise which psychologist H. Stephen Glenn and educator Jane Nelsen suggest is the sentence, "I feel _____ about _____ because _____." For instance, "I feel pleased about the way you straightened out the living room because the house will look nice when your aunt comes tonight." (The same formula is also very useful for expressing other feelings, and can be used when something your child has done has made you embarrassed, angry, disappointed, frightened, etc.)

3. Communicate with your child in other ways that build his self-esteem.

Why is self esteem so important? One of the strongest needs any human being has is the need to feel he is significant and needed. When a child doesn't feel important and of value to his parents, that's when big trouble starts. He may become depressed and withdrawn, or rebellious and angry, or he may turn to drugs, alcohol, delinquency, promiscuity, develop severe mental illness and even attempt or commit suicide. If his sadness and stress from not feeling worthwhile and of value to his parents is great enough, it can cause changes in his brain chemistry. Research has shown changes in brain chemicals occur when a person suffers depression, and these abnormal changes in brain chemistry have been found in the brains of suicide victims. (See Chapter 7.)

It is known that children learn better, behave better, and have more enthusiasm for school, work and life in general if they feel they are valued and loved by the important people in their life. But if they are criticized, not appreciated, or belittled, they lose their enthusiasm. After all, would you feel like putting forth much effort if you felt you would not be appreciated for what you did, but would be ignored, criticized, corrected or belittled?

So to build your child's self esteem treat him with kindness, respect, and the same courtesy you would show an adult. Don't shame, punish or correct him in front of others. Wait until the two of you are alone if you must correct your child. Then correct him without belittling him, insulting him or making him feel like a failure. And spend time with him doing things together that you can enjoy, anything from a walk in the woods to building a model plane.

Vicki Lansky in her book *Best Practical Parenting Tips* suggests some other ways of building self esteem in children:

- "Knock at your child's closed door and wait for an invitation to enter. Your child should return the courtesy for you."

- "Be aware of the tone of your voice when you call your child. A child can learn to hate his or her name if it seems always to be called in anger or in haste."

- "Take the time to introduce your children to others as you do adults."

- "Use a child's name a lot in conversation and make use of nicknames only if the child really likes them."

- "Make each child a SPECIALIST in the family—your favorite two-year-old, the exercise leader, or the nature scout."

- "Keep a regular baby drawer or box into which you drop an anecdotal record of your child's life several times a year...going through everything once or twice a year is fun for all."

- "Expect your children to do as much as they can, as well as they can, and let them know you do. But let them know that it's okay to make mistakes, too, and that mistakes—even Mom's and Dad's—show people ways to learn and improve."

- And Lansky's best suggestion: "Try to say at least one positive and affirming thing to your child every day."

4. Set limits on your children's behavior. Make rules, let children participate in making rules when possible, and stick to them.

Keep the rules simple and reasonable and make as few as necessary. And give children reasons for the limits you set and the rules you make. Don't just say, "Don't do this because I said so." Also be clear about the consequences that will follow if rules are broken, and stick to your guns. Don't let your child talk you into letting him get away with it if he broke a rule unless it wasn't his fault.

Dr. Benjamin Spock believes that parental hesitancy, indecision and lack of firmness in making children adhere to the rules parents have set is the main problem in child-rearing today. Children need parental guidance for their stability and security. Parents who don't set limits for their children may think they are being loving, but they are really damaging their children. Psychologists say such children will become anxious and insecure and will just increase their wildness, rudeness and spoiled behavior as if they were desperately trying to get their parents to take the reins and control them—which they are. It's often difficult to control children, and kids whose parents won't make that effort feel before long that their parents don't care enough about them to make the effort. Children brought up without rules and limits become selfish, destructive, have psychological problems, feel unloved, and have difficulty in making friends and getting along in society.

Limits must be set early, however, in fact when a child is two and three, according to child psychologists and pediatricians. Says Dr. T. Berry Brazelton, "Unless parents can accept the responsibility for limiting the child and for using appropriate punishment where it is necessary, they are deserting the child."

5. Empathize with your children when they have a problem.

Empathy is sensing how a person feels in a situation and showing understanding and appreciation of his feelings. It is different from sympathy because sympathy conveys the idea that you feel sorry for the person.

To empathize with your child, reflect back both the meaning of what he is saying and the feelings underlying his words, which often are expressed by his actions and body language, the process which we described earlier as *active listening*. And never tell him he shouldn't feel the way he does. For instance, if your son comes home from school bad-tempered, slams his books on the table and snaps at you, how should you respond? Should you tell him to go to his room until he can act pleasantly? If you do, you are not empathizing with him and helping him to communicate his problem and solve it. You are instead teaching him to suppress his negative emotions, which, if it becomes a habit, can lead to mental illness later in life. Instead, what you should say is "You seem angry about something." When he responds and you find the cause, you might give an example of a similar situation in which you felt the same way. Helping him express his anger helps him get rid of it.

Let's imagine your daughter came home late from school looking really sad and upset. The teacher had called, and you knew she had kept her after school. The worst thing you could do is begin criticizing and blaming her right away and make a comment like "The teacher said you had detention. What did you do wrong?" A comment like that would just make her angry and sadder, and turn off communication. Instead, start with a neutral comment like "What happened?"

"Mrs. Smith told me I was an air head and made me stay after school because I lost my reading book," says she. "And the kids all laughed at me."

"That must have embarrassed you." (picking up on her feelings)

"Yeah. It made me feel like a real jerk."

"Um. That's not a very good feeling to have. I remember once my second grade teacher called me four eyes when I started wearing glasses, and the kids laughed at me. I wanted to sink through the floor I felt so bad," (showing understanding of her feelings)

"It really wasn't very nice of my teacher to say that."

"She wasn't very considerate of your feelings,"(rephrasing what she meant). "I found your reading book, by the way. It had fallen behind your bed."

After a little more discussion, you might ask, "What do you think you could do so that something like this doesn't happen again?"

"I guess I could make sure all my books were piled on the table before I went to bed at night." (solution arrived at)

Handling a situation like this with empathy builds closeness and understanding between a child and parent. It encourages a child, helps your child deal with unpleasant emotions and find solutions, and makes her feel she can talk to you about problems she has.

6. When a child misbehaves, find out why before you punish.

Dr. Melvin Lewis of the Yale Child Study Center stresses this general principle of discipline. Perhaps there is a valid reason for your child's actions and no need to punish. If you see your son fighting with another boy, for instance, don't just punish him for fighting. Find out who started it. If he did because he didn't like something the other boy said to him, he is at fault. But if he was hit first and was defending himself, it's the friend who should be punished.

Most children misbehave because they feel people don't care about them and consider them important. They want to belong, to be noticed, to be loved, to be significant. If a child doesn't get enough positive recognition, he'll misbehave to get some attention, even if it's negative attention. Sometimes children misbehave because they are angry and want to get back at someone (usually their parents). If you can figure out the reason behind the misbehavior, you are more apt to find the way handle it successfully. (For more information, see the Misbehavior chapter.)

7. Treat your child with kindness and respect.

Get rid of the idea that you have to punish a child to make him behave. Parents who follow the "spare the rod, spoil the child" adage, child behavior specialists have found, generally produce children with behavioral, emotional or psychological problems. You don't raise a child to be capable and responsible and to feel he is a worthwhile individual by hitting him, belittling him, humiliating him or punishing him harshly. Parents need to be firm, true, but they also must be kind, understanding and respectful toward their children.

8. Demonstrate by your own behavior the kind of behavior you want in your child.

Children learn to behave by copying the way their parents behave. Many studies have shown that children who have been abused often grow up abusing their own children. Nursery school director Josee Bancroft observes that children learn by imitation and "children who are shouted at, treated harshly, slapped, not listened to, etc., will learn to treat others that way."

So if you want your child to grow up kind and respectful, treat him, other family members and friends with kindness and respect. If you want him to take responsibility for his actions, admit his mistakes and learn from them, you do the same. If you want him to grow up loving, give him love.

9. Instead of punishing children, use natural or logical consequences whenever you can.

Punishment usually is not a very effective way to discipline children because, although it may work temporarily to stop misbehavior, it makes the child angry and often makes him want to do something to get back at his parents. So he is likely to misbehave again. Then his parents punish him more severely, and the cycle goes on and on. Or if punishment is frequent or severe, some children will react by becoming fearful, withdrawn and timid. Studies have shown that children punished severely, especially with physical punishment, are more likely to get in trouble in school, bully other children, become delinquent or turn to drugs, alcohol or promiscuity as teenagers, or suffer from depression, phobias, or other psychological problems later in life. (See pp. 54-58)

Children can often be disciplined more effectively by using natural or logical consequences. Educator Jane Nelsen describes this method in detail in her book *Positive Discipline*. A natural consequence is something that naturally follows an action. If you leave the box of popsicles on the kitchen table, they melt. If your child doesn't want to wear boots to school when it snows because it's not "cool," his feet get wet and cold. If your daughter leaves her doll out in the yard and it rains, it gets wet and ruined. She won't do it again.

Natural consequences can't be used when they would be dangerous to your child or to someone else (for instance, if your toddler is about to touch a hot iron or if a child is throwing rocks at another child), or when the natural consequences of a child's behavior wouldn't be important to him (for instance, if he treks mud in on your kitchen floor). In such cases logical consequences can be used. Logical consequences involve another person and are logically related to the misbehavior. For example, if your child treks mud over your floor, a logical consequence would be for you to have him wipe it up and clean off his shoes. Logical consequences should always be fair, be administered kindly but firmly, and without laying a guilt trip on the child. You don't say to your son who trekked mud on the floor things like "How can you be such a slob?" or "Don't you have any consideration for how hard I work to keep this house clean?" A respectful way to treat him would be to say "You'll need to clean the mud off the floor and your shoes before you have dinner." Then make sure this is done before you serve him dinner. Making him clean the whole kitchen, however, would be too severe and be an unfair consequence.

You should also explain to your children before you use logical consequences what they are and give some examples. You can also sometimes give a choice of a consequence to stop behavior you don't want. For instance, if a child is making a racket blowing a horn in a room full of adults, you can call him over and ask if he would rather have you take the horn away from him or play with it in another room where the noise he makes won't disturb people who are talking.

It may take a while to get get used to using logical consequences, but they are effective in many situations and will help your children develop responsibility, respect, and self discipline. And the method leaves children with a sense that they have been treated fairly, rather than with a desire to get even with punishing parents.

10. Criticize the child's behavior, not the child.

For instance, if a child misbehaves, don't say, "You're a bad boy." Instead, say something like, "When you play with your fire truck in the kitchen, water gets all over the floor. Now let's get a rag and wipe it up." Be especially careful to avoid using words or phrases that label a child negatively, for instance, "You're a weakling," or "You're too sensitive," or "You're such a slob." Even if they are said jokingly, and even if the child is not conscious of being hurt or angered by such remarks, there is evidence now that negative words can subconsciously affect the mind, and such labels may damage his sense of self worth.

Yale psychiatrist Bruce Wexler had people listen to pairs of words in which one had a positive or negative emotional connotation and the other was an emotionally neutral word that sounded like it, such as hug and tug or kill and till. Then he measured their subconscious responses through brain waves, smiles, frowns, heart rate and descriptions of their own thoughts. By using a special computer Wexler was able to give his subjects one of the words in one ear and the other in the other ear at exactly the same time. The result was that the person was only conscious of hearing one word and had no idea he had been given two words. About half the time the person heard the neutral word. But his subconscious thoughts showed reactions to the emotionally charged words even when the person was only conscious of hearing the neutral word.

When Wexler paired the words gore and door, for example, one subject said he only heard the word door. But when asked to describe his thoughts after hearing the word, he said he thought of someone walking through a door with blood on him. The psychiatrist also found that his subjects' biological response to negative words they didn't hear, such as activity in their frowning muscles, "was just as great as to consciously processed negative words." His experiments show how negative words and experiences affect both the mind and the body and suggest how in some people they may even lead to psychosomatic illnesses.

11. Use a time out, rather than a spanking if your child misbehaves.

Make your child sit apart from other children he is playing with, or send him to his room or another room away from the family for a specified time or until he feels he can control himself.

Discuss why the child is being punished before using time out, advise teachers at Spring Glen Church Nursery School in Hamden and others. Tell him the time out is to help him control his angry feelings. But they stress it is also most important to let the child know he is loved even if he is being punished. "Being supportive and building a positive self-image is extremely important," says director Louise Miller.

Some parents put children in their rooms for a time-out for a specified amount of time. Others tell the child he can come out when he feels he is ready to behave nicely. If you use a time out with a young child, it should be only a few minutes long. If a child won't go to his room for a time out, you may have to firmly lead him there. If you have told your child he must stay in his room a certain amount of time, and he comes out, put him back, and keep putting him back until he stays the time you have set. But don't lock a child in a room because this will frighten a child.

If you send your child to his room for a time out, don't worry if he reads or plays with toys he has there. You are not trying to make him feel imprisoned or miserable. You just want to stop his bad behavior. Time outs are one of the best ways of showing a child you can control his behavior in a calm, respectful manner, without hitting, yelling, or anger. After a time out, you should always talk with a child about the behavior that prompted it, how it can be avoided in the future, and encourage him, perhaps by an arm around the shoulder and a suggestion of some activity for him.

12. Shift the locus of control of behavior to the child whenever possible, so that you are not in the role of parental oppressor.

Psychologist H. Stephen Glenn and educator Jane Nelsen stress the concept of shifting from an external to an internal locus of control. To do this, set limits and rules with a child at a calm time and be clear about what will happen if the child CHOOSES not to abide by the rules. If a child breaks a rule, ask why, and if there is no good reason, say you are sorry he CHOSE to break the rule and CHOSE a certain punishment instead. Then calmly carry out the consequence you have specified. For instance, you might set a rule that there is no television watching until all homework is done. You might check with your child when he comes home from school about the homework he has and how long it will take. Then if he dawdles and plays all afternoon and wants to watch a program after supper, say, in a friendly, matter-of-fact manner, "Sorry, but you chose not to do your homework this afternoon and not to watch television."

13. When a problem arises with your child, decide if the problem is one that primarily affects the child or you and respond accordingly.

Psychiatrist Foster Cline notes that a major cause of friction between children and parents is that parents often are not able to distinguish between what is the child's problem and what is their problem. For instance, laziness, fights with other children, bad grades and a poor choice of friends are all the child's problem. But something like refusal to do chores and talking back to parents is the parents' problem because it affects them directly.

Cline says parents should handle things that are basically the child's problem by listening and being empathetic, showing concern and love; not rescuing the child but letting him experience the consequences of his behavior; and asking "What are you going to do now?" However, parents shouldn't say directly to the child "That's your problem" because this seems uncaring and cruel. If parents get angry at the child in problems of this type, it only makes the problem worse. In problems that do not affect the parent directly, give advice without orders if it is wanted, for instance, by saying "I notice that you may be having a problem making that model (or whatever). Would you like my suggestions?" If your child says, "No," say nothing. If he says, "Yes," give your opinion, but don't lecture.

However, in problems that affect the parent, anger may be appropriate. But parents should avoid the word "you" in such situations ("You shouldn't do that"; "You're a bad boy"; "Don't you do that again.") because it only provokes resentment and more controversy. Instead, the best way to handle problems that affect the parent directly, say Cline and psychologist Thomas Gordon, is to give "I" messages, such as, "I really get upset when you play that music so loud because I can't concentrate on my work." Use the "I feel...when you...because" pattern. For instance, "I feel annoyed when you leave dirty dishes in the sink because it gives me more work." After your "I" message, wait for a good answer from your child. If he doesn't come up with a good answer, ask if he has a solution to the problem. If he has no solution, you may then have to give him a choice, such as, "You can either do your chore now, or I will deduct 50 cents from your allowance."

14. Instead of punishing misbehavior, try to redirect it into contributing behavior.

For instance, if a child does something disruptive, have him make up for it by doing something to contribute to the household. For instance, if he writes on your wall, have him do something to make up for it that will make you feel better, such as washing that wall. If he is fighting with his sister over a game, have him show his sister how to play it.

15. Instead of nagging, decide with your children what consequence will follow if they fail to take responsibility for their things or their household chores. Then, if they don't, calmly let them take the consequence.

For instance, if your child has a habit of leaving his toys and things all over the house, set a rule that anything not put away by the time he goes to bed, you will pick up. To get it back, he will have to do a special chore, pay a small amount from his allowance, or wait several days. Find a special place, like a chest you can lock, in which to put these things. If it's your son's job to feed the cat and he doesn't, his consequence might be to wash dishes that night, or he might get docked so much from his allowance.

The important thing in doing this is to keep nastiness and sarcasm and an "I told you what would happen" attitude out of the whole situation. Be kind, calm and unperturbed. If your son left his basketball in the middle of the living room floor last night, and he just HAS to have it because his friends are outside waiting to play, say something like, "That's too bad. I know it must be really disappointing not to have the ball. But you remember we agreed you would have to wait three days to get it back." And go calmly about your business. Your children may storm and fuss when the consequence falls, but after a while they will see you mean business. They will pick up after themselves, and remember their responsibilities, and you won't have to nag.

16. Adapt child-rearing methods to the temperament of the individual child.

Children with different temperaments need to be handled differently, mental health specialists say. Temperament is the style of behavior a child has, and the way parents respond to his temperament helps influence whether the child's behavior will be normal or deviant, say psychiatrists Alexander Thomas and Stella Chess. The two psychiatrists followed 136 children from 80 families for more than 20 years to determine the effect of temperament on mental health and how best to handle children of different temperaments. They found the temperaments of children usually fell into one of three categories: easy, difficult, and slow to warm up. Difficult children had irregular sleeping and eating patterns, reacted with angry protests to new situations, and were likely to have temper tantrums when frustrated. Easy children had regular habits, adapted easily to new situations and were generally cheerful. Slow to warm-up children adapted slowly and were apt to withdraw quietly from new situations. This and other studies suggest temperament is in part genetically determined. The researchers found most behavior problems arose because parents did not know how to handle a difficult or slow-to-warm-up child. Easy children didn't create problems. Slow-to-warm-up children must be allowed to adapt to situations at their own speed, they said. With a difficult child parents need to wait out his negative moods calmly and not get angry, but set safety limits and repeatedly explain the rights of other children and not let him infringe on these rights by his behavior.

Yale psychologist Edward Zigler stresses the importance of adapting child management methods to the child's temperament. "For example," he says, "parents who have slow-to-warm-up children should not pressure them to accept and adjust to new situations quickly, for this may only strengthen their fears and tendency to withdraw." But they should not go to the other extreme and give in to the child's fears and overprotect him. Instead, the parents should anticipate the child's fears and encourage him that he will be able to adapt.

If they don't, Zigler notes, their child may turn out like a slow-to-warm-up boy in Thomas and Chess's study called Bobby. If Bobby rejected any food, his parents didn't give it to him again. If he didn't want to mingle with the children in the playground they kept him home. At age 10 he had no friends and only ate hamburgers, hard-boiled eggs and applesauce. Another boy named Norman was easily distractible and not able to study for long hours. But his hard-driving father did not take his temperament into account, called him irresponsible and pressured him. As a result the boy develop tics and later became depressed and dropped out of college. But parents of a difficult child called Carl were able to anticipate his frequent outbursts, be patient with his tantrums, encourage and reassure him, but not give in to his demands, said Zigler, and he did not develop a serious behavior problem. In general, the child specialists say, remember not to pressure a child to do what he is temperamentally unable to do.

17. Use rewards, but not bribes, in disciplining children.

What's the difference? Rewards are reinforcements for good behavior and are given after the behavior. A bribe is a reward promised if a child will stop a negative behavior or to prevent bad behavior, explains psychologist Louise Bates Ames. Behavioral psychologists know that reinforcements are necessary to teach children the way we want them to behave. Young children need some real things as rewards sometimes, like a piece of candy or new toy. But even more important all through a child's life are rewards such as a hug, a pat on the back, a smile or words of praise, says psychologist Martha Smith. Don't get in the habit of giving gifts and rewards, however, only when a child achieves something or behaves well, she warns, because the child may think he is only worthwhile if he behaves a certain way or accomplishes something. Give your child little gifts sometimes just for the heck of it.

18. Set aside a regular time to spend with each child which is special.

For younger children try to do this every day, and with older children at least several times a week. For some children the best time might be when they come home from school and want to tell you all about their day and the problems they had or the good things that happened. Or it might be for 15 minutes or so at night when you tuck you child into bed. Ask about any difficulties your child might have had that day, anything especially nice that happened to him, anything he is looking forward to or worried about, or anything interesting he learned. You might share some of the things that happened to you that day. Or take some time to do something together you both like. For a small child this could be reading a story together or playing a game. With an older child you might go shopping together, play tennis, go out for an ice cream sundae, go to a movie together on a weekend, or just spend some time talking and sharing your experiences in the evening.

19. Give children choices, even young children, because children need practice in making decisions.

Even small children can be given practice in decision-making by asking them, for instance, whether they want a ham and cheese or a peanut butter and jelly sandwich for lunch. But make sure the choices you give small children are easy ones that they are capable of making, says nursery school director Josee Bancroft, such as asking them which story they want you to read to them (if you have several out to choose from) or if they want to color or play with playdough. And don't give them a choice if they really don't have one and are going to have to do something. For instance, don't say, "Do you want to eat?" when you really mean "It's time to eat dinner."

Giving children choices is a good way of avoiding the "No's," obstinacy, and disobedience that directing and giving orders often produces. For instance, if you take out a dress for your preschooler to wear and tell her to put it on, you may very well get a "No. I'm not going to wear that." But if you take out two, and ask her which dress she wants to wear, she is likely to choose one and put it on readily since she has participated in the decision-making. If you ask your teenager whether he wants to put out the garbage or sweep the kitchen floor as his daily chore for the week, you are likely to get more compliance than if you just tell him to put out the garbage.

20. Don't expect things of children that are beyond their age level.

Most children, for instance, aren't toilet-trained until two or three. Toddlers can't sit still long and usually can't concentrate on any game or toy for more than a few minutes. Nor can they understand other people's feelings, realize how another child feels if they take his toy, or understand the idea of sharing. Don't expect two or three year olds to sit quietly and be quiet through a long church service because they need to be active and to talk. Get a good book on child development or refer to the table at the back of this book for a general idea of what children do at what age so that you don't pressure your child to do something he is not yet capable of doing.

SOME GUIDELINES FOR MANAGING TODDLERS

Early childhood specialists have some other guidelines to help parents manage toddlers and preschoolers:

1. If you want to speak to a small child or make friends with a child who doesn't know you, squat, kneel, or sit so that you get down to his level. It's much easier for a child than talking to someone who is towering above him, and it promotes closeness and friendship. And don't try to talk to a small child or give him orders from across the room because he isn't likely to pay much attention.

2. Use positive directions. Tell the child what he can do, rather than just what he can't do, say teachers in the former Title XX Early Childhood Program at Fairfield University. Instead of saying "Don't throw your football in the living room," say "You can throw the football outside. You can throw your whiffle ball in the house."

3. Guide through orienting instead of directing, the teachers advise. Say "The boots go in the closet," not "Put away your boots." Say "There are two blocks left under the couch," rather than, "Put away those blocks."

4. Help a toddler physically to stop doing something that could be dangerous. For instance, if he is climbing on a counter, lift him down and find something else interesting for him to do.

5. If you have to modify a child's behavior try to redirect it rather than stop it if possible. For instance, if a child is writing on a table with crayons, give him a big piece of paper to write on instead, and explain clearly the reason, such as "Writing on the table makes the table get messy."

6. Don't use the word "No" too much. It's easy to do this, especially once a baby starts getting around and getting into things. Use it if a toddler reaches for something that could injure him, such as a knife or a hot stove, and either remove the object or physically move the child away. Distract him by finding something else for him to do. Say "No" firmly also if a child is doing something that could hurt someone, such as throwing blocks. But try not to say no every time the toddler picks up something in your house or someone else's, or he is likely to get frustrated and irritable at being stopped from exploring the world around him and may start having tantrums.

Also, be consistent about the things you say "No" for, and explain why you are saying "No." For instance "Knives can cut you and hurt you." Sometimes you can redirect behavior instead of saying "No." For instance, if your child has pulled and scattered the clean clothes from your laundry basket all around, say, "We fold the laundry and put it in piles on the bed," and show her how to put the handkerchiefs in one place, the socks in another, etc.

7. Instead of trying to change a toddler's behavior, try to eliminate the situation causing the problem. For instance, separate toddlers who are starting to argue or fight with one another. Move things they are getting into out of their reach instead of constantly telling them to leave the things alone.

Twenty Methods of Discipline to Avoid

The television program, "20/20," on January 17, 1988, devoted a large part of its program to discussing why two million teenagers have left home and millions more have turned to drugs and alcohol. The startling statistics are "evidence of something going wrong" between parents and their children, said moderator Hugh Downes. Although some of these children have run away or turned to drugs because they were beaten or sexually abused by their parents, many others have done so because they were targets of verbal and emotional abuse. Their parents would say things to them like "You're pathetic," "You can't do anything right, "I wish you were never born," or similar words "as hard as a fist," Downes said. Mental health specialists "20/20" consulted for the program noted that an occasional outburst from a parent who becomes angry doesn't do the damage, but a continuing pattern of communication that humiliates children and shows lack of regard for them undermines a young person's sense of self worth. Because they feel worthless, children who are the brunt of this kind of communication drop out of school, run away, or take drugs and alcohol to ease their pain.

On the program was a mother identified as Bobbie and her daughter Carla, a teenager who had become an alcoholic. A therapist in a rehabilitation program to which she was sent insisted that the whole family be involved and found at the root of the problem was a communication problem between mother and daughter. "It was all those years of not knowing how to talk to Carla or to any kid," said Bobbie. "I didn't know how to parent."

"We didn't have a relationship at all. We didn't talk," said Carla. The program made the point that the message parents must get across to their children is, "I care about you, I care for you, I care what you do." As co-anchor Barbara Walters noted, it's not just what you say, but sometimes what you don't say that can be damaging. In conclusion, the moderators stressed that a child can deal with anger, but not insult—that saying "You're wrong," to a child is accepted, but saying "You're stupid," does damage.

The program graphically illustrates that there are some forms of discipline and communication that must be avoided in raising children. Psychologists and psychiatrists agree that certain forms of discipline should not be used with children because they are physically or psychologically dangerous to them. Parents who use these methods can provoke destructive emotions in their children that are likely to surface later as resentment, rebellion, delinquency, anger, withdrawal, or even in mental illness such as depression if the pattern is habitually followed. Dr. Albert Solnit, former head of the Yale Child Study Center, is one psychiatrist who says certain forms of discipline can cause psychological or developmental damage to a child. When he sees a parent on the street hit or yell at and humiliate a child who is fussing or misbehaving, "I feel like going up and saying `Don't do that. You're going to have trouble later'," he said.

Methods of disciplining that can be physically or psychologically damaging to children include the following:

HARSH PHYSICAL PUNISHMENT

It should be obvious that beating, paddling, or any other form of harsh physical punishment should never be used on a child. It constitutes child abuse, a crime punishable by law. Not only is there physical danger to a child so treated, but the psychological danger is even greater. Such treatment, instead of producing conformity, is more likely to produce hatred and resentment of the parent, which will generalize to hatred and resentment of other authority figures.

In past generations, many parents thought children had to be punished severely to make sure they wouldn't turn out bad. Today many studies have found that harsh punishment harms, rather than helps, a child. Not only can it lead to rebellion and delinquency, but it can also cause devastating psychological problems later in the child's life.

Many studies have shown that children who are abused are more likely to become violent, delinquent and criminal. Dr. Dorothy Otnow Lewis, a psychiatrist on the staff of New York University and Yale University, did a study of 97 jailed male juvenile delinquents in Connecticut. She found that 78 had committed violent acts, and 75 percent of those had been abused. But of the 19 incarcerated delinquents who were not violent, only 38 percent had experienced abuse.

Lewis also did a study of nine juvenile delinquents who later in their life were charged with murder and found that seven of the nine had grown up with extreme family violence and repeated beatings. In another study of 15 death row inmates she found most had violent or troubled childhoods, several had been beaten on the head as children, and five had attempted suicide in childhood or adolescence.

Marie Balter's life is also living proof that harsh punishment can cause severe psychological problems. Her story was told in a television documentary entitled "Nobody's Child" and written up by Michael Ryan in *Parade* magazine. Balter was confined for almost 20 years in the locked wards of a state mental hospital. She finally recovered after treatment and became a public relations official in the Massachusetts mental health system. Balter battled panic disorder and harrowing terrors that incapacitated her until she finally regained her sanity. The cause of her illness had its roots in her family history. An adopted child, she was frequently locked out of the house, locked in the basement, or even tied to a post as punishment for offenses she supposedly committed.

Balter's is not an isolated case. A landmark study by S.J. Holmes and N.L Robins indicates that children who are punished harshly are more likely to suffer from depression or alcoholism later in life. The two researchers compared 100 subjects who had suffered from either alcoholism or depression sometime in their lives with 100 control subjects who had not suffered either condition during their lives. They interviewed them in detail about their home lives between the ages of 6 and 12.

They found that unfair, inconsistent and harsh discipline, such as being punched or hit with a stick or belt, was strongly associated with major depression or alcoholism later in life. The investigators found that 41 percent of parents of depressives and 40 percent of parents of alcoholics usually used harsh physical punishment to discipline their children compared to only 14 percent of parents of the control group. They also found that harsh, inconsistent and unfair discipline predicted alcoholism or depression no matter what the individual's sex, their parents' psychiatric history or the severity of behavior problems in childhood. Holmes and Robins say their findings indicate "a very powerful role indeed for parental disciplinary practices in the genesis of psychiatric disorder."

Sometimes the stress of bringing up small children becomes too much for parents and they will lose their temper and hit their children. To help a parent control this impulse, The National Committee for the Prevention of Child Abuse developed a list of 12 things to do if you think you are about to hit or abuse your child:

Twelve Alternatives to
Lashing Out at Your Child

1. Take a deep breath. And another. Then remember that you are the adult.
2. Close your eyes and imagine you're hearing what your child is about to hear.
3. Press your lips together and count to 10. Or better yet, to 20.
4. Put your child in a time-out chair (Remember the rule: one time-out minute for each year of age).
5. Put yourself in a time-out chair. Think about why you are angry: Is it your child? Or is your child simply a convenient target for your anger?
6. Phone a friend.
7. If someone can watch the children, go outside and take a walk.

8. Take a hot bath, or splash cold water on your face.
9. Hug a pillow.
10. Turn on some music. Maybe even sing along.
11. Pick up a pencil and write down as many helpful words as you can think of. ("You're a good kid. You try your best." These are the kinds of comments suggested by Joy Byers, coordinator of the committee's public awareness department.)
12. Write for parenting information to The National Committee for the Prevention of Child Abuse: Parenting, P.O. Box 2866, Chicago, IL 60690.

In other words, says the committee, stop using words that hurt. Start using words that help. And when you are angry, take time out. Don't take it out on your child.

A word of warning: if you find that you are hitting your child too frequently, and especially if things are getting too much for you and you feel you may really hurt him, call the local Parents Anonymous chapter in your neighborhood. Its number should be found in your phone book or through your area HELP line or mental health center. You will find you are not alone, and help is available.

SPANKING AND HITTING

Most parents still believe it's necessary to hit their children at times in order to bring them up properly, according to a University of Minnesota study cited by noted pediatrician Benjamin Spock during a talk at the Yale Medical School in 1985. But Spock said, "We're bringing up gentle thugs by whacking them all the time." He noted that a supervisor displeased with an employee's behavior doesn't hit him, and said children should be treated with the same respect. He believes elimination of physical punishment will result in better values and more emotional stability in children.

Many other child behavior and mental health specialists say spanking is psychologically damaging. Yet even though child specialists have warned of the dangers of spanking for years, parents are still hitting and spanking their children, sometimes even babies six months or younger. It is not only emotionally harmful to spank a baby that young, who needs love and care and cuddling to build a sound personality, it is also pointless. A baby that young doesn't have the mental ability to make a connection between the pain a spanking parent is inflicting on him and something he has done. Parents who hit babies this young can use help and should contact Parents Anonymous or a mental health professional.

Slapping the baby's hands and saying "No" when he touches something he shouldn't isn't a good practice either, say child behavior specialists. As babies learn to crawl and then walk, adults usually encourage their efforts to get around and explore their environment. Suddenly hitting a child for doing this sends a contrary message and confuses and upsets the child. If parents use this method a lot, they will squelch his natural curiosity and are likely to make him timid and fearful of venturing into new situations.

The late John Rowland believed that parents spank a child for one of six reasons: (1) They don't know any other way to control their children and perhaps were spanked themselves as children; (2) They are not getting along with each other and are taking it out on the child; (3) they are unhappy themselves and feel inadequate; (4) They believe other people, such as their relatives, think they should; (5) They want quick results; (6) They are having a temper tantrum themselves. If a parent does get at the end of her rope and spanks a child, the important thing is for the child to know she still loves him despite the spanking, the psychologist noted.

Instead of spanking a baby or toddler who is getting into things, child behavior specialists suggest using distraction or substitution. If a baby picks up something he shouldn't touch, just hand him something that will be more interesting to him and take what you don't want him to have out of his other hand. Or hold out your hand and say, "Thank you." A baby will often give you the object. Or suggest that he put down what he has picked up so you can show him something interesting. It worked with my two-year-old granddaughter when she grabbed my glasses one day. My first reaction was to take them out of her hand. but she held on to them and cried. Then I said, "Oh, look, there are birds on the porch. Let's put these down so we can go outside and see the birdies." She put the glasses down on the table at once and took my hand to go outside. Of course, the best thing is to put away things that you don't want a child to get into.

What about spanking a preschool or older child? Spanking is no way to discipline a child or teach any child anything, according to the National Association for the Education of Young Children. When adults hit children, discipline has already broken down, the association notes. Hitting a child just sets a bad example. It is thus an especially poor way to punish a child who hits others. "You do not hit children when you want them to stop hitting," says Jeannette Stone in a booklet published by the association.

New Haven pediatrician Morris Wessel says that the "spare the rod, spoil the child" philosophy that is part of American culture "encourages many parents and other adults caring for children to spank, hit with the hand, belt, paddle or throw a child against a wall when disciplinary measures appear to be necessary." He recognizes that parents who discipline this way may be at their wit's end and lose control of themselves because they are so frustrated with the child's behavior. Although an occasional slap on the bottom is not likely to do any serious psychological harm to a child, Wessel stresses that spanking, beating or inflicting any other kind of corporal punishment in general only serves to confuse a child. "All he knows is that adults, whom he loves and trusts are attacking him, sometimes in an angry and violent manner. The immediate effect on the child ranges from mild embarrassment and feelings of worthlessness to permanent physical and psychological harm," Wessel writes in an article in *Pediatrics*. He adds that physical punishment, although it may temporarily improve the child's behavior, is not effective in helping him establish self-control and self-discipline in the long run.

This is because physical punishment impairs his trust in individuals he looks to for love and guidance and because it teaches him a dangerous lesson—that might makes right. He gets the message that "size, brawn and position in the adult world entitles one to inflict pain on younger and smaller individuals." And it teaches another dangerous lesson, Wessel adds, that when he becomes an adult and gets angry about something, physical violence is an accepted solution to the problem. Psychiatrists have found again and again that people who were hit and beaten as children become adults who discipline their own children the same way.

Instead of physically punishing a child, Wessel says adults should realize that when a child's behavior is exasperating, it may be perfectly natural for his stage of development, or it may be a sign of some problem that's bothering him. The toddler that pulls everything out of a kitchen cabinet is just exhibiting curiosity that's natural for his age. The older child who won't go to bed at night or who is defiant may be reacting to some stress in the family, some tension between his parents. Spanking and physical punishment won't solve the problem. Instead, parents have to find out what's causing it, talk about the child's feelings, then make clear rules about how the child should behave and withhold privileges if the child fails to live up to them.

Wessel is not alone in his views. The American Psychological Association, the American Public Health Association and the National Education Association have all taken positions against the use of corporal punishment.

A 22-year-study by Rowell Huesmann and Leonard Eron at the University of Illinois-Chicago found children who were spanked or physically punished at home were more likely to be aggressive and bullying at school. And the study found that the young bullies grew up to be less successful than their non-aggressive classmates. They were less likely to hold professional jobs and were more likely to be unemployed or in jail. "What you're doing when you're spanking them is showing them the way you get what you want is by hitting," Eron said. Commenting on the study Dr. Derek Miller, a psychiatry professor at Northwestern University Medical school, said the results were not surprising because the chronic stress these aggressive children are under at home or in society makes it much more likely they will be underachievers.

EMOTIONAL ABUSE

Emotional abuse is a pattern of parental behavior that impairs the development of a child's sense of self and self worth and his social competence. The definition is based on that given by James Garbarino, Edna Guttmann and Janis Wilson Seeley, specialists in child development and family studies, in their recent book *The Psychologically Battered Child*. They say there are five main types of emotional abuse:

Rejecting - refusal by the parent or adult guardian to acknowledge the child's worth or his legitimate needs. This can include refusing to touch the child or show affection, not acknowledging the child's accomplishments or belittling them, frequently using labels such as "dummy" or "stupid," humiliating the child or being excessively critical, and excluding the child from family activities.

Isolating - cutting the child off from normal social experiences, preventing him from forming friendships. Leaving him in his room for long periods, prohibiting him from playing with other children, forbidding him to join after-school activities, clubs, etc., are examples.

Terrorizing - verbally frightening the child, bullying him, giving him the idea the world is a fearful and hostile place. It can include threatening the child with extreme punishment, setting expectations the child can't meet and then punishing him for not meeting them, teasing and scaring young children, frequent raging at the child, threatening to expose the child to humiliation or ridiculing him in public.

Ignoring - depriving the child of needed stimulation and responsiveness, stunting his emotional and intellectual development. This can range from total disregard of the child and his physical and psychological needs to not talking to the child, emotional coldness, or comments that keep the child at a distance or make him feel he doesn't belong, such as, "Don't climb in my lap. You will get my skirt all mussed up." or "I don't want to hear any crying. Go someplace else if you're going to cry." Not protecting the child from threats or not intervening when the child needs help are other examples of ignoring behavior. Sometimes a parent's psychiatric problem, such as depression, can make the parent neglect and ignore the child, the authors observe.

Corrupting - "mis-socializing" the child, encouraging him to engage in antisocial, destructive behavior, such as sexual activity, drug abuse, assaulting other children, stealing or other criminal acts, making the child unable to develop normally socially.

Studies of children in several different cultures who grew up with rejecting parents show they develop the same impairments despite cultural differences.

Rohner and Rohner found that children whose parents rejected them either by being hostile and aggressive or by being indifferent to them and neglecting them had impaired self esteem. They were either excessively dependent on their parents or were emotionally unstable, unresponsive, and tended "to perceive the world in negativistic terms," Garberino, Guttmann and Seeley noted. Children who are psychologically neglected in infancy don't thrive and may even die. As noted earlier, Dr. Rene Spitz, studying 91 infants in orphanages who were not picked up and given attention, found that more than one third died despite good food and medical care.

Garberino, Guttmann and Seeley cite 20 cases of children who were emotionally abused and describe the psychological consequences. One is Jon, age four, who was either teased in front of other people by his father or ignored by him. The father often put him in "double bind" situations in which the child couldn't win no matter what he did. When they played games Jon's father would call him an egghead if Jon won and a dummy if he lost. He'd call him over for a hug, then push him away when he responded and tell him not to be a sissy. The father in this case, according to the authors, terrorized his child by teasing him and also ignored him, because he paid no attention to him except to attack him. The psychological damage done to Jon from this kind of treatment is already evident, they report. Jon is tense and tongue-tied at home, sucks his thumb, has begun to stutter, and in nursery school alternates between being aggressive and whiny.

Another case they describe is Teddy, who lived in foster homes for five years, then returned to live with his mother and stepfather at age seven. The stepfather made Teddy ask permission for doing anything, even sitting down or going to the bathroom. He refused to let him play with other children or join the Boy Scouts. When he needed help with his schoolwork, his stepfather would ridicule him and call him stupid. The terrorizing, rejecting and isolating resulted in Teddy being rushed to the emergency room at age 11. He had swallowed a can of turpentine. Health care workers thought it was a deliberate suicide attempt.

SHAKING A BABY

Some parents get so provoked at a baby that won't stop crying that they shake the child, unaware of the tremendous damage this can do to an infant. Shaking a baby can cause brain damage, retardation, and even death.

Shaking an infant can result in blood clots on the brain, bone fractures, compression of spinal discs and eye hemorrhages, according to a study by three Yale physicians. Shaking an older child is also a poor method of discipline because it does not teach good behavior, but only builds anger and resentment.

THE THREAT OF ABANDONMENT

Sometimes a parent becomes so exasperated because her child is acting up in a store that she threatens to leave him there. Such threats should not be used, psychiatrists say, even though the parent doesn't mean them. And certainly a parent should never leave a small child alone or disappear even for a minute or two when he is with the child. Threatening or pretending to leave a child if he doesn't do something you want can terrify the child. Fear of abandonment is the greatest fear in a child because he knows he is absolutely dependent on his parent to live. Children who fear their parent might abandon them can suffer from anxiety, stomach aches, school phobia, nightmares and sleep problems, and other emotional problems. It has also been found that children whose parents die or leave them in childhood, or who are afraid a parent will do so if they don't behave perfectly, are more likely to suffer from anxiety or depression as adults and see the world as a fearful, frightening place.

YELLING

Although all parents are bound to raise their voice and yell at their children at some time or other when the children's behavior becomes particularly exasperating, regularly yelling at children is a poor way of disciplining them. After a while, they may just tune out the yelling and ignore the parent. However, the yelling may still be causing some psychological damage. Children whose parents yell at them a lot "usually end up feeling bad about themselves and their parents," says Colorado psychiatrist Foster W. Cline. If the parent who is yelling is the same sex as the child, the normal and healthy identification that a child should have with a parent as the child grows up may not occur. The child may subconsciously decide she doesn't want to be like Mommy.

SHAMING A CHILD OR DAMAGING
HIS SELF-ESTEEM

Making a child feel guilty because he is angry or afraid of something or doesn't measure up to your expectations can be psychologically damaging to the child, according to mental health experts. We all feel angry or afraid at times. Allow your child the right to such feelings and help him verbalize his feelings so he can work his way through them. Making him feel guilty because he is angry at his teacher or afraid of the dark will only make him keep his feelings inside himself. If he is often treated this way, ultimately he may turn these feelings of anger and guilt against himself for not living up to his parents' standards, or not being good enough, and the result may be depression, severe mental illness, maybe even suicide.

Shaming a child "makes him more angry and afraid and tends to exaggerate other conflicts between the parent and child," says Dr. Albert Solnit, the former director of the Yale Child Study Center and the commissioner of mental health in Connecticut. It may also cause the child to bury his fears, make him more anxious and increase his fear of separation from his parents, says the psychiatrist.

Shaming a child by punishing him in front of others is also damaging. It isn't an effective way to teach him anything because it will only make him more angry and resentful at you for embarrassing him. Sometimes parents shame a child for not living up to their expectations when their expectations are unreasonable for a child his age. The father who calls his four-year-old son a sissy because he is afraid of a big dog, and the mother at the beginning of this book who shamed her three-year-old daughter because she feared putting her face in the water are examples of this type of parent. Such parents can do significant psychological damage to their children.

Shaming a child by consistently giving him the idea that he is not living up to your expectations will damage his self esteem and can lead to an inferiority complex that can hurt him all through his life, according to mental health professionals. It can also make a child angry, resentful, guilty and depressed, and these feelings may go with him into adulthood. So if your child isn't living up to your expectations, find out why. If his marks aren't as high as you think they should be, for instance, perhaps he is in a class that is too advanced for him and he doesn't have the capacity to keep up. Instead of shaming him for his failures, find out why he is having difficulty and help him. Most important, reward him for his successes, and they will multiply.

EXTENDED SILENCE

This can cause psychological damage to the child in some circumstances, according to Solnit. If the mother does not talk to the child, but is still communicating her love and concern in other ways, for instance by giving him food and taking care of him, the child can probably weather extended silence for a few days, says Solnit. Also, an independent older child might be able to tell the parent it is not nice or kind of her not to talk to him, and just decide he will talk to his father or other family members instead. He had one case like this, says the psychiatrist. The child was able to weather his parent's extended silence because he had a warm relationship with his grandparents and was precocious. However, his relationships with his peers suffered and he did not socialize well with children his own age.

Some children, however, may feel so guilty if a parent does not talk to them for a long time that it will damage their self esteem and they may beg the parent to talk to them. In such cases, Solnit says the parent has "interfered developmentally" with the child. Most damaging probably is the parent who ignores and does not talk to the child because she is severely depressed or has other psychological problems. For the child, "it really means being cast loose," he says. In this case, "some friend or family member needs to help." The child's pediatrician might also be enlisted to talk to the mother and tell her she may be conveying things to the child by extended silence that could be damaging, Solnit comments. He could also encourage her to explain why she won't talk to the child, and suggest better ways of handling problems with her son or daughter.

PROLONGED ISOLATION

Although a time out, sending a child to his room for a short time for misbehavior, is a good form of discipline, leaving a child alone for a long period or locking a child in a room alone should never be done because isolation is frightening to a child. It suggests that his greatest fear, the fear of abandonment by his parents or caretakers, may be coming true. Prolonged isolation is a devastating type of discipline and a form of emotional abuse. It should never be used.

TELLING A CHILD HE IS BAD OR NO GOOD

If a child misbehaves, label the action as bad, not the child. Telling a child he is bad destroys his self worth and self esteem. Yet many parents, from the time the child is a toddler, make the mistake of telling him he is bad, instead of telling him what he has done is wrong. For instance, if your preschooler comes home with his friend's truck, and you find he just took it, don't call him a bad boy. Tell him people cannot take things that don't belong to them, and make him return it.

Psychologist H. Stephen Glenn and educator Jane Nelsen say generalized condemnation should be avoided in dealing with children. Instead, they advise using the sentence "I feel _____ about_____ because_____" to express displeasure with a child's behavior. This gives the child good clear feedback. For instance, "I feel upset when you leave your things all over the living room because it makes the house look messy if someone stops in," is a much more effective form of communication than "You're such a slob. Pick up your things." The first invites the child to do something that will make you feel better; the second produces resentment and often no action.

COMPARISONS WITH OTHER CHILDREN

Don`t compare a child with others, such as his sisters or brothers, and especially not in his presence, because if you indicate he is not measuring up, it can damage his sense of self worth. It makes a child unhappy and hurts his feelings if you compare him with someone else and indicate he isn't as smart or as popular or as likable as someone else. We know enough not to talk that way with our adult friends. We should be as considerate of the feelings of our children as we are of our friends. Also, sometimes a child isn't very good at something because he just hasn't matured enough or hasn't had enough instruction or practice. But if you tell him he is not as good Joe or Johnny at sports, arithmetic, etc., he is likely to accept that evaluation for a long time, and it may influence his direction in life.

SARCASM, RIDICULE, PUT-DOWNS AND ADULTISMS

Ridicule and sarcasm can do tremendous psychological damage to children. However, many people use put-downs and sarcasm on their children without being aware of it. Their parents used such comments, they hear other parents using them, so they don't see anything wrong with them. Most of us, in fact, have probably said to a child of ours, or heard another parent say, "You're always getting into trouble", or "Can't you do anything right?" or "You're such a crybaby!" But such comments can give a child a poor self-image. They may also become self-fulfilling prophecies. The child who "can't do anything right" will accept that assessment and perhaps become even more careless, and the "crybaby" even more babyish.

Psychologist Louise Bates Ames in one of her columns gave a whole list of putdowns that should be avoided in talking to children, among them:

"That was a stupid thing to do."

"Can't you remember anything?"

"You are totally helpless!"

"Look what you made me do!"

"I can't ever trust you."

"Can't you move any faster?"

"You have a terrible disposition."

Adultisms are similar to putdowns. Glenn and Nelsen call them a major barrier to effective communication with children. They define adultisms as statements in which an adult forgets what it is like to be a child and then expects the child to think, act and understand as an adult. Some examples they give in their book *Raising Children for Success* are "Why can't you ever...?" "How come you never...?" "How many times do I have to tell you?" "When will you ever grow up?" "Surely you realize.." Adultisms, they say, make children feel frustrated, hostile and angry. They can destroy a child's belief in his own capabilities and his significance.

Any comments such as put-downs or adultisms that imply that the child is ALWAYS untrustworthy, inattentive, helpless, slow, childish, or not acceptable for some other reason can be devastating to the child`s self esteem and make it more difficult for him to see himself as likable and worthwhile. Children who grow up not liking themselves and feeling they have little value grow into adults who are unhappy, insecure, and sometimes mentally ill. Because the concept a child has of himself generally lasts into adulthood, child specialists say putdowns which make a child feel inferior and unworthy can ultimately handicap him for life.

Instead of using sarcasm, putdowns, and adultisms, Glenn and Nelsen advise using language that indicates respect for the other person. Beginning with the phrase "What was your understanding of..." is a good way to do this. For instance, instead of "Why is your room always such a mess?" you might ask, "What was your understanding of what I meant when I asked you to clean your room?"

TELLING AND ORDERING

All of us do this to some extent. We tell our children what to do. "Put this away." "Pick up your toys." "Don't forget your books." "Do your homework." Some of this is probably unavoidable, especially when your children are small, and it is certainly the simplest way to deal with them. And many parents direct and boss their children because that's the way they were raised. But ordering children to do things doesn't work. It leads to resistance, anger, defiance because people of any age resent always being told what to do. Children will defy the directing parent one way or another just to show their independence and their annoyance at being treated like they can't think for themselves. They may just ignore the directing parent, not "hear" things she says, do things differently than they know she wants, pick up just a few things in their room, or maybe even actively rebel by answering back or taking out their frustration on a sibling or playmate. And children who are always being directed aren't likely to develop the initiative to do things on their own around the house. They may also find it difficult to make decisions on their own as they grow up.

How can you handle children without directing? Instead of giving a command, try making a suggestion. Instead of ordering them to do a task, encourage them to contribute to the household. For instance, in place of saying, "Pick up your toys," say something like, "Daddy is bringing a friend home for dinner. If you moved your trucks from the living room to your room so they don't trip over them, it would be a big help to me." Instead of ordering a small child to wash his hands, say "We wash our hands before eating so we don't get dirt on the food we are going to eat." With small children, the key can be letting them think they are making the decision. Instead of "Go to bed," you might say, "Do you want to take your teddy bear or your Mickey Mouse doll to bed now?" And don't order children around and then give in when they won't follow your orders, and do what needs to be done yourself. That just sets the state for continuing disobedience and arguments, and they will pay even less attention to your commands.

MAKING EXCUSES FOR A CHILD

Sometimes people think they are being good parents if they come to the defense of their child if he has done something wrong. For instance, if a teacher calls a parent and says Johnny hasn't been handing in his homework, and Johnny hears mother tell her "He doesn't have to do homework. He's only in grammar school. He needs time to play outdoors," this sends a strong message to Johnny that he can get away with all sorts of things. Mom will come to his defense. Teachers I have talked to say parents often do not make children take responsibility for doing their schoolwork. I myself in some church school teaching I did recently was told by one of my students that she didn't have to do an assignment I had given because her mother said she didn't have to do it. It's no wonder SAT scores are going down and so many children graduate from school without even being able to read and write decently. If parents don't make children take responsibility for something as vital as their education, it will hamper the young people all through life.

Making excuses for your child instead of letting him suffer the consequences of his behavior can seriously harm the development of good character in your child, say child behavior experts. One of the best ways a child learns to become a responsible, confident adult is by experiencing the consequences when he doesn't do what he is supposed to. If parents keep getting their child off the hook when he misbehaves in school, lies, steals, or whatever, the child will grow up more vulnerable to bad influences because he will figure someone will always set things right if he gets into trouble. Instead of making excuses for their child, parents need to sit down and talk with him if he gets into trouble, find out why, what his feelings are, and discuss how he can remedy the situation and prevent it from happening again.

When raising my own children, I saw a good example of the damage a parent can do by refusing to allow a child to suffer the consequences of his bad behavior. A neighbor's child took my son's tricycle without permission and broke it. When I went to speak to his mother about the situation, she was immediately on the defensive, insisted her son hadn't done it and wouldn't even call him out of the house to ask him about it. By her actions she prevented her child from learning valuable lessons about private property, about making reparations for damage he might do, and about taking responsibility for his actions. Her children were later in trouble with the police for vandalism.

STIFLING CHILDREN'S EMOTIONS

Comments like, "We don't get angry in this house" or "Go to your room if you can't talk nicely to your brother" are damaging to children because they squelch normal emotions. In time, children who are told what they can and can't feel will hide their emotions, deny them, or perhaps eventually not even recognize what they are feeling. A Connecticut woman, for example, grew up with a very domineering father who would insult her mother. She would get angry at him, but her mother always told her to be quiet and not say anything. By the time she was an adult, the woman did not even realize it when she was angry. She always seemed quiet and easy-going. But she was subconsciously turning her anger inward against herself and she finally suffered from a severe depression which required psychiatric treatment.

Children need to be able to learn about, understand and identify their own emotions so they can learn how to handle them. When your child is experiencing a negative emotion, such as anger or fear, what you need to do, child specialists say, is get him to talk about his feelings and what caused them, listen with empathy and understanding, label the emotion he is feeling, and, if possible, explain how you felt the same way in a similar situation. This prevents him from feeling guilty about his negative feelings and suppressing them instead of dealing with them.

For instance, if your son has just finished making a model airplane and his little brother comes over and plays with it and breaks it, he is likely to get furious and hit him. In this case, you should NOT hit your older son or tell him to go right to his room. Instead, show empathy for his emotions, but make it clear hitting is not allowed. You might say, "I can understand why you are angry at George. You put a lot of work into the airplane, and I'd feel angry too if someone broke something I made. But you cannot hit when you get mad. Then suggest that he go off by himself and calm down, and you will talk with him about the situation later. There is no point in trying to solve a problem when someone is full of anger. Later, after anger subsides, is the time for discussion and a clear setting of rules of behavior for both children, with the understanding of what the consequence will be if they do not adhere to the rules.

Adults can help children identify and control their emotions by asking them, if they come home upset about something, "What happened?" "What's the matter?" and similar questions. As they talk over upsetting situations with you, they will learn about different ways they can respond if they get angry, and they will develop self-control.

Adults can also help children learn about emotions by identifying their own emotions clearly. If you are angry about something, say "I'm really angry about..." and then talk about the situation more with whomever is involved when you have calmed down. And avoid blaming others for your emotions by using phrases like, "You made me mad" or "You upset me." If we take responsibility for our own emotions our children will learn to take responsibility for theirs.

DOUBLE BINDS

Putting a child in a "damned if you do, damned if you don't" situation can be tremendously damaging emotionally to the child, mental health experts say. Psychologist Donald Grinder gives an example: a child in the family is regarded as a misfit because he is not socially successful and has no friends. One day he comes home for dinner 15 minutes late because he was enjoying the company of a new friend, but is punished for it. The message that would come across to a psychologist from such a situation is that the family really doesn't want the child to develop social skills because he is needed at home to take care of his parents. It's possible, he says, that if a child in such a situation has social success and is off with friends a lot, the family will fall apart.

Some research has found that children could become schizophrenic if they are raised in a "double bind" environment, where they face conflict or censure in whatever choice of behavior they have.

FRIGHTENING A CHILD

Never say or do things that could frighten a child. Don't even say something you don't really mean but which could frighten a child if he took it literally, such as "I'm going to kill you if you do that again," or "I'm going to break every bone in your body." Frightening a child builds anxiety, timidity and insecurity that can last through his teens and adult life.

THREATENING

Parents who often use threats with their children can make children timid and submissive, or rebellious and hostile. A threat also tempts a child to test the parent—to do what he has been warned not to do, just to see if the threat will be carried out. In general, avoid the word "if" when you are telling a child a punishment will result from a certain behavior, says psychologist Donald Grinder because it makes the statement into a threat. For instance, saying, "If you are not home by 11:00 you won't be allowed to go out for a month" is a threat and a form of intimidation and is likely to provoke resentment in the child, particularly when you carry out the punishment. Rephrasing the statement slightly by using the word "when" instead of "if" can change the whole tone of the situation, Grinder notes. He recommends that parents tell the child something like, "When you are home on time this will happen... When you are not home on time, this will happen..." It gives him a choice and lets him choose the consequences, says Grinder, and it takes the onus off the parent and frees him from the "bad guy" role. (See *Shift the Locus of Control*, p. 46).

CRITICIZING AND BLAMING

Parents who frequently criticize and blame their children can do significant psychological damage to them. Comments like, "why can't you sit up straight?", "Your hair really looks a mess", ""You don't know what you're talking about", "If you failed the test, it's your own fault", can really hurt a child. Such negative communication makes children feel stupid, inferior, and bad. If used frequently, this type of communication damages a child's self-esteem and can lead to strong feelings of inferiority. It may even lead eventually to a full-fledged depression.

Criticism also makes children angry and may cause rebellious and defiant behavior. And it stops communication between parent and child because it teaches the child to keep his thoughts and feelings to himself. It also destroys closeness between child and parent because frequent criticism will drive a child to look elsewhere for people who will give him the acceptance and affirmation he needs. As a teenager, he may even turn to the very type of peer group that the parent with his criticism has been trying to keep him away from, such as youths who drink, take drugs, or get in trouble with the law.

It's good to have high expectations for your children, but constantly pointing out to them when they fail to meet your goals or standards will just make them feel inferior, resentful, and depressed. In fact, such an attitude may well prevent them from fulfilling the expectations you have for them. If they feel they can never satisfy you, before long they are apt to stop trying. Criticizing when children fall short of high standards also soon cuts off communication between the child and parent because who wants to confide in someone and be close to someone who is always saying you are not good enough?

Instead of expecting perfection, praise your children's accomplishments and improvements, no matter how small, and keep your mouth shut about what hasn't been good enough. For instance, if you want your small child to learn to set the table, and she puts the forks on the wrong side, don't criticize her for it, but praise what she has accomplished, saying something like, "you put a knife and fork at each place. That's good." Another time, before she begins, you can ask her to please put the forks on the left of the plate. Use the same attitude towards your child's schoolwork. Praise accomplishments; don't nag about mistakes and failures.

LAYING GUILT TRIPS ON CHILDREN

"Your father and I work our fingers to the bone so you can go to a private school, and you bring home papers like this full of mistakes!"

"Why didn't you call if you were going to be late for dinner? You know how I worry."

"Your teacher called and said you took another boy's lunch money. How could you bring such shame on our family?"

Comments like these lay guilt trips on children, and guilt trips can be psychologically devastating. The child gets the message from these that it's his job in life to always please and be grateful to his parents for all they have done for him. If he makes mistakes or doesn't do just what he is supposed to , he is conditioned to feel guilty.

Certainly a child needs to feel some guilt occasionally when he has deliberately done something he knows is seriously wrong. But loading a child with guilt feelings can make him grow up with so sensitive a conscience that he can become neurotic, say mental health experts. He is likely to live a restricted life as an adult and not be able to really feel free and able to enjoy life. He may even develop obsessive-compulsive behavior, phobias, or depression.

Further useful information on methods to avoid in managing children can be found in Thomas Gordon's book, *Parent Effectiveness Training*. He lists the "Typical Twelve" ways that about 90 percent of parents respond to their children—ways that he says can be destructive and stop communication.

Are You Driving Your Children Crazy?

Rosalyn was 13 when she was admitted to the Yale Psychiatric Institute. She wouldn't speak, was anorexic, had delusions of persecution and had tried several times to commit suicide. She was hospitalized after she climbed on the roof of her house one day and wouldn't come down because she was afraid of being poisoned.

George was a problem to his parents from the time he was born because he was an overactive, colicky baby. When he was three, his behavior was so bad that he was expelled from nursery school. He fought with other children and with his sisters, hit and bit them, and by the time he was admitted to elementary school his behavior was uncontrollable. At eight he had to be admitted to the Yale-New Haven Hospital Child Psychiatric Unit.

Rosalyn and George both had average or above average intelligence and no brain damage. They came from intact families and were not neglected, beaten or abused. What led to their mental illness, according to the psychiatrists who treated them, were damaging kinds of communication and discipline used by their parents.

Mental illness is widespread in America today. About one in every six Americans is suffering from mental illness in any six month period, and almost one out of four people will suffer from mental illness sometime in his or her life, according to a National Institute of Mental Health study. At least 15 percent of American adults, or 27 million people, need psychiatric treatment. Some 13 million people experience anxiety disorders, such as phobias, panic disorders and obsessions and compulsions. More than 9 million Americans suffer from depression in any six month period. An estimated 1.3 million people suffer from schizophrenia, and 7.5 million children suffer from mental illness.

Even very young children can suffer from depression, psychiatrists have found, and the problem is more common than people have thought. In such cases the children have been abused, severely neglected or subject to more than normal stresses. Dr. Javad Kashani and researchers at the University of Missouri-Columbia studied 109 preschool children and found one who was severely depressed and eight others that had some symptoms of depression. He found that stressful events were more common in the lives of the depressed children than in the lives of the other children.

Why does all this mental illness occur? More and more evidence is accumulating that many emotional and mental illnesses people experience may have their source in childhood, in the damaging patterns of communications their parents used with them. This doesn`t mean that if you occasionally lose your temper with your child, don't pay attention to what he's saying, or call him lazy or bad, that you are going to cause serious damage to his personality. It is a PATTERN of poor communication, of unreasonable expectations or damaging methods of discipline used over a period of years that can cause problems. Yet, how can this be true when research has linked many mental illnesses to abnormalities in brain chemicals?

BIOCHEMICAL CAUSES OF MENTAL ILLNESS

Psychiatrists know that many mental illnesses are caused by an imbalance in certain chemicals in the brain called neurotransmitters. These chemicals help transmit impulses from one nerve cell to the next. About 20 of these neurotransmitters have been discovered, and researchers know that too much or too little of some can result in a specific mental illness. For instance, anxiety disorders and panic attacks are linked to too much norepinephrine, a brain chemical produced in greater amounts when one is faced with a situation that demands fight or flight. Imbalances in other brain chemicals may also be also involved. Medications which restore the balance of some of these neurotransmitters, such as certain antidepressants and a combination tranquilizer-antidepressant called alprazolam, can relieve the symptoms of anxiety and panic attacks. In weeks, when combined with supportive therapy, they can cure people who have been housebound for years because of agoraphobia and panic attacks.

Norepinephrine imbalance is also involved in depression, but more important is a lack of sufficient serotonin, another brain chemical that helps produce calmness, serenity, and sleep. Dr. John Mann and other researchers from Cornell University Medical College recently showed that levels of norepinephrine and serotonin are reduced in the brains of people who commit suicide. They studied brain specimens collected during autopsies from 21 suicide victims and 21 people who did not commit suicide. The specimens were taken within 24 hours of each person's death. Other researchers have found lower levels of breakdown products of norepinephrine and serotonin in the fluid bathing the brain and spinal cord of suicide victims. Antidepressants can help restore the balance of these brain chemicals in people who are depressed or suicidal.

Schizophrenia, a serious mental illness in which the person sees or hears things that aren't there, has delusions, or becomes withdrawn and incoherent, in some cases is linked to an over-supply or overactivity of a third brain chemical, dopamine. Anti-psychotic drugs work by suppressing the activity of this brain chemical.

But how do the brain chemicals get out of balance? Some people think there may be a genetic reason, that certain genes or defects in genes could make a person vulnerable to particular mental illnesses. There is considerable evidence that mental illnesses such as depression, panic disorder, and schizophrenia tend to run in families, and that mental illness in general is found more frequently in families of a person with a psychiatric illness than in families of persons without mental illness. Richard Livingston, a psychiatrist at the University of Arkansas, recently studied families of 12 children suffering from anxiety disorders and 11 children suffering from depression. A social worker and a psychiatrist obtained information about 127 relatives of the youngsters and found that 70 percent of their parents, siblings, aunts or uncles suffered from some emotional disorder, with depression and alcoholism especially frequent.

Dr.Russell Noyes Jr. of the University of Iowa College of Medicine found that agoraphobia, the fear of leaving one's home, also runs in families. He found that 11.6 percent of relatives of agoraphobics were at risk for agoraphobia, and 30.8 percent of male relatives of agoraphobic were at higher risk for alcohol abuse. Studies by Myrna Weissman when she headed the Yale Depression Research Unit have also shown that depression runs in families.

But this doesn't mean these emotional disorders are necessarily inherited. Some may be genetically caused, but many can be caused or triggered by environmental influences.

ENVIRONMENTAL CAUSES OF MENTAL ILLNESS

Many cases of mental illness may well have their roots in destructive patterns of communication from parent to child passed down from generation to generation. Physicians know that a person's emotions and what is going on in his mind can affect the function of many organs and systems in his body, a relationship sometimes called the mind-body continuum. Fear and anxiety, for instance, cause a surge of adrenaline that leads to a rapid heartbeat, increased sweating, cold hands, and other manifestations of the primitive *fight or flight* response. "Almost every week I see typical examples of anxiety and emotional upheavals affecting many bodily functions. Emotional upset almost always leads to gastrointestinal, cardio-vascular or sexual difficulties," says psychiatrist Foster Cline. In childhood he says the mind-body continuum is even more important. Adults may say a situation makes them sick to their stomach, but a child often does develop a stomach ache if he is afraid to go to school for some reason. What the adult expresses sybolically in words, the child still experiences literally in his body. Thus, situations which cause stress, which provoke anger, sorrow, fear, frustration, may change the balance of complex neurotransmitter systems in the brain, leading to physical or psychological symptoms.

There is evidence from animal experiments that this can happen. French biochemist Paul Mandel has shown that levels of serotonin and another neurotransmitter called GABA can be changed in rats by altering their environment, and the change is accompanied by changes in their behavior. Both of these brain chemicals tend to calm or dampen emotions. Mandel found that rats that are genetically more violent have low levels of these chemicals. But he was also able to make both calm and violent rats more violent by stressing them by putting them in isolation. When he did this, he found that the GABA and serotonin levels dropped in both groups. When he put the rats in overcrowded conditions, the levels of these chemicals rose and they became more passive. And Mandel also discovered that the levels of these chemicals would drop and the rats become more violent if they just saw other rats acting violently.

There is no indisputable laboratory evidence that stress alters the brain chemicals of humans in a way that could impair their mental health, says Yale psychiatrist Selby Jacobs. But he comments, "most of us believe that repetitive developmental experiences and stresses can, in fact, influence brain physiology creating vulnerability for mental disorders in adulthood." And even though some people may be more vulnerable to mental illnesses because they inherited a particularly sensitive brain chemistry system, psychiatrists and psychologists now think that the illness itself is often triggered by environmental stresses, such as loss of a loved one, lack of parental love, or by years of stress through childhood because of the way a person's parents talked to him and disciplined him. Even parents who love their children sometimes use patterns of communication that are emotionally damaging because they don't realize it. Often they are just communicating with their children the same way their parents communicated with them.

Words can be devastating. The words parents speak to their children, the attitudes they exhibit toward them, the patterns of communication they use, have the power to make a child either happy and secure or anxious, depressed, or defiant. Many parents probably injure their children psychologically to some extent by the words they use although they have no idea they are doing this. New Haven pediatrician Robert LaCamera, speaking at a panel discussion on "The Abused Child" sponsored by Yale-New Haven Hospital in 1985, said that three times in the previous week there were parents in his office who were shouting at their child "Don't do that! You're no good." He called such communication "emotional abuse." Parents who threaten to leave their child in the doctor's office because the child is misbehaving are also abusing the child, said LaCamera, a clinical professor of pediatrics at Yale University School of Medicine.

Such methods of discipline, which damage the child's self-esteem or prey upon his greatest fear, the fear of being abandoned, are psychologically damaging, he asserted. "And such emotional abuse occurs all the time." But he believes that most parents who emotionally, or sometimes even physically abuse their children are not evil people. They do so because they are under stress, because they don't realize they are being abusive, or often because they don't know how to control the child and need help.

In some cases parental words and attitudes can be so damaging they can even drive a child to suicide or murder. Rosalyn, whose case was described above, was on constant suicide precautions at the Yale Psychiatric Institute yet managed to mutilate herself several times in suicide attempts. It took two and a half years of treatment before she reached the point where she didn't want to die.

What was so horrible in her family life that life itself became unbearable to her? It was not because Rosalyn was beaten, physically abused or sexually molested by a parent. According to Dr. Ira Levine, deputy director of the institute, it was because there was a major flaw in communication in the family.

"There was extreme domination by one parent with a subsequent sense that one couldn't speak in an open way about problems that were there," said Levine. Also, "there was an enormous emphasis within the family of everyone looking good to the outside," he added, so Rosalyn felt she could not talk about her feelings to anyone.

When she was admitted to the institute Rosalyn was diagnosed as suffering from extreme depression, anorexia nervosa, a borderline personality disorder and a learning disability even though she had a high IQ. Even after she was released from the hospital, she made several more attempts at suicide and had to be rehospitalized once. It took years of psychotherapy and medication, but she was finally cured, Levine said.

An even more bizarre and horrible case occurred in February, 1986, in New Britain, Connecticut. A 17-year-old youth, who had been an altar boy, stabbed his mother to death and also attacked his 15-year-old brother with a knife. His parish priest described the boy's mother as a "wonderful" person, but according to an Associated Press story, a neighbor said the mother "used to treat the boys as if they were mud under her feet. She was yelling at them all the time."

CHILDHOOD COMMUNICATION PATTERNS AND DEPRESSION

Jacobs has seen evidence from his patients that depression can be caused by events that occur during a child's developmental period. Sally, a woman about 30 with three children, came to Jacobs suffering from severe depression. He traced it back to patterns of communication in the family when she was growing up, even though she had a good relationship with her parents. Sally's father died when she was 13, but she pulled through that without any psychological problems. But after her mother died, she plunged into a deep depression and couldn't pull out of it.

"She had learned to deal with death when her father died with a stiff upper lip, don't-let-you-get-it down attitude," he said. Sally's mother was a tough woman who didn't express much feeling and she communicated the idea to Sally that "to show feelings was viewed as a failure," Jacobs said. But these methods didn't work when her mother died, and she felt guilty because she couldn't cope. Jacobs had to help her express her real emotions through psychotherapy and also treated her with antidepressant medication. Her spirits lifted and she was able to resolve marital problems her depression had caused and manage her children better.

"Developmental events can lay down emotional pathways and may result in biochemical processes that set the stage for reacting to experiences in adulthood in a certain way, specifically with depression," Jacobs observes. He has found that people who are depressed seem to share in common a certain way of thinking about experience and coping with problems. They all tend to exhibit a "learned helplessness." Psychiatrists used to think that the loss of a parent in childhood caused adult depression, but when cases didn't reflect this, they thought it was more likely to occur when there was an uncaring parent or a family situation that caused the child to fear the loss of his parent. "A child might learn living in this kind of family that it's not possible to make secure, nurturing relations with others," says Jacobs, and despair of doing so in adulthood.

Psychiatrist A.T. Beck says that a certain type of negative thinking precedes depression and can lead to it. This negative mind set has three aspects: the view that the person is inadequate, defective, deprived, worthless and thus lacks the capability to achieve happiness; the idea that the world is putting excessive demands on him and putting obstacles in his way so that he's bound to be defeated in trying to find happiness; and the idea that the future only holds continuing suffering and failure. Beck says this negative mind set has its origin in childhood experiences. Studies have also shown that children who are physically or verbally abused, or disciplined harshly, are more likely to develop depression later in life.

CHILDHOOD COMMUNICATION
PATTERNS AND ANXIETY

Yale psychiatrist Scott Woods also says that abuse and ridicule of a child often seem to be at the root of another psychiatric disorder in adulthood known as generalized anxiety disorder. It is the most common psychiatric illness. Symptoms include a constant feeling of tension, worry, feeling rushed and anxious. Physical symptoms can accompany it, ranging from headaches to stomach aches, diarrhea or constipation, sweating, insomnia and dizziness.

Other researchers agree. "A variety of environmental stressors occurring during childhood and later life—predominantly disturbances in interpersonal relationships—have been found to be responsible for the emergence and maintenance of anxiety," say Dr. Rudolf Hoehn-Saric and Daniel R. McLeod of Johns Hopkins University School of Medicine.

ANOREXIA AND PARENT-CHILD RELATIONSHIPS

Anorexia is also linked to disturbances in parent-child relationships. Anorexia is a sometimes fatal psychiatric disorder in which a person refuses to eat because she considers herself too fat even though she may be thin to the point of emaciation. Margo Maine found that it was most common in girls whose fathers were cold, distant and self-centered (see Chapter 8, page 84).

CHILDHOOD COMMUNICATION PATTERNS AND BEHAVIORAL PROBLEMS

Behavioral problems in children have also been linked to poor and inadequate communication on the part of their parents. Researchers have shown that behavioral problems occur more often in children of adolescent mothers, and behavioral scientists from the University of Rochester and Cornell University recently found out some reasons why. They studied 30 adolescent mothers between the ages of 15 and 20 and found that the younger mothers were less accepting of their children, less cooperative, less likely to speak to their children, and more impatient with the children's desire to explore their environment, which squelched the child's natural curiosity. They concluded that the behavioral and learning problems some children have in their early school years may have their roots in the poor communication and attitudes of an immature mother.

CHILDHOOD COMMUNICATION PATTERNS AND SOCIOPATHIC BEHAVIOR

Sociopathic behavior also has its roots in adverse childhood experience. British psychiatrist Michael Rutter says anti-social personality disorder almost always begins in childhood and is associated with the lack of loving maternal care. Colorado psychiatrist Foster Cline has worked for 20 years with severely disturbed children, children who lie, steal, set fires, sometimes even kill. These children got this way, he has found because they never bonded as an infant with at least one significant adult. This is usually because their parents neglected, abused, or abandoned them or for some reason did not give them the love and care they needed. (See pp. 15-17.)

CHILDHOOD COMMUNICATION PATTERNS AND SCHIZOPHRENIA

Even though there is substantial evidence from twin studies that there is a genetic basis for some schizophrenia, many psychiatrists believe that environmental stresses can trigger the illness in a person who has a biological tendency toward the disease. Many researchers have found that parents of schizophrenics use certain typical patterns of communication that are destructive and confusing. M.T.Singer and L.T.Wynne, who have studied communication patterns in families of schizophrenics since the 1960s, believe that "the parents of schizophrenics show communication deviances that have permanently impaired their children's ability to focus attention on the meaning of verbal communications and which predisposed these children to the development of schizophrenia." They found two typical patterns of deviant communication by the parents. Their communication tended to be either vague or fragmented, meaning they did not complete what they were going to say.

Dr. Marvin Goldstein at the University of California at Los Angeles studied children who developed schizophrenia even though their parents had no mental illness. He found two typical ways in which the parents talked to the children. First, their communication was disordered. "They would stop a thought in the middle, appear to disqualify things just said or contradict themselves," he said, so that it left family members "confused about what was real and not real." Second, they used a negative method of disciplining. "When a child caused a problem," Goldstein said, "instead of criticizing his behavior they would verbally attack the child, telling him he was bad or stupid and damaging his self-esteem."

Rutter says there is evidence that certain childhood experiences may play a part in schizophrenia, manic depressive disorder, anti-social personality disorder and emotional disorders of children. Although researchers believe there may be a genetic predisposition to schizophrenia, it isn't genetically caused because only 10 percent of schizophrenics have a schizophrenic parent, Rutter reports. He says it has been shown that "poor family communication combined with hostile or critical patterns of interactions" makes schizophrenia worse. "Accordingly, it seems plausible that intrafamilial hostility and poor communication might also be implicated in the genesis of the disorder."

A professor emeritus of psychiatry at Yale, Dr. Theodore Lidz, also corroborates the connection between disordered parent-child communication and schizophrenia. "We've never seen a schizophrenic patient who's come from a reasonably stable family. There's always a disturbance in the communication in these families," he said. Dr. Joaquim Puig-Antich also comments that "critical, hostile, or overly involved relatives may contribute to a (schizophrenic) patient's relapse" and notes that some psychiatrists are trying to prevent relapses in such patients through family therapy and educational programs with family members.

I have referred to all these research studies not to worry parents unnecessarily, but to point out how important the words are that we speak to our children. But parents and the words they use are not the only factors that affect the way a child will turn out. Psychologists and psychiatrists point out that many other things have an influence on the development of the child's personality, such as school, friends, television, the social level of the family, and in fact, the child himself.

THE CHILD'S TEMPERAMENT AFFECTS COMMUNICATION

Children are born with different temperaments, a number of studies have shown, and the child's temperament has an influence on how parents react to him and interact with him. Investigators A. Thomas, S.Chess and H. Birch have found three general types of temperament in children. Some are easy-going, others respond slowly to things and with a low intensity, and the third kind are *difficult* children. These children tend to cry a lot, seem generally unhappy, are irregular in feeding and sleeping schedules and are slow to accept new foods or changes in routines. Yale psychologist Edward Zigler, in describing these findings about temperaments in children, says the different temperaments are observable in newborns and stabilize by about four months. And he notes, "Just as a parent's behavior influences that of the child, a child's behavior influences that of the parent." Difficult children, for instance, "may arouse negative responses in parents which may, in turn, have detrimental effects on the children's psychological development."

George's case is a good example of this—the child mentioned at the beginning of this chapter. Granted he was a difficult child. He had slightly abnormal brain waves that resulted in an occasional mild seizure and was overly active, but Dr. Joseph Woolston, director of the psychiatric unit, said the major factor contributing to his out-of-control behavior was his mother's way of disciplining him. "His mother would hold back punishment until she got very angry. Then she would yell, scream and overdo it," he said. "But then she would apologize profusely, kiss him, and undo the punishment."

A handsome child with brown hair and dark eyes, George came to the psychiatric unit with virtually every label in psychiatry from conduct disorder to schizophrenia, Woolston said. His parents had tried everything from food allergy evaluations to megavitamin diets to individual therapy in an attempt to improve his behavior. He also was put in a class for emotionally disturbed children, which helped, but when he was put back in a regular classroom he fell apart again and was put in a another psychiatric hospital for a week. His behavior only got worse, and finally his parents brought him to Yale-New Haven Hospital.

George was in the children's psychiatric unit there for nine weeks. At first his behavior was so bad that the staff couldn't get him to sit in a chair for a five-minute time out when he got out of control, a typical method of discipline used. He had to be taken directly to the unit's quiet room when he became unmanage-able, a small room with just a rug and carpeted bench with windows through which the staff could check on him. "He had temper tantrums at first, but after a few days he began to accept it," Woolston said. George also liked the reward cards the hospital used on which his behavior goals were listed and his behavior rated daily. Good behavior earned stars, which could be cashed in for rewards. Woolston and his staff also worked with George's parents to show them better ways of handling their son. And when the parents visited, which was required, they were left in charge of their son, although staff members were nearby to call on if needed. "The turning point came when he put himself in the quiet room one day," Woolston said. And when George left the hospital he insisted that his parents create a quiet room for him at home.

Woolston had noticed that George never looked at people when he first came to the hospital, but by the time he was discharged he was looking at people directly. Woolston asked him why he had avoided looking at everyone before. "He told us he knew everyone was angry at him, so he couldn't bear looking at them. But now he was sure they were not angry, so he could bear to look at them." Although George needed a special education classroom and he and his family had to continue therapy, his behavior was controllable both at home and in school once his parents were shown better methods of communication and discipline.

Zigler warns that parents of difficult children must be careful that their own behavior doesn't become as negative as their children's, or a vicious cycle may result which can lead to increasing tension and maladjustment in children. He says an important principle in parenting is that child-rearing methods should be adapted to each child's temperament. (See pp. 48-49.)

THE STAGE MOTHER TYPE OF PARENT

Parents who use their children to fulfill their own unachieved ambitions can also cause emotional damage in their children. The stage mother who drives her daughter to become an actress, the jock father who was a football star but has no use for a son who can't make the team and would rather spend his time on music —these parents can be tremendously damaging to their children's self-esteem and cause them psychological problems later in life. Dr. Earl Patterson, a Meriden psychiatrist, calls such children *tool children* because they are used as tools by their parents to build their own self-esteem and are not valued for what they are themselves. Dr. Benjamin Spock, the noted pediatrician, believes that fathers who run Little Leagues and similar organized sports for children may cause emotional damage to the children on the team by harsh criticism and pressure, and urges downplaying such competitiveness.

Arnold is an outstanding example. A very bright, college educated young man, he was so depressed he was suicidal when he came to see Jacobs and had to be hospitalized. His first bout with depression occurred, he said, when he realized in his early teens that he was a homosexual. He knew this was totally unacceptable in his family. The family was Catholic and his father was severe, authoritarian, and an athletic type who was an executive in a major corporation. He never provided any affection. Despite his son's scholastic achievements, when Arnold didn't show an interest in sports, his father "disinvolved himself from the young man" said Jacobs, and Arnold "felt he was fundamentally flawed." His mother had psychiatric problems, was distant and uninvolved with Arnold.

Unable to accept his homosexuality, Arnold became involved with women as a teenager and got a 16-year-old-girl pregnant. She died in childbirth. Arnold 's father adopted the child, but was so horrified he treated Arnold "basically as a nonentity. He was totally ostracized," said Jacobs. He was treated as if he was not the father of the child and had no say in what happened to him. "It tells you a lot about how this man was treated through his childhood," said the psychiatrist. Arnold revealed his homosexuality to his family in his 20s and experienced more rejection. What finally triggered his suicidal depression was the death of his homosexual lover.

Another example of the damage pressuring parents can do was revealed in a letter to Ann Landers from a California reader in April, 1986. "My brother was pushed to incredible limits by our parents," she wrote. "From the day he was born, no matter what he did, it was never good enough. He finished second in his class at Yale. When he was one year away from getting his Ph.D in physics, my mother told him, 'I want to introduce you to my friend, but don't tell her you don't have your Ph.D. yet. I said you already have it.'" Her brother, said the letter writer, "developed severe psychological problems and has been institutionalized for the last four years."

Recently a New York City prosecutor who became famous for prosecuting drug cases was found to be addicted to cocaine himself and to have stolen money and even cocaine that was evidence in his cases because of his drug habit. He was tried and imprisoned. He and his parents were interviewed on a television program. From the time that he began school the prosecutor had been at the top of his class. He was a workaholic. He turned to drugs, he said, because he never felt worthwhile for who he was, only for what he did and could achieve. Where did he get such a poor sense of self worth? The program gave a hint. The lawyer is reading and studying in prison now and trying to help other addicts. When asked if he could forgive him, his father, who used to introduce the young man as "My son, the prosecutor," answered, "Maybe, but he would have to work harder."

OTHER CAUSES OF MENTAL ILLNESS

There are other childhood experiences besides lack of love, poor parent-child communication and poor methods of discipline that can also lay the groundwork for certain mental illnesses. Chief among these are loss of a parent and separation of parents. British psychiatrist Michael Rutter says researchers have found evidence that parental loss in childhood predisposes a person to suffer depression as an adult because it makes him vulnerable to later stress. Parental loss sets the stage for a feeling of helplessness and an inability to control bad events that happen to them which contributes to low self esteem. But Rutter says more recent studies indicate that it is not parental death so much that sets the stage for adult depression, but rather "a serious lack of adequate parental affection and loving care in childhood that predisposes to depression." Other researchers have found that separation from a parent or the death of a parent can contribute to panic disorder later in life, although heredity and a biological vulnerability may also play a part.

Anti-social personality disorder, which usually starts in childhood, is most likely to persist if it starts early, occurs in different settings, if peer relationships are poor, and if there are severe abnormalities in the way the family functions, such as lack of affection, strife, and poor supervision in the family, says Rutter. In addition to lack of affectionate maternal care, he said researchers found this disorder was also linked with loss of the natural mother, usually through foster placement. One of the researchers Rutter cites, J. Bowlby, believes that an upbringing that lacks secure loving relationships creates a mind set that makes a person lack self worth and blame himself for later losses and failures to establish affectionate relationships. Such research, says Rutter, suggests the possibility "that adverse experiences in childhood may have long-term effects."

All this doesn't mean that every case of mental illness has its roots in the availability of parental love and support or the way the individual's parents communicated to him or acted toward him as a child. In some cases brain injury, neurological disorders, and biochemical abnormalities that occur for no apparent cause can lead to mental illness. But there is enough evidence from years of study by mental health professionals that a person's mental health as an adult often hinges on the words his parents speak to him as a child.

Some mental health experts now believe it is possible to prevent mental illness by reducing stress and by helping people develop competence early in life. Parenting classes, parent-aide programs for parents at risk of being abusive, programs to prevent drug and alcohol abuse, and this book are part of a movement to prevent mental disorders through public awareness and community education.

The Importance of Fathers

A child needs a father as well as a mother for the best and fullest development of his personality. This doesn't mean a father who just spends a few minutes with him in the evening and whose communication is mainly directing and correcting. It means a father who is deeply involved in the care of his child from the time he is born, who helps bathe, change and feed him and spends time cuddling and holding him. This early interaction is important in making a man feel confident as a father and in fostering warm and loving feelings for his child, say child behavior specialists. It is also important for his wife, because she needs a break and someone else to take over for a while after spending most of her time caring for a demanding infant.

A father is also vital as a child grows to set limits on his behavior in a firm but just way, to give love and help, to educate, and to be an example for his child. A father also helps children develop their sexual identity. A son learns what a man is like from his father, and a daughter's future relations with men—what she thinks of them and how she acts towards them—have a basis in the relationship she had with her father.

Fathers are just as important as mothers in influencing the development of their child's personality, psychologists are beginning to realize. They have found that young infants bond to their fathers as well as to their mothers. This bonding begins about the middle of the first year of life, even though the average father interacts with the infant only about 10 hours a week, according to Yale psychologist Edward Zigler and Rose Cascione. But the interaction between fathers and their children is different. Mothers tend to play conventional, gentle games like peek-a-boo, while fathers play more vigorous and physically active games. Mothers also hold their babies more to care for them, but fathers were likely to hold them "just to play with them or to satisfy the babies' desire to be held." This difference, he says, may broaden the children's social and intellectual abilities.

Zigler and Cascione say research by a number of investigators has shown that fathers treat the sexes differently from mothers, especially after age one. They seem more attentive to sons and are less involved with daughters, and as a result children develop a preference for the same sex parent. This may help the child develop his sense of gender. They note that other research has revealed that boys may become deficient in adjusting to their sex roles when their fathers are absent in infancy.

Zigler and Cascione say that fathers "who are highly nurturant enhance masculinity in sons and femininity in daughters." They note, "Girls with absent fathers may not develop an adequate female role and as adolescents may have difficulties in their relationships with men." Another study they cite found that maladjusted children who are very aggressive tended to have weak fathers, but children who were shy and had inferiority feelings had dictatorial fathers who were insensitive to their children and their feelings.

They note that fathers can also compensate for the limitations of the mother. A study was done of how three-year-old children whose parents had different parenting styles adjusted to nursery school. The investigators found that children had a difficult adjustment whose parents were not very nurturing, but were either very strict or very lenient. But when either the mother or father was really nurturant, the adjustment was much better.

Both boys and girls need fathers who are warm and affectionate, but it has been found that a daughter especially may suffer psychological damage if her father is often absent and is unaffectionate and unconcerned about her. A recent study has found that lack of a father's love may be linked to anorexia, a strange illness affecting many young people today, especially girls. Anorexics see themselves as too fat even though they may be skin and bones, and they starve themselves, sometimes to death. Margo Maine, assistant clinical director of the Eating Disorder Service at Newington Children's Hospital, studied 39 anorexic adolescent girls and found that 36, or 92 percent, said their relationship with their father was distant. The girls felt their fathers were absorbed in themselves and unable to deal with feelings. The girls all had low self esteem and were more sensitive to the culture's emphasis on thinness and were more likely to see emaciation as beautiful, she said. Maine acknowledges that other factors play a part in a complex disorder like anorexia. But the psychotherapist believes love and acceptance by her father can help prevent such disorders and help a daughter "see herself as OK no matter what she weighs."

Good fathers have several basic traits, according to psychiatrists and psychologists. They spend lots of time with their child. Good fathers are home with their children most evenings from the time they are infants and play with them regularly and enjoy them. They also know how to communicate with their children, to listen to them, empathize with them, understand their point of view. They don't lecture and criticize. They go to events at their children's school and sometimes take their children to doctor visits, music lessons, Little League games, etc. Good fathers do not discipline their children harshly, they understand they won't always obey, and they treat their children fairly. They earn their children's respect by setting a good example, listening to them, having time for them, and loving them. Good fathers raise children who are responsible, capable, well adjusted, and who are likely to be more successful academically than children of absent or uninvolved fathers. Studies have shown that children who have attentive fathers are often half a grade ahead of their classmates in their ability.

Some Special Helps for Working Parents

When both parents work full time, raising children can be a real challenge. They come home from work tired, yet they are faced with household chores, meals to prepare, and children who also are tired and demand and need attention and love. How can working parents manage everything and still give their children quality time? Noted pediatrician T. Berry Brazelton has some suggestions:

- Make it a point to get close to your children as soon as you get home. Sit with them in a rocking chair or hold them on the couch and talk about your day.

- Involve your children in what you do when you get home, so that you all have as much time together as a family as possible. Let them share in chores, housework, meal preparation as soon as they are old enough, so you feel you are all working together to accomplish what needs to be done.

- Set aside some time on the weekend for a family celebration or some special family fun.

- Make sure you spend time alone with each of your children at least once a week doing something special with the child. Remind the child during the week about the special time coming up.

When children are tired at night and when they have been away from their parents all day, they are more likely to fall apart, act up, and behave wildly. Working parents sometimes feel guilty about disciplining their child when this happens, but the child needs limits, says Brazelton. But discipline should be teaching, not punishment. Holding and calming a disruptive or hyperactive child, making him take a time out and isolating him from the rest of the family for a short time are the forms of discipline Brazelton recommends. After this, he says parents should sit down and discuss why they have had to set limits and stop the way the child was behaving.

Morning can be difficult also. Children do not want to be separated from their parents, and so may dawdle, refuse to dress or eat breakfast to put off leave-taking. But the parents are under pressure to be at work at a certain time, so mornings are likely to end in a hassle with them screaming at the kids and the children in tears. To help make mornings easier, Brazelton says:

- Get up earlier.

- Spend some time with the children, sitting and talking with them before having them get dressed.

- Help them choose what they will wear.

- Talk out feelings about the separation ahead and remind them you will all be together again at the end of the day.

- When you are ready to go, gather up the children, but expect they will still be uncooperative and angry because you are leaving them.

- Don't sneak out of the house or day care center where you are leaving your child. Always tell the child you are going and say goodbye.

Getting children to go to sleep is also harder for working parents. Because working mothers do feel guilty about leaving their children, they may find it hard to be firm about bedtime, observes Brazelton. They also may feel they need to go to the child every time he cries out at night. But the pediatrician says children have to learn to go to sleep by themselves and sleep through the night. A regular routine before bedtime and a special comforting object, a lovey blanket or stuffed animal, will help the child get to sleep. As for waking at night, he advises parents to wait five minutes, and if the child doesn't calm down, then go in, find out what's wrong, comfort and reassure him and give him his lovey blanket or animal to get him back to sleep. But child behavior specialists say don't take the child in your bed and don't get in the habit of giving him a bottle or letting him get up, walk around and play. (For further information see Sleep Problems.)

Family meetings can be a big help for all families, but especially for families in which both parents work. It's a good idea to hold a family meeting once a week to air any problems that have been bothering family members and to resolve any conflicts, according to a number of psychologists and child education specialists.

For each week's meeting there should be an agenda of topics family members think need to be discussed. Some families keep a sheet of paper on their bulletin board or refrigerator door on which any family member can write down something he thinks the family needs to talk about. Difficulties with siblings, chores that don't get done, problems at school, plans for weekend excursions or trips are all subjects that might be discussed at a family meeting. One person is in charge, usually mother or father, but children who are old enough can also be given turns leading the meeting. It's important to give each family member a chance to talk during the meeting about anything of concern to him. The family discusses each problem or concern that is raised and comes up with possible solutions, then decides on one that will be tried. It's nice to end the meeting by having some cake or ice cream or doing something that's fun, like playing a game together.

Family meetings give children a sense of importance and control over their environment which helps them develop self esteem and a sense that they are capable people. They build confidence, mutual respect, and problem-solving abilities. They also make children feel they are part of the family and build a sense of unity as a family. In addition, these meetings are useful to make rules for the family and to solve behavior problems that arise in raising children. And they also teach a family to work together. "Families that have regular family meetings in which the children are actively involved have a substantially lower rate of vulnerability in the human service, criminal justice, and social welfare systems," say psychologist H. Stephen Glenn and educator Joel W. Warner.

PART II

COMMON PROBLEMS THAT ARISE WITH CHILDREN AND HOW TO HANDLE THEM

Anger

Anger in children should not be punished and should not be ignored, but it must be dealt with satisfactorily when it occurs or it can cause problems throughout life, say experts in health and mental health. Dorothy Noyes Sproul, public health expert, believes there is "no single fact more important than this for preventive psychiatry and the future of mankind."

Anger is a perfectly natural reaction in a child and in fact begins to occur soon after birth. The loud, insistent crying of a baby that usually occurs every few hours is really anger. Psychiatrist Foster Cline calls it a "rage reaction." The baby "rages" because something is wrong—he's wet, uncomfortable, or usually hungry—and his cries are his only way of getting something done about the situation. It is vital that parents respond to these regularly occurring bouts of crying and do what is necessary to calm the baby, whether it be giving the infant a bottle, changing him, rocking and soothing him. It is through this early interaction that the baby learns to trust and love. He senses that his wants will be taken care of, that the world is an okay place, and he develops a feeling of security. If the parents don't respond to the baby's needs, this rage reaction can persist in later years in the form of severe emotional or behavioral problems or sociopathic behavior (see pp. 15-17).

How do you help a child older than an infant to deal with and get rid of anger and other negative feelings? If a child a year or two old seems to get angry a lot, try to figure out what things provoke his anger and then reduce such situations as much as possible. Children this age generally get angry if you stop them from doing something they want to do, if they try to do something and can't manage it, or if you try to get them to do something they don't want to do. So childproof your house as much as possible so you don't have to stop your child from touching things, and help him with things he can't manage. If your toddler gets angry when you try to dress him, acknowledge his angry feelings by saying something like, "You're angry because you don't want to get dressed." Then hug him and distract him with a song or story or something to look at while you get the job done. In general, calm him by cuddling him and distracting him rather than getting upset with him, yelling at him or telling him he's a bad boy.

How do you handle anger in an older child? First, never tell a child he shouldn't be angry, child development experts say. This will make him feel ashamed or guilty about having angry feelings and will cause the child to suppress his anger rather than talk about it and learn how to handle it. And it will just result in more negative feelings because he will have guilt as well as anger to deal with. Also, parents should not be overly strict and moralistic and reject the child, tell him he is bad, or punish him because he is angry. Nor should they say they don't want him around and send him to his room. And obviously you should not hit a child when he gets angry because this just shows him you have also lost control and when he's bigger it's all right to hit when he gets angry. A parent also should not try to squelch a child's anger to avoid a scene if the child is angry at the other parent or some other relative. All these approaches will just have the same result—they will make the child suppress his anger, and it will cause trouble later. A child who is forced to suppress his anger may become a submissive adult who may not even be aware of his emotions. But these suppressed emotions are likely to result in depression or other psychological problems in the course of his life, mental health experts have found.

What should the parent do when confronted with an angry child? First, label the emotion, with a comment like "You're angry about something." Then, child development experts say, ask "Why?" or "What happened?" Listen carefully to the child's explanation because by doing so you acknowledge that you think his feelings are important and you allow him to vent some of his anger verbally. Avoid the temptation to interrupt with comments that make him feel guilty about his anger, such as "You shouldn't have done that," or "You're too sensitive." Nursery school director Dolores Andreucci stresses that it's very important to find out what the child is angry about and "take it from there."

After finding the reason, let the child know that you would also probably feel angry in the same situation. Hamden nursery school director Louise Miller and her teachers suggest saying "It's all right to be angry. Sometimes I am too, but we cannot hurt others (if the child has struck out in anger)." Or you could say, "I am sorry that you're angry, but I love you."

Then tell the child that after he feels calmer you will talk with him about how to deal with the person who provoked the anger and how to handle such a situation next time. Before you do, however, you need to help the child get rid of his charged-up, angry feelings. One of the best ways is by physical activity. You might suggest that he whack the ground hard with a stick or bat, throw a ball hard against the wall, or run around the house half a dozen times. Punching an old pillow, stuffed animal or punching bag can help, especially if he pretends he is hitting the person who made him angry. But it must be made clear that hitting the person who caused the anger is not acceptable. You could also give the child some crayons and suggest that he make a picture to show how mad he feels.

Laura Spencer of the Stork Club Child Care and Development Centers in Connecticut stresses that when a child is displaying feelings of anger it's important for the parent or adult supervisor to go to him and express a desire to help him. "Communication is the pathway for ventilating such an emotion. Through communication the child is beginning to deal with the feeling, and with the help of a teacher, the child should feel much better," she says. She also finds that a group discussion is useful after the problem is resolved, with children sharing what makes them angry and how they should deal with it.

It's important for your child to learn to express his anger with words. If he comes home angry at someone, suggest he pretend the person is standing there and tell him what he thinks of him. If he uses swear words, tell him that's okay, but he should go off by himself to do so because most people don't like to hear those words. Encourage him to tell people when he feels angry at them (even when he feels angry at you, his parents), rather than hit someone or sulk or throw things around. You can't allow him to carry his angry feelings into wild behavior, such as hitting and kicking others or throwing things around because a child will only feel guilty and frightened if his parents let him get out of control. But remember, it's important to show your child you accept him even when he has angry feelings and he's not risking the loss of your love by becoming angry. Your big job as a parent is to guide him into acceptable ways of expressing his anger.

After the child has vented his angry feelings and has calmed down, you need to talk to him about how to handle the problem that provoked the anger. Discuss what happened and the reason for his anger. Have him think of other ways he could have acted to prevent the situation that led to his anger, or other ways he could have acted when he became angry. If another child makes him angry, for instance, he could let the other person know how he feels and make it clear that he does not like what the child said or did. He might ask the other child then to explain why he acted as he did. Or he could just pay no attention and walk away. Or he could ask the child to try and work out a solution to their problem with him if a disagreement between them makes him angry. If another child is repeatedly taunting your child or making him angry, however, you or your child's teacher need to step in and make the other child understand such behavior will not be tolerated.

ANGER AND OUT-OF-CONTROL BEHAVIOR

Many professionals who work with children suggest a "time out" for children who become angry and exhibit rough or out-of-control behavior. This can be done by having the child sit in a chair away from other children in the room, or it could be done by sending him to another room until he calms down. Josee M. Bancroft, a day care center director, says time out should be used only if the behavior doesn't stop after the adult has explained why it is not appropriate. Then when the child returns to the group, the adult should discuss the behavior of the child and why it was not good. Calling a time out is especially recommended if there is a power struggle between the child and an adult.

Dr. Joseph Woolston, director of Yale-New Haven Hospital's children's psychiatric unit, uses a series of time-outs with children in the unit. When out-of-control behavior first occurs, his staff will remove the child from the group and have him sit in a chair for five minutes. This is done not as punishment, but as an attempt to "interrupt escalating behavior," he says. If this doesn't work, the child will be put into the quiet room, a small carpeted room with a bench and two windows through which the staff can look in. If necessary, the door is locked. The child may yell and scream, but not get attention. Occasionally a severely ill child that gets completely out of control and is injuring himself in the quiet room may finally have to be restrained in a bed by a staff member until he quiets down. But along with the time-outs the staff gives each child a daily reward card and increasing freedom as his behavior improves. The card has three or four behavior goals the child is working on. He's rated three times a day, earns stars for good ratings, and for a certain number of stars gets a reward.

Most of the children admitted to the hospital unit have many problems, "but the most common thing that gets them in is out-of-control behavior," says Woolston. Combined with this often are inability to pay attention and learning disabilities, but some also have a neurological disorder or other medical problem. Woolston insists that the parents be involved in the treatment of their children because he says an important goal of the treatment is "to teach parents to communicate with their children better." He and the staff spend about two weeks meeting with the parents, learning about their child's problems and their method of interacting with him. When parents visit, they are completely in charge of their child, but they are prepared for this by coaching from the treatment team in how to handle the child. If parents and the child's school are not involved, he says "the likelihood positive changes will be generalized after hospitalization is very small."

Woolston says parents of such children may not be to blame for the child's psychiatric problem, but by the way they handle the child "may encourage it to continue." He notes that many of these children are difficult to handle because they are active, distractible, easily angered. Parents need to "put a lid on the child's behavior very early," and deal with them firmly and consistently, but often they don't know how, says the psychiatrist. They try to be "nice people" and tell the child over and over to behave until suddenly one of the parents loses his or her temper "and mirrors the child's loss of control," and the situation just grows worse. "The problem is circular," he says.

A wild, out-of-control child is really a frightened child, according to Woolston. Children he sees, he says, "are afraid there are no limits to their behavior. We show them no matter how out of control the child gets, we have a way of keeping him in control." He says his staff usually has to impose control on a child once or twice. After that, "we tell them what our response will be, and it's totally up to the child."

He says the methods he uses on children with psychiatric problems are also useful for parents to use on normal children who become very angry.

A bulletin from a teachers' center at Fairfield University suggests good ways to handle a preschooler who is angry enough to act out in a way that could be dangerous:

Move physically toward the child and make eye contact.

Describe what you see and don't give orders. For instance, "You really are angry."

Ask: "Do you need my help to keep you safe?"

Give directions about what to do, not what not to do. For instance, say, "blocks are for building," rather than "blocks are not for throwing."

Help him physically to regain control by removing him from the area if necessary, with words like "I'm not going to let you hurt anyone," or "I'll help you gain control."

Children who have frequent angry outbursts may need professional help because abnormalities in brain chemistry may be contributing to the problem and medication may be needed. Family therapy may also be required because tensions within the family or unsatisfactory ways of dealing with the child by the parents may be provoking the anger.

ANGER BETWEEN PARENTS AND CHILDREN

There are bound to be times when your child gets angry with you—when you forbid him to do something he wants, take away a privilege, perhaps when you don't keep a promise. What do you do? First, try to prevent anger in your child by not being overly strict and dictatorial. Instead of always telling your child to do something, ask politely and try to give your child choices when you can, for instance about what family chores he would rather do. Show your child the same respect you want him to show you. If he is angry, take the time to hear his side of the story and try to see his point of view. Keep calm and don't raise your voice even if you start to get angry at him. And let him know it's all right for him to get angry at you because you get angry at people too. If he speaks disrespectfully to you, don't slap him. Just make it clear you don't want him to talk that way to you even if he is angry.

Psychologist Thomas Gordon recommends that when you get angry it's useful to give "I" messages that center on the way you feel and why, a process he describes well in his noted book *P.E.T. Parent Effectiveness Training*. Some child behavior specialists, such as Dr. Foster Cline, Dr. H. Stephen Glenn and Jane Nelsen, suggest using the verbal pattern "I feel...about or when.....because." For instance, "I feel annoyed when you make so much noise because I can't hear Dad on the telephone." Or "I get upset about your leaving your dirty dishes around after a snack because it makes me feel that you consider me like the maid in the household." By using this technique Cline says you are not telling the child what to do, but it's pretty clear to him what he should do if he has any consideration for the way you feel. If you have been loving and considerate to your children, it is likely that they will be considerate of your feelings too. Encourage your children to use this same pattern for telling you about their feelings.

It is as important for parents to control their anger around children as it is for them to teach their children self control because parents who can't control anger produce children who can't either. If you do lose your temper and say things that hurt your child, apologize, and require the same from your child if he does this. It's not going to undermine your authority if you apologize, psychologists say. On the contrary, you are setting a good example for your children if they lose control or make a mistake.

Bad Children

It's almost inevitable that sometime in your child's life he is going to encounter "bad" children—children who fight, bully other children, lie, swear, take other children's things, and generally make life unpleasant for those around them. This can occur in the neighborhood, at school, at camp, in the playground, or just about anywhere children get together. The problem is what to do about the situation.

When your child is a preschooler, don't feel you have to go run to your child's defense the first time another child gives him a shove because your child has to learn how to deal with such a situation himself. But if another child hits your child and hurts him or seems to bully and push around other children quite a bit, you need to take action. He must be told firmly that such behavior is not allowed in the group. Try to shift the locus of control to him (see p. 46) by telling him it is his choice whether to behave with consideration for others and stay and play with the children, or to fight and bully people and be sent home (or be sent for a time out in another room). Try to realize that the reason a bad child behaves the way he does is often because there is something wrong at home. Perhaps his parents are abusive or don't get along, or perhaps they are excessively strict and demanding with the child at home, or perhaps they neglect him. By allowing him to play with your child in your home or yard with good supervision and firm, fair and kindly discipline, you may be able to manage him. But if the bad child often makes your child unhappy or hurts him, you may have to forbid the child to come into your house or yard to play.

When your child is older and is playing in other children's yards or goes to school, the problem becomes more difficult. To some extent, it is out of your hands because your child will have to learn for himself how to deal with bullying, aggressive, and cruel peers and schoolmates. However, if someone at school is consistently making your child anxious and unhappy and he doesn't know what to do about it, you may have to meet with the teacher or principal and together plan what steps to take. One parent did this very effectively when his daughter was being harassed in high school by a group of students (see Harassment by Other Children). If a bad child is making life miserable for your child and other children in the neighborhood, you may eventually have to meet with the child's parents and tell them that you would like to have young Joey play with your child, but unless he stops fighting, bullying, or whatever, he is not going to be welcome in the group. Going in the company of several other parents is much more effective than going alone, for it is easy for Joey's parents to just blame your child for the problem if you are alone.

Suppose your child is the "bad" child? First of all, don't tell him HE is bad. Tell him rather that certain behavior of his is bad. If you tell a child he is bad often enough it destroys his self esteem. He feels guilty and inferior and he may decide he might as well act badly because everyone thinks he is bad anyway. Don't hit your child if he is bad, for many studies have shown that children who are hit and disciplined harshly often take out their anger on other children by hitting and bullying them. Don't threaten him that something terrible will happen if he is bad, for instance that he will be put in jail, because this only serves to add another fear to the child's underlying insecurity, guilt and anger.

It also is not wise for a mother to threaten that she will tell his father that he has been bad boy when Daddy comes home, and he'll get it from his father. This puts the father in the position of punisher, and he then has to punish a child for something that happened when he wasn't even around. Each parent must take the responsibility to punish the child, if it is necessary, when the misbehavior occurs. Finally, never tell your child you are going to leave him because he is bad or misbehaving. This is terrifying to the child because he is so completely dependent on his parents.

If your child is bad, what you have to do is figure out the reason why. Have you been neglecting him and not giving him the time and attention he needs? If so, his bad behavior may really be a cry for love and attention. Have you been pressuring him too much perhaps? Discipline that is too harsh and strict often produces children who rebel. If they are hit often at home, they are likely to hit others when they are away from home. Or perhaps you have not been clear in setting down rules about the kind of behavior your expect of your child. If so, it is time to sit down with him, tell him the rules of behavior you expect him to follow, and the reasons for these rules. Then explain calmly that if he chooses not to follow them, it means he will be sent to his room, not allowed to go out or watch television, or will have some other privilege taken away. When your child is bad, also take the time to ask your child what's the matter and why he misbehaved. Then listen, and if he talks about something that is bothering him, try to work out a solution to the difficulty with him. But it is important always to set limits and follow through with the consequences that you have explained will follow breaking your rules of behavior, stressing that he chose to break the rules, and so must take the consequences. Be calm and be encouraging, saying that next time you hope he will make a better choice.

Bad Dreams

What do you do if your child wakes up at night crying because he has had a bad dream? You go to him, of course, hug him and comfort him, and tell him it was only a dream, that everything is all right. Don't encourage him to get up and come into your room. If he does climb in bed with you, hold him a minute or so, then take him back to his bed. If you let him stay in your bed, you may start a habit that is hard to break, child behavior specialists say. He will want to come sleep with you every time he has a bad dream, or perhaps even when he is upset or wakes for some reason. If he is still upset and won't settle in his own bed, sit in his room a while, or lie down next to him in his bed until he calms down and gets back to sleep. Leaving a night light on in his room may also make him feel more secure.

Children can have dreams that wake them and bother them as young as age two and three. Too much excitement or rough play before bedtime, travel, unusual sights, television shows with a lot of noise and violence, a brief absence of a parent, tension in the family or upsetting experiences can cause a child to have bad dreams, psychologists say. If your child seems to have them a lot, something may be frightening him, or there may be stress in the family that is bothering him or perhaps too much pressure on him from his parents. You may need to take your child to a mental health specialist to see if there is something you don't know about that is causing his bad dreams. It's important that the cause be found so he can have a good night's sleep.

Nightmares are often caused by emotional conflicts the child is having, says pediatrician Richard Ferber, and a child who awakens frightened from a nightmare needs comfort and reassurance from his parents.

Night terrors, however, are different from nightmares and are caused by a partial awakening from the deepest phase of sleep, according to Dr. Ferber, a pediatric sleep specialist. A child having a night terror will thrash around, sob, and sometimes scream, but he does not respond to comforting and may even push his parents away. He also has no memory of the incident when he does awaken. Dr. Ferber advises not waking a child, particularly a younger child, having a night terror, just to watch him and let it run its course. If the child gets up or is in danger of hurting himself, however, you need to step in and gently try to calm him and get him back to bed.

Bad Manners

Most parents want their child to have good manners and be courteous because courtesy is important in helping them get along with people throughout life. People are more friendly towards persons who are polite and think more favorably of them. So you want your child to learn to thank people when he is is given something, to say please when he is making a request, to shake hands when he meets someone and say he is glad to meet them, and to practice similar courtesies that put other people at ease and create a favorable impression.

It's easier to try to prevent bad manners by teaching courtesy than to try to correct bad manners once a child has gotten in the habit of acting discourteously. Courtesy takes a long time to learn, but it's important to start teaching it as early as possible, even as early as two or three. The best way to teach it is to set a good example yourself, say child care experts.

Get in the habit of saying "Please," "Thank you" and "Excuse me" when talking to your children, and wait for them to do the same before you respond. If you want your child to do something, for instance, don't just say "Set the table," but rather, "Would you please set the table?" And be sure to thank your child when he does it. Teach him to say "Pardon me," instead of "What?" if he hasn't heard something by doing this yourself. Show him how to shake hands with people and greet them, then introduce him to people you meet and let him practice his skills. Insist on good table manners for the whole family. Get your children in the habit of asking to be excused when they have finished their meal, instead of bolting from the table.

The teaching of manners should be done at home, not in public. Parents should not remind a child to say "Please" or "Thank you" in front of other people once the child is past toddler age. This can be annoying to adults and embarrassing to the child. If a child does not thank someone who hands him a gift, or if he reaches across the table for the mashed potatoes at Aunt Susie's, tell him about it when you get home and ask him to do better next time. If there are some bad manners that are typical of children in your family, such as interrupting or putting elbows on the table, you might work out a signal, perhaps rubbing your nose or hitching your shoulder, that you can use when you are invited out.

Children should be taught also to show their appreciation for gifts and to acknowledge gifts that are sent to them by writing thank-you notes, something that unfortunately is becoming a lost art. Even if your son doesn't really like the sweater Grandma sent, it's important that he write and thank her, or at least call and thank her. He doesn't have to lie and say how terrific he thinks the sweater is. He merely has to thank her for being so nice and sending him the gift.

If your child acts rudely and unkindly in your presence, this should not be tolerated. You need to step in immediately, take him aside and tell him what he did was rude and unacceptable behavior. Explain the polite way he should have behaved, and insist he stop being inconsiderate and rude. If he says he was just acting the way his friends do, tell him that people in this family don't behave that way. They treat others with politeness and consideration. Explain that people will like him more and he will get along better in life if he treats people politely.

Bedwetting and Soiling

Parents should not get uptight if their preschooler wets the bed at night. Complete bladder control takes longer for some children to achieve than others. Bedwetting occurs frequently among two- and three-year-olds, and some four- and five-year-olds still wet the bed sometimes.

You should never punish a child who wets the bed, warn child care experts. Nor should you belittle him or call him naughty or a baby. The child who is trained doesn't want to wet the bed, but can't help it. Punishing him is not going to solve the problem and is only going to make him feel more guilty and anxious about something he can't help.

Why do some children wet the bed at age three, four or even older, and what can you do about it? In many cases the preschool child who continues to wet at night may just sleep so soundly he doesn't wake up enough to sense he has to urinate. Bedwetting is also more likely if parents have put pressure on their child to become toilet trained, say child behavior specialists. In fact, pediatrician T. Berry Brazelton has found that children whose parents did not pressure them to sit or stay on the potty seat tended to train themselves by two and a half and seldom wet the bed (see Toilet Training).

Bedwetting that occurs regularly after age five may have physical or psychological causes. It's a good idea to consult a pediatrician, or better yet, a urologist, and make sure there is not something physically wrong which is causing the problem. In about 10 percent of cases there is an organic cause, some urinary or neurological problem, according to Dr. Foster Cline. My own daughter had to urinate every hour or two when she was six or seven although she seldom had accidents at night. We brought her to a urologist who found she had an overgrowth of tissue around the opening of her bladder which was preventing her from emptying it completely. Minor outpatient surgery cured the problem. Nursery school director Sue Marcio had a child whose parents spanked him when he wet the bed until a physical examination revealed the child had an unusually small bladder.

Emotional tension is one of the major causes of bedwetting in a child four, five or older, according to mental health experts. The child is often anxious about something, perhaps tension and arguments between his parents, a parental separation, too much pressure from parents, a new baby in the family, or pressure or problems at his day care center or school. Sometimes children who continue to wet or have accidents past school age are really angry at their parents but are afraid to express this anger because of fear of losing the parent. If you have checked to make sure no physical problem is causing the bedwetting, it might be wise to consult a child psychiatrist or psychologist to see if something is bothering your child. If there is discord in the family, a lot of arguing and bickering between you and your spouse, or an event such as a separation that might be distressing to your child, a family therapist may be of help.

"Studies have found that there is often a definite correlation between urinary incontinence and coercive training, unwantedness, parental anger, and frustrated demands," says psychiatrist Foster Cline. If children continue to wet the bed past preschool age he believes general aspects of the parent-child relationship need to be explored by a therapist or counselor. A counselor can help shed light on whether parental anger and frustration may lie beneath the surface of family relationships and be causing anxiety in the child. A therapist may also help parents to recognize how they are expressing their anger in ways that might be disturbing to their child. Therapy may also reveal whether there is a control battle going on between the parents and their child. Enuresis (bedwetting), says Cline, "is often a subtle control battle which the child will win because he 'can't help it.' As long as the parents are invested in having a dry bed, the battle will go on and the child will continue to 'win' while his self-image continues to suffer." If bedwetting becomes a control issue with an older child, he says parents should recognize that the problem is the child's, not theirs, and have the child take care of changing himself and his sheets if he wets. But for parents of bedwetters of any age, he says not to feel bad about your child's bedwetting, and don't make the child feel bad about it. Recognize that it is a problem that will be resolved, and the resolution will happen sooner if parents help the child feel as good as possible concerning the problem of wetting.

To help a child remain dry at night, child care specialists have these suggestions:

- Make sure your child goes to the bathroom just before he goes to bed.

- Before you go to bed, wake him and take him to the bathroom again.

Explain beforehand that you are going to do this to help him stay dry through the night.

- Limit what he drinks in the evening.

- Put a flannel-covered waterproof pad on his sheet. Explain that this will prevent your having to change the whole bed if he wets.

- If he wants you to help him stay dry at night, try setting a clock radio to waken him in about three hours so that he can get up and go to the bathroom. If that works, you can set it gradually later and later until he gains control through the night.

- When your child does wet, just change the child, the rubberized pad, or the bed, if necessary, without grumbling and without making the child feel guilty. Reassure him that he will gain bladder control and stay dry at night. Some child behavior experts recommend that a school-age child who wets the bed change the bed himself without the parents getting involved and making him feel embarrassed.

If these methods don't work, you can try a conditioning device, psychologist Louise Bates Ames suggests. These devices consist of a pad of material which is treated so that a buzzer or bell attached to it goes off as soon as a drop or two of urine hits the pad. The buzzer wakes the child, but after a time the sound of the buzzer becomes connected with the feeling of a full bladder, a process called conditioning. Then the full bladder alone is enough to wake him before he starts to wet. Ames says this probably shouldn't be tried before age six or seven because many children normally wet occasionally until this age. And if it doesn't work after two weeks, she suggests it be put away with the comment that the child probably isn't ready for it yet. Psychologist Lee Salk doesn't recommend conditioning devices, however. He says he has had men who were impotent as patients whose impotency seems to be related to the use of these in their childhood.

An antidepressant medication called imipramine has also been found to help some children stop wetting the bed. A method called "tangible rewards with fading" devised by child psychiatrist Stuart Kaplan has also been quite successful and was described by Mary Jo Kochakian, *Hartford Courant* Family Affairs writer, in her column. In this method the pad and warning bell device is used, but parents and child also agree on certain rewards for dry nights and penalties for wet nights. Rewards might be toys, going to bed later, a special time with a parent. Penalties could be limiting television, going to bed earlier, etc. Parents are told to praise the child for dry nights but just show mild disapproval if he wets, for instance, by saying, "I see you wet the bed; that's a shame. I hope things go better tomorrow." After 14 consecutive dry nights, the warning device is removed. Then a procedure he calls "fading" begins. For each dry week there is a day off the reward-and-penalties program. Of the children using this method in a study, 85 percent were dry for two weeks compared to 67 percent who used the bell and pad alone, and there were fewer relapses. Other mental health experts, however, do not believe punishment should be used at all with bedwetting because feelings of guilt and fear can become connected with urination, which may increase anxiety and make the problem worse.

Kaplan, a clinical professor of psychiatry at Columbia University, doesn't believe children younger than six need to be treated for bedwetting because the problem often disappears as the child grows older. Other child behavior specialists agree that parents don't need to be worried about bedwetting in a preschooler, but if it persists into elementary school years, they should seek help. The first professional to consult is their pediatrician, then a urologist if a physical problem is suspected, or a family therapist or child psychologist or psychiatrist if discord and emotional tension in the family could be contributing to the problem.

Biting

Babies will bite on things from the time they start teething, around three to five months, until they have cut all their baby teeth. The baby wants to bite on something because his gums are bothering him, and he may bite your finger if it is close to his mouth. The baby should never be punished for this because it is a normal reaction. Just give the baby a teething ring to chew on. After the baby's teeth have come in, he usually loses the urge to bite.

Some children, however, may begin biting others again around the age of two or three. They realize that they have a formidable weapon, their teeth, and when they get angry at another child, they bite him. How do you handle biting? Child care specialists say you should make it clear to the child that biting hurts the other person and is not something that people do. If it is repeated, they advise a time-out—removing the child from the group for a time. Nursery school director Dolores Andreucci of Guilford says to a child who bites, "See what you've done. You hurt Janie (or whatever the child's name is). She's your friend. You don't bite. It hurts." If the child bites again, she will send him to a time out chair or room and repeat the message. "We don't do this to our friends. It's painful. It hurts."

Nursery school director Louise Miller of Hamden uses similar methods, telling the child biting hurts and saying, "Animals bite. People do not." But she observes it is usually a phase that passes.

Nursery school director Sue Marcio shows the child what he has done and says "You bit Johnny, and see how he's crying and how hurt he is." She makes it clear to the child that biting hurts "and it's not something we do to our friends." Then she will have the child sit in a chair away from the rest of the group for a time out. When he returns to the group is up to the child. She tells him to let her know when he is feeling happy again.

Teachers at the Stork Club Child Care Centers in Connecticut say the parent should tell the child how serious biting is, what will happen if the skin breaks and the danger of infection from germs. They also suggest having the child who bit wash off the bite with warm water and removing the child from the group using a time out period.

When one child bites another, the first thing you should do is separate the two and comfort the bitten child, says Jeannette Stone in a publication of National Association for the Education of Young Children. Make sure the child is all right and that an antiseptic and bandage are applied to the bite. But you also must make it clear to the biter that biting is not allowed, using words such as, "I will not permit biting. It is dangerous." Then she suggests getting the children involved in a soothing activity, such as playing with sand or water.

Should you ever bite the child back or encourage the bitten child to bite back? Child care experts say no. "Biting a child back is one of the worst things you can do," says Marcio. The reason is obvious. Children learn by imitation. Just as a child learns when he is spanked or hit that hitting is a way of expressing anger, he may also learn that biting is acceptable if an adult does it to him. Stone agrees, noting that biting is wrong, destructive and dangerous, and is "wrong for everyone at all times".

Cheating

When a child is in kindergarten or first grade, he may not understand what cheating is, and so he may not realize it is wrong if he copies something from another child's paper or if he moves an extra space in a game. It's important for parents to explain to their child at this age what cheating is and that it is wrong. When your child begins having written assignments in school and homework, it's a good time to explain that he should not copy what another student has written if he does not know the answer or has not done the assigned work. Explain that this is not honest because he is taking credit for someone else's idea or information. Also, if he does not understand something and copies another person's work, the teacher cannot help him because she doesn't realize he needs help. Explain also that teachers will punish a child they find cheating. They will give him no credit for the work, and will most likely let his parents know about it.

Children in the early elementary grades may also cheat at games because competition is keen then and winning a game is important at that age. If you find your child cheating at a game, don't humiliate him in front of others or punish him harshly. Take him aside and explain that this is not fair to the other players and people will not want to play with him if they think he cheats. If it happens again, you need to stop it right away. If you are involved, it will be effective if you just stop the game and say you do not want to play anymore. You will play another time only if you can be sure he won't cheat.

If your child seems to be cheating repeatedly, it may be that you have been emphasizing the importance of excelling too much, of getting all A's in school, of being at the top of the class. Your child may feel that if she isn't perfect and doesn't bring home 100s, she will risk losing your love. You need to back off a bit and let her know that it's all right to make mistakes, that everyone does. Tell her it's a lot worse to bring home an A on a paper in which she copied someone else's work than a B or C on a paper she did all herself. Perhaps competitiveness and the importance of winning in sports has been stressed too much in the family. If so, you need to make your child realize that playing a game well and fairly is what's important, that cheating to win is wrong. You need to show her you appreciate her efforts and love her whether she wins or loses a game, whether she gets A's or C's in school.

Another reason a child may cheat is if parents compare her with another sibling or another child who consistently does better in school or better in sports and competitions. A child may also cheat because he is having trouble understanding the work in school and doesn't want to be embarrassed (and possibly punished) for bringing home a report card with bad grades. If you think this is the reason, talk to your child's teacher and see if she can give her some extra help. Take time to help her yourself with homework. Help her learn techniques of studying, such as making a check in pencil near important items in her text for review, or jotting down notes on key information to help her study for tests.

If your child actually copies something from a book and passes it off as her own composition, you need to explain that although you can use other people's ideas, copying what they have written word for word and pretending you have written it is wrong. This is called plagiarism and is taken very seriously in school. In high school and college it usually results in a failing grade.

Most important, child development experts say you should deal with cheating as soon as it occurs. Don't ignore it or joke about it, or else it may develop into a habit with your child. And finally, be a good role model yourself. If your child sees you cheating at games, in business, on your income tax, or whatever, she is not going to think cheating is all that bad, and she's likely to do it when she thinks she can get away with it.

Chores

It's important to give children chores to do around the house because it makes them feel they are making an important contribution to the family and gives them a sense of responsibility and belonging. It also makes them feel capable and builds their self esteem when you praise them for jobs well done. Children as young as three or four can be given a simple chore to do, such as setting the table or putting away their clean clothes. Child behavior specialists say it's a good idea to start this young because children of this age are interested in what their parents do, and often follow them around imitating their activities. They want to help and feel needed. Take advantage of this natural interest by giving your child a little chore or two to do each day, such as setting the table.

Even a two-year-old who follows his mother around wanting to dust or vacuum or cook like she does can be given a simple chore to do, such as dusting a table or putting away the silver from the dishwasher. The mother who squelches the two- or three-year-old's natural interest in helping around the house by telling him he is too little and to go off and play starts very early to make him feel incapable. When she does want him to help when he's older, he very likely won't want to be bothered.

As your child gets older, he should be given more age-appropriate chores as part of his responsibility for the smooth running of the household. Once he starts elementary school, he should be able to keep his things picked up and his room neat, feed the dog or cat each day, or dry the dinner dishes. By the middle elementary school years, children should be able to wash and dry the dishes, help vacuum, put out garbage, help with yard work such as weeding and raking.

It's important, however, to train your child in the way you want the chores done. He may not understand what you want done when you say "Do the dishes" or "Clean your room." He may think cleaning his room just means dusting and vacuuming, not clearing out dirty socks from under the bed or putting away clothes and toys scattered around. Or your daughter may not realize doing the dishes means washing and drying them, wiping the table and counters and putting the dishes away. You might ask her first what she thinks you mean by the task you have asked her to do. Then explain clearly and show her how you would like things done.

If a chore is not done completely or to your satisfaction, don't immediately criticize because your child will get the idea she can't do things to please you and she won't want to help you. Don't immediately point out something she has forgotten to do. Compliment her on what she has done well, but don't add, even though you might be tempted, "but you didn't..." Instead, ask if she thinks she might improve on the way she did the job. Or later ask her to do some part of the job she neglected, such as putting out the napkins, if she forgot that in setting the table. And one thing you should never do is redo the job in front of your child if she hasn't done it well. That will only make her feel incapable and not very worthwhile, and you can be sure she won't want to do that job for you again. If you have to improve on what she has done, wait until later when she is not around.

It's generally not a good idea to pay a child for doing chores. It's important for your children to participate in the work of the household, say child development experts, and help with things like dishes, cleaning, yard work, watching younger children, so that they feel they an important and necessary part of the family and are needed in the running of the household. This is one way in which you can help build responsibility and self esteem in your children. Occasionally, however, payment may be warranted if you have asked your child to do a special or difficult job. But in general the payment you should give is thanks and appreciation for his help, and perhaps a hug.

WHAT IF YOUR CHILD WON'T DO HIS CHORES?

Don't expect that your child will always remember his chores.Every parent at some time or other has a problem getting a child to do his chores. The first thing to do is remind him if he has forgotten a chore that the job is part of his responsibility towards the smooth running of the household.

To prevent noncompliance:

- Make it clear at the beginning of each week what chore every child is to do. Don't just think of a chore for your child to do when he walks into the room. Give children a choice of the chores they would prefer to do. If one objects that he gets stuck with the same unpleasant chore each week, such as taking out the garbage, rotate the chores each week. Or, to distribute chores fairly among several children you might write down with them all the things that need to be done, put them in a bowl, and then let everyone, Mom and Dad included, pick one or two at the beginning of each week. Or you could post a list on the refrigerator and have everyone move along one or two on the list each week.

- Tell children how long their chore should take. Dishes and room cleaning, for instance, should be able to be done in half an hour, but if a chore will take a long time, break it up into sections so the job doesn't seem too much to your child.

- Be clear about when and how often the chore is to be done, for instance, every evening or every Saturday morning.

- Give children some leeway about when they want to do their chore when this is possible, for instance, before or after supper.

- Set a consequence that will follow if the chore is not done. You might allow one reminder. Consequences could be no television that night, an extra chore the following week, no permission to go to a game that the child might want to attend, etc. Decide with your children what the consequence will be.

- Use the "As soon as" technique if a chore isn't done. For instance, if your child asks for something, such as help with homework, a shirt she wants ironed, etc., say, "As soon as you do (your chore) I'll do it."

Above all, don't yell and nag. That doesn't work. And don't do the chores assigned to your child without withholding some privilege from him. Otherwise he will figure you're not really serious about his doing chores, and he'll goof off.

Climbing

Young children usually love to climb up on things and climb over things, so it's a good idea to have playground equipment in your yard or take your child at times to a nearby playground or school yard where he can satisfy his climbing urges. Obviously, you have to be nearby and watch a preschooler carefully when he is climbing to catch him if he falls and make sure he doesn't get hurt. If your child starts climbing on things indoors, you need to decide what you will allow him to climb on, such as an old, soft couch or old chair, perhaps, but make it clear he cannot climb on other things. If he gets up on your kitchen counter, for instance, say "You can climb on the couch and chair downstairs, not on the counter."

Company-Caused Problems

Sometimes children tend to act up when company comes, and of course this can embarrass parents and make guests uncomfortable. How to handle it depends on the age of the child. You can't expect a child under four to willingly allow his parents to spend a lot of time talking to company. After all, his parents are the center of his world, and he's going to get mad if they ignore him. So prepare ahead of time for the situation. Try to entertain at night rather than during the day unless your guests are family members or friends who will enjoy taking time to play with your child and will take him out in the yard for a walk or give him attention when you are too busy as hostess to do so. If you have a small child and must entertain during the day, plan ahead to take turns with your husband, with one devoting some time to the child while the other entertains the company. Have the child's toys handy in a corner of the room or in an adjoining room so he can be near you and still be able to amuse himself playing. Explain if the child is old enough that company is coming and you want the child to meet the guests and talk to them a little, but after that you would like him to go play because the grownups want to talk. Having the child help you prepare by doing some simple tasks like setting the table also will make him feel he is included in the day's events.

Never send your child off as soon as guests arrive because he will feel you don't want him around for some reason and this will damage his self esteem. When the guests arrive, introduce the child to them, and talk about him a little. Perhaps ask him to show them a favorite toy or a picture he has colored. If he has helped you, be sure to point out to the guests what he has done in front of him. But don't make the mistake of having him perform for them—sing songs or read or recite—(unless they are doting grandparents or aunts)—because this makes him the center of attention and he is likely to want to keep on being the center of attention. Also, parents who have their child show off a lot give the child the idea he is worthwhile to them only because of what he can do, rather than for himself alone, and this can be damaging to the child's emotional development, say child behavior experts.

If a small child starts pestering you or the company, ask her to go play with her toys for a little while because mother and the guests want to talk. You might promise to color a picture with her after you have finished talking. And you should fulfill that promise and give her that time and attention when she asks. If you are not willing to devote some of your time to your small child when you are entertaining during the day, arrange to have a sitter come to play with her and take care of her.

With an older child explain ahead of time also that the company is coming and that after he talks to them a while you would like him to go outside or to his room or the playroom and play. Explain that this will be more fun for him because he will get restless just sitting around and listening to grownups talk. Teach him ahead of time how to greet guests, shake hands and say he is glad to meet them or see them. Make sure you introduce him as soon as the guests come. Don't talk on and on with them ignoring him, and then finally introduce him. You would be uncomfortable and feel left out if someone acted like that to you, and your child will feel that way too. If you are entertaining at night, explain ahead of time that you would like the child to get ready for bed after he has met the company and visited with them a little while. And when the time comes, see that he does go to bed even if you have to go up with him.

If your child does act up with company, don't yell or shame him. Take him aside and tell him that is not the way to act around company. If he has been rude—for instance, if he said irritably to talkative Mrs. Worthington, "Stop talking,"—explain that this is rude and hurt her feelings. Ask him to apologize. If he starts misbehaving and getting out of control, don't yell or hit him and don't ignore the situation. Tell him in a calm but firm voice to go to his room until he is sure he can behave better. If he hesitates, take him to his room.

Conflict

CONFLICTS BETWEEN PARENTS AND CHILDREN

No matter how patient and understanding you are with your child, there are bound to be times of conflict—times when he feels he needs to behave a certain way, but his behavior is interfering with your needs. What do you do about conflict?

First of all, don't get uptight about it and think conflict must be avoided no matter what. Accept the fact that conflict is bound to occur in any family and it is not necessarily bad. Learning to deal with conflict in the family can prepare a child for dealing with the conflict he is bound to face in the world. In fact, mental health experts say a family in which there is no conflict may be a troubled family because either the parent is very harsh and domineering and the children are afraid to counter him in anything, or else the parent is uncaring and can't be bothered disciplining the children. In both cases the children will suffer. With a strict, authoritarian parent, they are likely to become either submissive adults who repress their own feelings and desires, or else they are likely to rebel and try to dominate others as their parent did them. With overly lenient parents psychologists say they are apt to grow up spoiled and selfish, yet insecure because deep down they have a sense their parent didn't care enough about them to set the limits they needed on their behavior.

When there is conflict in a family, most parents will either assert their power to win the battle, like the authoritarian parent, or cave in to the children's demands and let them win. The authoritarian parent says things like "Pick up those toys this minute," "Stop bothering your sister, or I'll send you to your room the rest of the night," "Do your homework or you won't go out with your friends at all this weekend." Or worse yet, he hits the child who disobeys him. The lenient parent, perhaps after a half-hearted attempt at giving his child some guidance, takes the attitude, "Oh, I don't care. Do what you want."

Although there are times when a parent has to be authoritarian, for instance if the child starts to do something dangerous, the authoritarian method when used regularly doesn't work. The child will turn off a dictatorial, directing parent after a while and pay even less attention, so the parent has to threaten, nag and punish even more. Or if the parent is a harsh disciplinarian, the child may comply, but will be filled with suppressed anger, which he is likely to take out on his peers, or which can damage his emotional health in later life (See Anger).With a lenient parent the child is apt to throw tantrums, be unmanageable and self-centered and have difficulty getting along with people. If one parent is authoritarian and the other very lenient, it's even worse, according to child mental health specialists. Such inconsistency leads not only to family tension, but is likely to produce a difficult and disrespectful child who may develop behavioral or emotional problems.

Psychologist Thomas Gordon says that when there is conflict, parents need to get rid of the idea that either they or the child has to win. He recommends that the parent and child solve the conflict together, using what he describes as the *no-lose* method of conflict resolution. He describes his method in detail in his excellent book *P.E.T. Parent Effectiveness Training*. In brief, he says you need to tell a child when he is behaving in a way you disapprove of, but instead of ordering the child to do something, the parent should state clearly what the problem is and ask the child's help in solving it. Then the parent gives an "I" message explaining how he feels about the child's behavior, how it is affecting him, and what his needs are. For example, "I get upset when I see your books and clothes lying all over the living room when I have just cleaned it and picked up so it will look neat when Daddy comes home." This is more likely to result ultimately in cooperation and a better relationship than if you said "Pick up all your junk in the living room. Why do you always make such a mess?"

Then ask your child to talk about his feelings and his reasons for acting the way he did. Through discussion you can usually get to the reason behind the child's disturbing or disobedient behavior. Maybe he was in a hurry to go out and play and there was not enough room in the closet. Then ask the child how he thinks the problem can be solved. Both parent and child should give suggestions about what can be done to resolve the problem until they decide on the best solution. Maybe a chest for books in a corner of the living room and hooks behind the kitchen door would help him be neater. Try out the solution. If it doesn't work, look for another. Resolving conflicts this way promotes a caring, friendly relationship between the parent and child, while the other methods often result in hostility and annoyance and turn off real communication between the child and his parent. Also, since the child has participated in coming up with a solution to the problem, he is more likely to carry it out.

Here's an example of how the method works from *P.E.T. Parent Effectiveness Training*:

Dad: I have a need for us to work out something about bedtime. (I-message) Each night Mother or I or both of us have to nag you and worry you and sometimes force you to get you into bed at your regular time, eight o'clock. I don't feel very good about me when I do that (I-message) and I wonder how you are feeling about it.

Laura: I don't like for you to nag me...and I don't like to go to bed so early. I'm a big girl now and I should be able to stay up later than Greg (reason behind her actions coming out).

Mother: You feel we treat you the same as Greg and to do that isn't fair. (active listening-acknowledging daughter's feelings)

Laura: Yeah, I'm two years older than Greg.

Dad: And you feel we should treat you like you're older.(active listening)

Laura: Yes!

Mother: You have a good point. But, if we let you stay up later and then you fool around about going to bed, I'm afraid you'll really be very late getting to sleep. (I-message)

Laura: But I won't fool around—if I can just stay up a little longer.

Dad: I wonder if you might show us how well you can cooperate for a few days and then we might change the time.

Laura: That's not fair either!

Dad: It wouldn't be fair to make you earn the later time, huh? (active listening)

Laura: I think I should be able to stay up later because I'm older. (Silence) Maybe if I went to bed at eight and read in bed until eight-thirty?

Mother: You would be in bed at the regular time, but the lights could stay on for a while and you could read?

Laura: Yeah, I like to read in bed.

Dad: That sounds pretty good to me—but who is going to watch the clock?

Laura: Oh, I'll do that. I'll turn the light off right at eight-thirty!

Mother: Sounds like a pretty good idea, Laura. Shall we try that for a while?"

The parents, who were in one of Gordon's PET classes, reported they had very little problem with Laura at bedtime after that.

Gordon says parents should not try to use this method to resolve conflicts that involve the child's personal tastes, however, but only conflicts that are affecting other members of the family. For instance, if it is the style for boys to wear Mohawk hairdos in your town, you're not going to change your son's mind by using the no lose method. But the style of his hair is not really interfering with your life in any way or conflicting with your needs, so don't make an issue of things like that.

CONFLICTS BETWEEN CHILDREN

You should not rush in and try to solve the problem if your child gets into an argument with a sibling or another child, say child behavior specialists. Otherwise your child will get in the habit of running to Mommy to solve all his problems. Let the children try to work it out themselves. If a fight starts, of course, you will have to move in. If you see that the problem is getting worse and might end up in a fight, try to get the children to use the *no-lose* method of conflict resolution. State what the problem is. Get each to express his feelings and his needs. Clarify what each says with active listening, repeating back their ideas and feelings. Then ask them what solutions they can come up with. Parents who use this method, Gordon says, find their children soon stop running to them to settle conflicts because they know their parents will just have them work out a solution on their own.

Crying

A sound that grates on anyone's nerves is the sound of a baby crying. It can be particularly aggravating if you don`t know what to do to stop the baby's crying. You really feel helpless.

Why does a baby cry? Crying is the only way a baby has to communicate. When a baby cries it is usually for one of the following reasons, according to child care experts: he's hungry; he's tired; he wants to be held; he wants to suck; he needs stimulation; he needs to burp; he needs his diaper changed; he has colic; he's sick, or he's uncomfortable for some other reason.

WHAT DO YOU DO ABOUT A CRYING BABY?

First of all, pick him up, especially during the first month or two of his life. Don't worry about spoiling him if you do. A generation ago parents believed if they paid too much attention to their baby and picked him up when he cried, they would spoil him and he would want to be held all the time. But that's not true. Studies have found babies who are held more and have their needs attended to promptly usually cry less, especially in the first months of life.

Dr. Ronald Barr and Dr. Urs Hunziker of Montreal Children's Hospital Research Institute found that newborns who are frequently carried by a parent will cry less than ones who are infrequently carried. They studied 99 mother-infant pairs, randomly assigning them to a group that was asked to carry their baby at least three hours a day or to another group that received no such instructions. The parents were also asked to record their baby's behavior and their own. The infants were between three and twelve weeks old. The researchers found that the infants who were carried more cried 43 percent less overall and 51 percent less at night when measured at the peak crying age of six weeks. They also cried less at four, eight, and twelve weeks. "The relative lack of carrying in our society may predispose to crying and colic in normal infants," the physicians said.

In fact, researchers have found that holding and cuddling is necessary for a baby's survival and babies who are never held fail to grow and thrive and sometimes die (see p. 18).

After you pick the baby up, try to determine why he's crying. If you think he's hungry, feed him. If he's wet, change him. Try burping him, for a gas bubble may be making him uncomfortable. Does he seem too hot or cold? If he keeps on crying or seems unusually fretful for several hours, take his temperature for he may be sick. If he isn't feverish and you have taken care of feeding, diapering, burping and cuddling, put him back in his crib. Don't worry if he cries a little. He'll probably stop in a little while and go to sleep.

However, all of this doesn't mean that you must run and pick up your baby the instant he starts crying. Although you should pick up a newborn who cries promptly, pediatrician William A.H. Sammons thinks that once the baby is six to eight weeks old, it's sometimes a good idea to let him cry for a short time before picking him up. He believes this helps to teach the baby the beginning of self-sufficiency. In an interview with *The Hartford Courant* Family Affairs columnist Mary Jo Kochakian, Sammons said if you respond to your baby every time he whimpers he is really controlling you. But if you let the infant cry a little while, he may learn to calm himself by sucking on his fingers or toes or looking at something interesting. Most infants can develop the ability to calm themselves in some way by eight or ten weeks, Sammons says.

But the pediatrician warns that you shouldn't take this to mean you can let your baby scream anytime you don't want to bother about him. Rather, you should learn what your baby's different cries mean. He probably cries more loudly and insistently when he is hungry or in pain, and more quietly when he is just bored or fretful. You need to respond quickly to the insistent crying, but you can wait and see if he can calm himself during times of *low demand* crying. But when you try this, the pediatrician says to set a time limit, two, or five or ten minutes that you will let your baby cry, and if he hasn't calmed himself by that time, pick him up. If it takes longer than a minute and a half for your baby to calm down after you pick him up, he says you have probably waited too long. Sammons' views are explained in detail in his book *The Self-Calmed Baby.*

CRYING BECAUSE OF COLIC

Some babies cry a lot because they have colic, severe cramps in the stomach or intestines. Such babies often won't stop crying no matter what you do. If a baby cries violently, gets red in the face, and pulls his legs up, he could be suffering from colic. A baby who cries this way and cries for several hours during a day should be checked by a pediatrician. Colic usually occurs in the first three months of a baby's life and often occurs because the baby is allergic to her formula. Some babies are unable to tolerate formulas made with milk, and switching to a soy formula may help if your baby has colic. Burping the baby often, using bottles with plastic liners, and expelling the air from such bottles before feeding by pushing the liner gently from the bottom may help prevent the buildup of gas in the baby's stomach. Pediatricians also can prescribe a medication to mix with the formula to help prevent gas buildup.

The mother's own anxious feelings can sometimes contribute to colic and crying in infants, according to studies by Dr. Brian Forsyth at Yale. He found that mothers who had concerns about their baby's feeding in the day or two after birth were more likely to have colicky babies. And mothers who had a poor experience in growing up seemed to have babies with more colic problems the first few days. When he contacted the mothers again after four months, he found the mothers who were more anxious were still having more colic problems with their babies.

Forsyth notes that a baby's crying normally increases in the first six weeks of life and may reach three hours a day. He says it is important for pediatricians to tell new mothers this and talk to them about their anxieties, or else they may blame themselves and feel they are a failure as a parent.

If your baby isn't colicky and you have taken care of the obvious things, yet your baby is still crying, there are still lots of things you can do to calm him.

METHODS OF CALMING A BABY

Some methods of calming a crying baby parents have used for generations, such as walking or rocking the baby, singing to him, giving him a pacifier or rattle, or taking him for a ride in the carriage or car. Grandmothers also know that wrapping an infant securely in a receiving blanket helps calm him, perhaps because it's like the snug environment of the womb. I have found that if a baby keeps crying after you have fed and burped him and put him down, he often has another burp. Holding him seated on your lap with his tummy against your right hand as you pat him on the back with your left is often a good way of bringing up that burp. A baby swing also helps calm a fussy baby.

Another way to calm a fretful and crying baby is by massage. Rubbing the baby's back gently or stroking his arms and legs from his hands or feet upward can be soothing. Using a little baby oil while you do this can help. Cory Crock, who teaches an infant massage technique in Evanston, Ill., said in a *Chicago Tribune* newspaper article that parents who used it said their babies slept better, and it made them feel closer and more nurturing to their infants.

Some unusual items have been created to help calm a crying baby. Rock-a-Bye Toys produces toys such as stuffed animals and pillows that contain equipment which simulates sounds from the birth canal. The toys were developed by Dr. William C. Eller of Fort Lauderdale. He inserted a tiny microphone through a mother's cervix, recording the sounds heard by the unborn baby. It was found the sounds were calming to babies after birth. And a recording called "Baby-go-to-sleep" that contains nursery rhymes and the sound of a human heartbeat has been found effective in calming premature infants.

If nothing works, you may just have to put the baby in his crib or bassinet and let him cry. But check him every 10 to 15 minutes, and perhaps try holding him a little and burping him again. If crying goes on and on no matter what you do, it's a good idea to call your pediatrician. Sometimes a baby can have an ear infection or other medical problem causing pain, and the only way he has to tell you about it is by crying.

If you have a baby who cries a lot or who wakes you frequently at night with his crying, you may reach a point where you get angry at the baby and wish you had never had a child. You shouldn't feel ashamed of such feelings because many parents have them. But you should get help. Ask a grandparent or other family member or a friend to come in and help you with the baby a few times a week. Have your spouse take over the baby's care an evening or two a week and get out by yourself. Ask your pediatrician for advice. And if you begin to feel very depressed, develop insomnia, or feel as if you want to hurt the baby, get help immediately from a mental health professional. Your local hospital usually can refer you to a mental health clinic.

Don't be ashamed to ask for help for a mental health problem. Some mothers go through hormonal changes after childbirth that can make them feel severely depressed and unable to cope with a demanding infant. And the baby often seems to sense it if his mother is upset, and it makes him even more anxious and irritable. Sometimes mothers in this situation have become so distraught they have harmed their child. But help is available. Medication can lift depression and make such mothers able to cope with their baby and enjoy life again. Talking to a psychotherapist can also help a mother get to the root of just what is bothering her and find a solution to the problem.

CRYING IN OLDER BABIES AND PRESCHOOLERS

When babies get older, they may cry if a stranger comes near them, if they get hurt, if they hear a loud noise, if they are hungry or tired, or have a wet or dirty diaper, or if their parent leaves them with someone else. They may also cry if they are bored and want attention. Keeping them near you, giving them a toy, or talking to them or holding them a while will help in this case. So can having a sitter the baby knows, such as a grandparent, if you must go out.

When preschoolers cry, it is usually because they can't have something they want, or another child has taken their toy or has hit or pushed them, or they have hurt themselves. They might also cry because their mother has left them with a strange sitter, or because they crave some attention from their parent, or because they are tired or hungry. Toddlers and preschoolers are very active and need time during the day to nap, or at least to rest. If they miss their nap, they are likely to be cross and fretful later in the day.

If a child between one and three cries a lot, mental health experts say it may indicate that the parents are too strict and are stopping the child too often from doing what he wants. Children this age need to explore their environment, and the best thing to do is to put away things that are dangerous or should not be touched and let them explore, rather than to keep saying "No" when they reach for something.

Parents should never punish a child who cries or make him feel guilty about it because this can make him suppress his feelings, which can cause emotional problems in later years. Instead, they should try to find the reason for the child's crying and do what needs to be done to stop it and to prevent whatever caused it from happening again.

Ask a crying child to tell you what is the matter. Put your arm around him and comfort him at the same time. If he is crying because he is angry about something, show that you understand by labeling his feeling. Say something like, "I know you are angry about (mentioned what happened). How about telling me what you feel instead of crying?" You might also suggest that if he wants to get out his anger to go and punch his teddy bear or an old pillow or hit the rug hard with his hand.

Sometimes a child won't really know why he is crying. Maybe it's because he really wants your love and attention, and he should be given such attention. Or he may cry because he is tired. In such a case a parent should realize this and hold and soothe him, perhaps rock him, until he calms down and goes off to sleep. Even though he's tired, a child may cry and fight sleep because he doesn't want to miss what is going on around him, but a parent who is calm and holds and comforts the child can usually get him to relax and go off to sleep. If a child cries when put to bed, you may have to do other things to prevent it or stop it. (See Sleep Problems.)

CRYING WHEN LEFT AT NURSERY
SCHOOL OR DAY CARE

Joey, age three, was brought to nursery school for the first time. Even though his mother had told him all about it ahead of time and his father, who brought him, assured him he would be back at lunchtime to pick him up, Joey began crying uncontrollably as soon as he left. He wouldn't stop no matter what nursery school director Maureen Myers or her staff did.

What does a nursery school teacher or babysitter do in such a situation, and is there anything a parent can do to prevent it? What Myers did was call Joey's mother and let him talk to her. She felt he needed the reassurance of talking to his mother because he didn't seem to know where she was and worried if his father would be able to find her. The phone call helped some, but Joey still remained upset. Finally Myers called Joey's mother back and asked her to come in.

There are things you can do to make your child's adjustment to nursery school easier. First, visit the nursery school to which you plan to send your child and observe for an hour or so. Make sure the teachers manage the children well, do not discipline too strictly and do not criticize, shame or belittle the children when they don't do what is expected. Make sure the children are treated with warmth, caring and respect for their feelings and ideas. And make sure there are a lot of interesting things for the child to do. Then tell your child he will be going there and take him to visit. Let him meet the teachers and some of the children and play and take part in activities while you remain there.

On the first day of school some nursery school teachers want parents to leave as soon as they bring their children. But this is not always a good idea, especially if your child hasn't been with strangers much and is very dependent on you. If you think your child may become very upset if you leave on his first day at nursery school or daycare, ask the director to let you stay for a few days. You may have to leave for a short period at first and then increasingly longer periods until your child can adapt to being without you. Wait until he is calm and busy with some activity before you leave. Before you go, be sure to tell your child you are leaving and give him a kiss and hug goodbye. Never sneak away, because one of a child's worst fears is that his parents will abandon him, and if you sneak away, he may think this has happened and become terrified. Don't act overly anxious or worried about leaving your child, or this will make him more anxious. He may also get the idea then that by crying he can keep you there with him all the time. Be calm and reassure your child that you will be back by a certain time, for instance, before lunch or, if there is a clock, when the hands point to a certain numbers.

When I first brought my four-year-old son to nursery school, I found I had to stay with him, and after a few times there leave him for a short time and then gradually longer times to get him adjusted to being without me. The first day I brought him, the nursery school director told me to just leave him and go. I had my doubts, but considered her the professional, so I did what she said. Ten minutes later she called me and told me to come back because he was crying uncontrollably and was unmanageable. For several weeks either I or his older sister had to remain with him all through nursery school. Then we gradually left for a short time, then for longer and longer periods. It took a few months before he was able to stay alone all afternoon without one of us. If I had remained with him that first day, I'm sure he would have been weaned from mother's apron strings much sooner.

Myers used another technique that helped Joey. She called his mother the night after Joey's first day at nursery school and suggested that she have Joey bring something he really liked with him to nursery school, such as a blanket or a favorite toy. Joey appeared the next day with his rabbit, a real live one in a cage. "It did the trick," said Myers. "He cried a few minutes, but then he was okay." After that one time, Joey didn't even need to bring his rabbit and by the fourth session was adjusting well and beginning to take part in activities.

The director of the New School for Young Children in Hamden, Conn., Myers says that 90 percent of children will cry when their parents leave them at nursery school for the first time, but most stop in a few minutes. Since most come for the first time in the fall when nursery school opens, they are crying together, and she thinks this helps them because they see other children have the same feelings and fears they do. What made it especially hard for Joey was that he started in the middle of the term, and all the other children knew each other and were used to the school.

If a child cries when he is left with a babysitter or nursery school teacher, what the person should do is hold him and cuddle him, show she understands his feelings, and reassure him that his mother will always come back, say nursery school directors and teachers. Dolores Andreucci, director of Cradles to Crayons Day Care Center in Guilford, Conn., also tells the child that his mother will be back at a certain point in the day, such as right after lunch. Some day care teachers point to a time on the clock, which is also a good way of helping a child learn to tell time. Giving a child a toy or getting him to start an activity can also distract a child from his fears and help stop his tears. What the babysitter or day care worker should NOT do is tell the child to "Be a big boy and stop crying" because this will only make the child feel inferior as well as unhappy and make him more miserable.

Myers, who has an associate's degree in early childhood education, called in someone even more of an expert to do a workshop for her staff on managing children. Barbara Sherman of the Hamden Mental Health Center came and suggested another method for reducing children's separation anxiety when they are left at nursery school or daycare. Sherman suggested parents send a picture of one or both of them to school with the child, or even a picture of the family dog. Myers had one of the mothers whose son was anxious at nursery school do this. She put two pictures in his lunchbox. "When he got sad and wanted Mommy, I said, 'Go over and look in your lunch box.' It worked," she said. Sherman said the method even worked for her own daughter when she was a little over a year old. She had a favorite picture in her crib. When she was brought to a day care center and put in the crib there, she cried and screamed, but as soon as her favorite picture was put in the crib with her, she quieted down.

Mothers or fathers bringing their child to nursery school for the first time should expect that the child will cry for a few minutes and cling to them, says Sue Marcio, director of R&K Tiny Tots Nursery School in Hamden. She says a mother can reassure her child by saying "Mrs. --- can take care of you as well as I can," and by giving the child a time when she will be back. Marcio adds that the parent should keep telling the child all the wonderful things he will do in nursery school. Having the child bring along a stuffed animal or blanket that is special to him can also help ease the separation. She also suggests telling the child it is important for him to get to know and like another lady so that if Mommy gets sick or when she has to go to work there is someone to take care of him.

Myers stresses that the situation at home can influence how a child adjusts to nursery school. One four-year-old boy would always cry when he came to nursery school, and she found that his father was unemployed and his mother was working two jobs and was under a lot of stress. The father, who was home with the boy all day, also put a lot of pressure on him to learn his letters and numbers, behave well, etc. "As soon as the father went back to work, there was a remarkable difference in the kid," said Myers. He stopped his crying, his anxiety disappeared, and he began to enjoy nursery school. This child's parents also used to bribe him to go to nursery school, promising him a toy he wanted if he would go and not cry. Myers says parents should never do this. First of all, it doesn't work, but even worse, it can get the child in the dangerous habit of not doing what his parents want unless he gets something for it.

CRYING WHEN LEFT WITH BABYSITTERS

When a baby reaches the age of about six months he can differentiate his parents from other people and is likely to cry if strangers come near him, or even an aunt or grandparent whom he hasn't seen in a few weeks. And he's also likely to cry if his parents leave him with someone else. What do you do about this? First of all, get the baby used to staying for short times with one or two other people, such as a grandparent or a reliable sitter, early in his infancy. Always try to have someone the baby knows well stay with him when you go out. If you must get a different sitter, have her visit once or twice beforehand and play with the baby so your child can get to know her. If your baby suddenly wakes up to see a stranger taking care of him, it can be very frightening and upsetting to him, so try to prevent this. In fact, it's a good idea to have any babysitter come early so she can start playing with your child and taking care of her while you are still there. It makes your leaving easier for the child.

Some of the techniques used by the nursery school directors can also be used by babysitters. They should find out before the parents leave if the child has a favorite blanket or toy and where it is. Also, they should know what time the parents will be back and always have a phone number where they can reach the parent in case there really is a crisis. You should also tell the sitter the child's schedule, times for eating and bedtime, and suggest things that they can do with the child. Louise Miller of Spring Glen Church Nursery School advises that to deal with a child's separation anxiety babysitters should be supportive, warm and loving, and interest the child in something, such as a favorite book.

When you do have to go out, make sure you tell the child ahead of time that you are going out, where you are going, and when you will be back. Tell her who will be taking care of her and plan a special activity with her that she can do with the babysitter. If you are going to go out after she has gone to bed, be sure to tell her and let her know who will be staying with her. Again, never sneak away, or it can hurt your child's trust in you and make her feel frightened and insecure. "There is no fear as great and as deeply instinctive in a small child as that of being left alone," says Dr. T. Berry Brazelton, so it is vital that parents prepare children for separations and reassure them that they will return.

Before you go out it's a good idea to spend a little time with your child, cuddling her on your lap and playing or reading a little with her and the babysitter. Then give her a hug and kiss goodbye and reassure her you will be back before supper, or when she wakes up in the morning, or whenever, and the sitter will take good care of her while you are away.

Dangerous Behavior

What do you do about a child who does dangerous things—a child, for instance, who touches a hot stove, plays with knives or matches, or runs into the streets? Toddlers and preschoolers are apt to do dangerous things because they don't yet realize what is dangerous. As soon as you see a child of this age start dangerous behavior :

1. Tell the child at once to stop, using a word or two or a short sentence. ("Don't go in the street," "Stop!" etc.)

2. Speak clearly, firmly and loudly, but don't yell or sound angry.

3. Physically keep the child away from the danger. Hold him and keep him from running in the street, then lead him away from it. Move him away from the hot stove.

4. Tell the child how he can get hurt if he keeps on with what he started to do.

5. Teach the child when he is old enough to understand that some things are dangerous. Fire and stoves burn. Knives can cut him very badly. Pills should not be put into his mouth unless his parents or the doctor gives them to him, and only when they do, or he can get very sick. If he runs into the street without looking, a car could be coming and might hit him. Explain that all these things can hurt children so badly they have to go to the doctor or sometimes the hospital.

6. Make it clear the child is *never* to do certain dangerous things, such as run into the street or play with matches.

7. If your child disobeys, don't hit or spank the child, for this may encourage him to do it again just to get back at you. But do punish immediately by sending him to his room, not letting him play with his friends that day, or by giving some other punishment effective enough to make him realize you mean business.

Stork Club Child Care Center teachers and Louise Miller , director of Spring Glen Nursery School in Hamden, stress that you need to explain to the child why his behavior is dangerous, make him realize the importance and seriousness of the situation, and remove him from the area if you think he may continue his dangerous behavior.

But prevention of dangerous behavior is most important, says nursery school teacher Dolores Andreucci of Guilford. Parents need to be ever vigilant and keep children away from dangerous things. This was brought home to me vividly years ago when a neighbor sent her two-year-old son out in the yard to play in charge of his four-year-old brother. The children wandered over to the house across the street and started playing on the open wooden stairway. The little one was climbing up from underneath the stairway, got his head caught between two stairs and choked to death. The incident illustrates more than any words could that young children should never be left without supervision by an adult or responsible teenager, not even for a minute. Don't leave your infant, toddler or preschooler alone in a car, in the yard, or at home even for a minute or two. Not only will a young child be frightened to be left alone, but it only takes a minute for him to fall and get hurt, run into the road, get hold of matches, or be kidnapped by some mentally deranged person. In your home take precautions to prevent dangerous behavior by your child. If you have a toddler, put a gate at the top of a flight of stairs and devices that keep her from opening kitchen drawers or cabinets that contain knives, cleansers, or other things dangerous to children. Put medicines and cleaning agents on high shelves where children can't reach them.

If a child continues to do dangerous things when he is of school age and old enough to know they are dangerous, it is a sign that something can be seriously wrong in his home, with his early upbringing, or with his emotional state. He could be suffering from depression. Even young children get depressed, studies have found, and some children may get so depressed they may have suicidal tendencies and hurt themselves doing dangerous things. Help from a mental health professional should be obtained for a child who repeatedly does dangerous things. Both the child and the parents should have therapy to get to the root of what is causing his behavior.

When a child gets older, there are different dangers he must be aware of. As soon as a child is old enough, and especially if he is going to be alone at all after school, educator Barbara Brenner stresses that there are six safety rules parents must insist he follow:

- Never go anywhere with a stranger, no matter what the stranger says.
- Never open the door for anyone except people your parents have told you that you can let in.
- Never play with fire or use matches.
- Never play with sharp instruments, knives, or weapons.
- Never take medicine unless your parents or caretaker gives it to you and is home.
- Never change your daily pattern of activities without telling your parents where you will be.

It is wise to teach your child the first five even when he is as young as three or four years old.

Dawdling

Dawdling may begin in the preschool years when your child gets the idea there is a certain schedule you want him to follow—for eating, dressing, going to a daycare center, going to bed, etc. The way to handle it depends on the situation. If a child dawdles over eating, for instance, give him enough choices of nutritious food, then tell him he has a certain amount of time to finish because you need to clean up the kitchen. At the end of that time, say "Okay, I guess you don't want any more," and take his plate away. Don't give him anything else to eat until the next meal, or until a regular snack time. Don't make an issue out of eating. (See Eating Problems.) For a bedtime dawdler, be firm, put away toys with the child, shut off the television, and accompany the child to his room. Going through a pre-bedtime routine helps. (See Sleep Problems.)

The most common and most irritating dawdler, however, is the morning dawdler. If your child gets into a pattern of oversleeping, dawdling, and being late for school, you're not going to break the habit by constant nagging or by driving him to school whenever he's late. What you have to do is help your child to be on time. How do you do this? Child development specialists suggest:

1. Make sure your child has an alarm clock or clock radio, and make it clear that he is responsible for getting up and getting dressed when it goes off.

2. If he has not been getting ready in time, tell him he needs to set his alarm clock earlier and have him decide how much more time he needs.

3. Work out a routine with him for the morning, such as first washing, then dressing, then eating, etc.

4. Decide with him at night all the things he is going to need in the morning. Have him make a list. Have him choose the clothes he wants to wear and lay them out on a chair in his room.

5. Have him put everything he needs for the next morning, such as his books, homework, lunch money, perhaps hat and mittens, and his list, on a table near the door so that everything is ready for him when he leaves. Have him check the list just before he is ready to leave. He may need to get his lunch from the refrigerator, if you have packed one for him.

6. Don't allow television watching before school or nursery school.

7. Remind your child of time as he is getting ready in the morning, such as "It will be time for breakfast in 10 minutes." "We will have to leave in five minutes."

8. Don't dawdle and be late for things yourself, for he will feel justified in following your behavior.

9. If your child still continues to dawdle after you have given him all this help to get his act together, just let him be late and take the consequences, whether it be missing an event he wanted to go to, detention, or some other disciplinary measure given by his teacher.

Child development specialists also say you should not get in the habit of dressing a preschooler who dawdles once he can dress himself. This will just foster his dependency on you and make him feel less responsible. After all, if he knows Mommy will dress him eventually, he'll figure he might as well keep on dawdling. But make sure to train your child in what he must do to be ready in time. Make sure you teach him how to dress himself, tie his shoes, wash himself, etc. If he does have trouble with part of his dressing, such as tying his shoes, of course help him. If your child continues to dawdle about dressing himself, you may just have to take him to day care half dressed one day. Be calm about it, bring the rest of his clothes in a bag, and let him finish dressing there.

If a child continues to dawdle after you have tried these methods, it may be his way of telling you he is having a problem with school or nursery school. If you think this may be the reason for his dawdling, sit down and ask him if there is anything about school or nursery school that is bothering him, something that makes him not want to go. Try to draw him out. And if you find there is a problem, perhaps some child who is bullying him or a teacher who criticizes and embarrasses him in front of the class, do something about the situation. A preschooler may also dawdle because he doesn't want his parents to leave him. He may be afraid you won't show up and pick him up at nursery school some day. He may especially be afraid that a parent will go away and leave him if there has been discord and tension in the home. You need to talk this out with him and reassure him that you, his father, or a relative will pick him up every day and bring him home. Reassure him that the nursery school or daycare director knows where you are, has your phone number and can get in touch with you, if necessary.

A child may also become a chronic dawdler if he has parents who pressure him too much, who rush his development, and are too directive and critical. It can be his way of subconsciously rebelling because children don't dare defy authoritarian parents to their face. If you think you may have been doing this, ease off. Ask your child if he feels he has to do too much or do everything perfectly. Let him know you don't expect him to do everything right, that it's all right to make mistakes.

Destructiveness

Destructive behavior is fairly common among toddlers and preschoolers and is usually not something to worry about. Children this age may knock down a house of blocks that another child has built, for instance, crush a sandcastle a playmate has painstakingly created, or throw a toy or handle it roughly and break it. In such situations, don't hit the child or tell him he's a bad boy, child behavior experts say. Try to use logical consequences and constructive methods instead.

For instance, if your son has knocked down something another child has built, explain that it makes his playmate feel bad when he destroys something he has made. Ask him how he would feel if someone broke something he had spent a lot of time making and was proud of. Suggest that to make up for it, he help his friend rebuild the house or sandcastle. You might say something like, "Tommy, Susan spent a lot of time making that sandcastle, and she's angry that you smashed it. Let's help her build another one."

It's important, however, to step in and stop destructive behavior at this age. If a child doesn't learn as a preschooler that it's wrong to destroy someone else's work or property, he is likely to just go on smashing things if he gets angry or feels the urge to be destructive. If a preschooler continues to be destructive when you have told him it's wrong to destroy another's property and explained how the other person feels, you may have to take firmer measures. Many child behavior experts recommend a time out for children who are disruptive or unruly. If a child continues destructive behavior, sending him for a time out in his room or away from the other children is advisable. You might tell him that he needs to be away from other children for a while until he is ready to play nicely with them and not break or knock down things they make.

If an older child destroys something belonging to another person, the logical consequence is to have him use his allowance money to buy the person a replacement. If it is something that cannot be replaced, for instance, if your son deliberately destroys a picture your daughter has made, let him know that what he did was wrong, and discuss with the two of them what they think his punishment should be. You might give him a choice of one of two punishments discussed which you think are appropriate. In this way, he learns destructiveness does not go unpunished, but he is less likely to be angry and out for revenge than if you just said, "You're grounded for two weeks."

If a child frequently is destructive, however, his behavior can be a sign that there is stress in his life that has become too much for him and anger in him which he cannot handle. Such destructive behavior can be a cry for attention and help. Perhaps parents are always criticizing him, but giving praise and attention to his sister or brother. Or perhaps discord and arguments between his parents are contributing to the behavior. Children who are very destructive, who assault others, set fires, etc., have severe emotional problems which psychiatrists have found often result from the lack of bonding to at least one significant adult in the first two years of life. Such children as infants never had one person they could count on to answer their needs and they consequently grow up unable to love or trust people and lack a conscience (see pp. 15-17). In any case, if a child is chronically or severely destructive, it is wise to consult a school social worker or mental health professional to find out what is causing his stress and anger and how to resolve the problem.

Disobeying and Saying "No"

What do you do when a child disobeys and doesn't do something you have asked him to? First of all, don't get all upset about it. It's perfectly normal for children to disobey their parents at times, especially at certain ages. You have probably heard the phrase "the terrible twos." Two-year-olds often refuse to do what you tell them because this is the age when they realize they have a separate identity, and they want to make their own decisions. Disobeying and saying "No" is their way of asserting their newfound independence and is perfectly normal at this phase of child development. At this age a child gets into everything, may object to eating what you give him, sleeping when you want him to, and doing what you want him to do, and if you spank him, he may very well hit you back. Adolescence is another time when children are trying to find their own identity and want to be independent of parental controls.

What you should NOT do when a child disobeys is spank him, yell at him, or shame him because these responses are likely to make him more angry and defiant. He may obey for the moment, but is apt to defy you the next day, or else become sneaky and try to get away with things out of anger and revenge. Most parents have probably spanked a disobedient child at some time when they were at their wit's end, but spanking is a poor way of handling disobedience because it teaches the wrong lesson. It can give a child the idea that when he's bigger it will be okay to hit someone who doesn't do what he says.

How you handle disobedience depends on the age of the child, but for a child of any age the best thing is to try to prevent it as much as you can. So for a toddler or preschooler:

- Put away things you don't want him to get into so that you don't have to keep telling him not to touch things.

- Avoid using the word "No" as much as possible with a toddler because it's just a challenge for him to disobey. Save "No" for dangerous or serious things, and accompany it with action, such as moving him away if he starts to reach for a hot iron. If he reaches for a dangerous object again, remove him at once from the area, and put him in his playpen or in his room.

- Don't give your child a choice about something if you don't mean it. If you have his bath water drawn, don't say, "Do you want to take a bath?" because he may just say no, and then you'll get into a battle trying to get him into the tub. Instead, say "It's time for your bath now."

- Instead of giving an order, make a suggestion. Instead of saying, "Pick up the toys," say "Let's pick up the toys before Daddy comes home."

- Don't give ultimatums. If you say to a child, "If you don't get your shoes out of the living room by the time I count five, you'll get a spanking," he's likely to just defy you out of spite.

- Don't get into a battle with your child over eating or toilet training. You can't force a child to eat something or to go in the potty, so don't give orders in these areas. You will be just setting yourself up for disobedience and a power struggle, and you are bound to lose the battle, notes psychiatrist Foster Cline.

Teachers at Spring Glen Church Nursery School in Hamden have some other suggestions about preventing disobedience.

- Give advance notice of what you want, such as "In five minutes it will be time to pick up."

- Give praise along with a request, for instance, "You are so strong. Can you carry these three blocks to the box?"

If a toddler or preschooler does disobey:

- Use distraction, especially with a one to three-year-old, instead of an order. For instance, if your child refuses to come inside, take her by the hand and tell her about some game you are going to play with her as you lead her inside. If she keeps fooling around with the telephone, lead her to your pots and pans cabinet and show her how she can stack the pots inside one another. Pots and pans can sometimes keep a toddler amused longer than a new toy. If you distract her enough from something she is not to touch, she will get the idea.

- If a young child takes something she shouldn't, instead of saying "Give that to me," (which she will probably refuse to do), put your hand out and say, "Thank you." At the same time use distraction by giving her a toy or something else to examine.

- Stay calm and cool. Hostility and anger in your voice can provoke more defiance in a disobedient child.

- Don't have a confrontation every time your child disobeys your wishes. Some of the things you tell your child to do, he is not going to do. Don't be an autocratic parent and insist he jump to your every command. If it's not important that he do something, forget it. It gives a child a little feeling of autonomy and independence if he does what he wants sometimes. In fact, child behavior specialists have found that a child may become chronically disobedient if his parents are too strict and dictatorial. If you think this may be the case with your child, take time to find out your child's feelings about things and his wishes and interests. Show respect for him as an individual and for his feelings and needs.

- Be sure to give your child enough attention and praise. Children often misbehave because they aren't getting enough praise and attention. Since negative attention is better than being ignored, they may disobey just to have their parents pay attention to them.

- Show you are disappointed with the child when he disobeys. A teacher at a Stork Club child care center in Connecticut, says it is important to express your disappointment with the child's behavior when he does not do as asked and to stress the importance of cooperation. If the child still does not obey, she suggests using time out or taking away a privilege he has abused.

- If a child disobeys rules of behavior your have set, use a time-out. Dolores Andreucci of Cradles and Crayons Day Care Center in Guilford recommends sending a child who disobeys to a time out chair for a few minutes. If he still does not do as asked, she may have him sit in a cubby outside the main room, but still in view of teachers, for a short time. But she also uses another method which helps prevent disobedience. Instead of saying, "Pick up your toys," which is easy for a child to disobey, she will say "After you pick up your toys, you may join us at snack," or in storytime, or some other activity.

This is similar to a method I call the "stop his world" technique, one of the best ways I know of handling disobedience. It was suggested to me by a psychiatrist I consulted because I was at my wits end with my own four-year-old son, who had become completely unmanageable. Yelling did no good. He ignored it. Spanking didn't work. He hit me back. So I asked the psychiatrist what I could do when my son just wouldn't obey. He told me that if I wanted my son to pick up his toys, for instance, and he wouldn't, I should just tell him what I wanted him to do once, then go about my business and stop his world until he did. I asked what he meant. He said eventually my son would come to me and want something, a cookie, a story, the answer to a question. All I should say was, "As soon as you pick up your toys (or whatever), I'll give it to you (or read to you or answer the question)," and say nothing else to him, but answer each request the same way. It worked like a charm. I didn't have to yell or spank any more. It even worked during his teenage years, by which time he was aware of the method and would laugh and say "Oh, you're using the 'stop his world' technique." But he would still hang up his coat or do a chore that was requested when I stopped his world.

Yale psychiatrist Joseph Woolston agrees that this technique often works best with children who aren't doing things they are supposed to do. He considers such children harder to deal with than children who are doing things they are not supposed to do. For children who are doing things they are not supposed to do, he uses a time out—sending the child to his room or away from others in the group until he can act as he is supposed to. But for a child who won't do something an adult asks, he uses a "stop his world" technique. For instance, he says if a child is refusing to do his homework, parents can say, "As soon as you finish your homework you can start watching television (or do some other activity the child really wants to do)." By stopping a child's world, "you turn the situation over to the child. The longer he delays, the less he gets something," says Woolston, who heads the Child Psychiatric Unit at Yale-New Haven Hospital.

Psychologist H. Stephen Glenn and educator Jane Nelsen call this approach shifting the locus of control—creating an internal, rather than external control. It gives the child the choice of two behaviors, for each of which the consequences have been clearly explained. If he chooses the behavior that carries a punishment or a delay of some activity he wants to do, it is his choice. You are not in the role of the dictatorial bad guy. This way of handling disobedience is especially good with older children and teenagers. With an older child it's also important to listen to his side of the story and find out about his feelings and the reason for his disobedience. And instead of being an authoritarian parent who takes the attitude, "Do this because I say so," explain your reasons for wanting him to obey certain household rules and behave in certain ways.

SAYING "NO"

There is an age when some children seem to latch onto the word "No" and say it regularly when they are asked to do something. In toddlers of one to two years this is normal as they start to get independent, begin to be aware of their own individuality, and assert themselves. Thus parents shouldn't get unduly alarmed about it and see every "No" as an act of defiance. Some young children also say "No" even if they don't mean it, just out of habit. And some say it because their parents use the word a lot, and they are just copying what they hear. Harvard psychologist Burton L. White says that the negativistic period lasts from age 14-15 months to 24 months and may continue for a while even after that. "The likelihood that a child will comply with a request by his or her mother falls to less than 50 percent during this time," says White.

When toddlers say "No" a lot, parents should use the same techniques that they use for disobedience. Distract the child, use suggestions instead of commands, and just ignore the "No" and do what has to be done, whether it be dressing him, turning off the television, or whatever. Avoid confrontations, arguments and battles. Although firm discipline is needed during this period, child behavior specialists say it's all right to let a child occasionally have his way with a few "No's" on minor issues because it shows him you are willing to grant him some independence and some degree of choice in his life.

There are some other techniques you can use to cut down on the "No's" coming from your independent little boy or girl:

- Avoid asking toddlers questions that they can answer with "No". For instance, if you ask your child "Do you want to come say hello to Aunt Susie?" he's likely to answer "No". Instead, just take him by the hand and say "Aunt Susie wants to talk to you."

- Instead of ordering your child to do something, you can often get better results and avoid a "No" by a pleasant suggestion, such as "Let's put away the blocks before we go upstairs and have our bedtime story."

- In general, try to find methods to get your child who says "No" to do what you want without making him feel angry, frightened or guilty.

PARENTS WHO SAY "NO"

Some parents say "No" a lot to their child, and this is unwise. The word can quickly become meaningless when the child realizes his parents will say it frequently, but often not follow up to make sure he doesn't do what they forbid. Or else he will get confused if they sometimes mean the "No" and punish him if he disobeys, but other times say it and do nothing if he doesn't listen to them. Parents should use the word "No" as little as possible, but when they do, use it for something important and mean it. It should be used for dangerous behaviors, such as running into the street or reaching for a sharp knife, and for actions by the child that could hurt someone or do serious damage, for instance, if your preschooler is about to hit a playmate with his truck or whack your window with a baseball bat. You should take action at the same time, such as holding the child and moving him away from the street, or giving him a time out in his room for hitting or hurting someone. It's important to put a lid on this kind of behavior early, when the child is two, or it will become more and more difficult later.

It is really difficult to keep from saying "No" when you are around a young child all day because psychiatrist Foster Cline says a disciplinary or "No" situation occurs with a toddler every seven or eight minutes. In other words, the toddler's desires are thwarted in some way by his parent. But you need to find ways other than the word "No" to discipline. If a child is getting into something, move the object or the child instead of saying "No". Use distraction, substitution, time-outs and some of the other methods mentioned above. They take more patience, but they do work better in the long run.

Disrespect

It's easier to prevent a disrespectful child than to try to change a child who has become disrespectful. To prevent disrespect, you have to teach respect, caring and regard for others in your home from the time your child is a toddler. Respect for others—their feelings, their ideas, their possessions—needs to be the pattern you set and what your expect from other family members in your everyday family life.

You can teach respect for personal property when you see your child taking his friend's bike, for instance, by saying, "That's David's bike. You have to ask his permission to use it." Or if your daughter wanders over to your neighbor's yard and starts playing there, tell her that she is in Mr. and Mrs. Smith's yard, and she cannot play there unless they or someone in their family invite her there to play.

You can also teach respect for feelings and for persons through all sorts of situations in everyday family life. Teach your children not to barge into the bathroom or other people's bedrooms if the door is closed, but to knock first. Teach them not to interrupt when someone is speaking, to treat others courteously. If someone in the family is talking on the phone and your child is engaged in noisy play nearby, remind your child to be quieter so the person on the phone can hear. If Aunt Susie sends your son a gift, keep after him to write a thank you note. Try to develop empathy for others' feelings. Tell him Aunt Susie will be hurt if he doesn't write and say he got her gift. Ask how would he feel if he sent someone a gift and never heard from him. If he is mean to a playmate, tell him you don't like that behavior and ask him how he would feel if someone treated him that way.

To teach respect, it is also important to be respectful to your child. This doesn't mean letting him do whatever he wants. It means treating him with courtesy and concern for his feelings too. It means saying "please" when you ask him for something, just as you want him to say "please" if he asks for something. It means making time to listen to him, to be interested in his ideas. It means treating him with the same respect and consideration you would show to a friend or neighbor, even if your child is only three or four years old.

It takes time to teach respect, but the teaching needs to begin early and you have to keep at it. And the disrespect that many young people show to their teachers, other adults, and even their parents is evidence that respect and consideration for others haven't been taught very well in their homes.

If your child talks back to you and is rude or disrespectful, it's important to stop the behavior immediately. But don't yell, slap, or spank him. Such responses will only increase his resentment. Instead, tell him first that you do not want him talking to you like that. If you know what has irritated him, tell him you understand he is annoyed or angry at (whatever it is), but what he said was hurtful and disrespectful and not the way to talk to other people. If he got annoyed over something you asked him to do, explain why it is important for his benefit, for the smooth running of the household, etc. If he is disrespectful again, tell him firmly to leave the room and go to his room or somewhere else in the house because you do not want him around you when he speaks that way. Say that when he is willing to behave with respect and consideration for others' feelings, he can return. If you give a child a time out every time he speaks disrespectfully to you, he will learn that if he wants to be in your presence, he needs to treat you politely and respectfully. Since most children want to communicate with their parents and be with them, banishing them from your presence when they are disrespectful should be enough to stop the behavior fairly soon.

Submissive parents who let their children get away with being rude and disrespectful to them do their children no favors, and, in fact, do damage. Child psychologists and pediatricians say if parents allow a child to be rude and disrespectful to them, it can harm the child emotionally and psychologically. A child wants and needs limits on his behavior. He knows when he acts badly and disrespectfully, and if parents do not stop such behavior, he will continue it and probably increase it in an attempt to have them set limits. At the same time he will feel anxious and guilty because he knows his behavior is hurting his parents and is probably making them dislike him.

Parents who allow disrespect and bad behavior also make a child feel insecure about his parents' concern and love for him. When parents ignore a child's misbehavior, it sends the child the message that they don't care enough about him to make the effort to discipline him and teach him the kind of behavior that he needs to get along in the world. He thus begins to see himself as not very important, worthwhile, or lovable. And, of course, if his parents accept rude behavior, he will act that way towards others, and other people won't like him very much. Thus, his self-image will suffer even more.

If parents let their children be disrespectful to them, it also shows their children that they don't have much respect for themselves to allow themselves to be treated that way. So the children's opinion of their parents is likely to drop. But since children usually pattern themselves after their parents, they may grow up accepting inconsiderate and rude treatment from others as a normal part of life.

If your child consistently shows disrespect, it may be a sign that something is wrong in the home environment, say child care specialists. It may be your attitude toward him or the way you are raising him. If you ignore your child, or allow him to behave and talk disrespectfully toward you, or if you criticize, belittle and point out his weaknesses a lot, you may well end up with a child who is disrespectful to you and others and who is likely to get into trouble. Continuing disrespect, according to psychologist Lee Salk, is a signal that the child wants and really needs more discipline. If you find your child becoming increasingly disrespectful, it's a good idea to consult a family therapist to get to the root of the problem.

Doctor/Dentist Visits

It's the rare child who doesn't cry either before or during a visit to the doctor, but you can make things easier for your child if you prepare ahead of time. First, never tell your child you are taking her someplace else and then take her to the doctor's instead. You are really lying to her if you do this, and she may get the idea that lying is okay since you have done it and start telling lies herself. Also, this will make her lose trust and faith in you, and children need to be able to trust their parents. It will also make her more upset and angry when you do land at the doctor's office.

Instead, get her a book or two about a child going to the doctor's and read it to her before a regularly scheduled visit. Or keep it on hand to read to her if she starts to get sick and you will have to take her to the doctor's. When you leave, bring the book and remind her that you both will have to look for some of the things in the doctor's office which the book showed, perhaps his stethoscope or a thermometer. If your child has memories of previous doctor visits and injections and starts crying and worrying that the doctor will hurt her, don't lie and say he won't. Tell her that it might hurt a little if he has to give her an injection, but only for a very little while. Also, explain why you have to take her to the doctor—for instance, because he can find our why she isn't feeling well, or give her medicine to make her sore throat better. Many pediatricians have some interesting toys and books in their office, and you can remind her that she will be able to play with some new toys there, or that you will read her a new story.

Follow the same pattern of reassurance on dentist visits. Explain that the dentist needs to fix her teeth so that they will stay strong and healthy and so she can chew and eat properly with them.

If your child does cry and get upset in the doctor's office or on the way, don't tell her to stop crying and "Be a big girl." Child behavior specialists say this just adds guilt to her anxiety and can make her suppress her feelings, which can in time do psychological damage. To help a child learn to handle disturbing feelings like fear and anger, parents need to let the child express these feelings with words, tears, etc., show they understand what the child is feeling, and reassure her and help her cope with the feeling. So tell your child you understand it is scary for her to go to the doctor, that you were scared when you were little too. But reassure her that you will be there with her, and the doctor's purpose is not to hurt her, but to make her better or to keep her well.

Eating Problems

IN INFANCY

Eating problems tend to occur when parents worry too much about what their child is or is not eating. They can start in infancy if a parent tries to feed the baby more than he wants or tries to feed him when he isn't hungry, say child behavior specialists. If your baby loses interest in his bottle and there is still a lot of milk in it, don't try to force him to take more. It will just make him annoyed and irritable. If you keep doing this, he is likely to become even less interested in eating. Granted, it can be difficult if you have a baby who only takes half his bottle and wants to eat every two hours. But he may be the kind of baby who needs to eat little and often. Don't snap on the soles of his feet with your fingers or shake him if he falls asleep feeding to try to get him to take more. This is associating pain and discomfort with feeding. Instead, cuddle the baby and keep feeding time relaxed and comfortable. And take comfort in the fact that as he gets bigger, he will go longer between feedings and take more.

By about six months, most babies are ready for a regular three-meal-a-day schedule with solid food, even though they will still continue to take a bottle.

When a baby begins to take solid food, offer different kinds, but don't force any food on the baby that he doesn't like. Instead, wait a few weeks and try it again. Many pediatricians recommend baby cereal as the first solid food, but babies often like fruit better because it is sweeter. Mixing fruit with the cereal I found worked well for me. Don't feel your baby has to eat all the food you have put in his dish. Don't force him to eat more once he shows he is not interested—for instance, if he refuses to open his mouth. And don't play games and use all sorts of tricks to get him to eat because this is just likely to make him more resentful, and you may end up with a child who doesn't want to eat at mealtimes or only eats a few things.

Expect that a baby will take a long time to learn to feed himself and that he will get food all over himself and on the floor as he is learning. Give a baby a spoon when he can grasp and maneuver it and seems interested in trying to feed himself. But don't get mad if he drops his spoon, dish, or finger food on the floor or even throws it. The child usually isn't doing this to be bad; he may have just discovered gravity and is fascinated to find that things fall to the floor when he lets go of them. One mother I know says she just takes away the dish when she sees her son getting ready to toss it. Another puts the garbage pail next to her son's high chair and lets him empty his dish into it when he is finished eating. If he isn't done, it's too bad. He learns that once food goes into the garbage, he doesn't get it back.

Noted pediatrician T. Berry Brazelton makes the following recommendations about how to get children to feed themselves and how to avoid feeding problems:

- Start giving the child finger foods at about eight months.

- By one year let her choose what she wants to eat.

- If she won't eat vegetables, give her a multivitamin each day, make sure she gets enough milk and protein and don't hassle her about it.

- Expect her to play with food between a year or two.

- Don't make an issue of food.

IN PRESCHOOL YEARS

If a child won't eat a certain food, child care experts agree that you shouldn't make a fuss about it. Just try giving it to her again a few days later. You may have to do this a couple of times, but probably your child will eventually try it. But don't put pressure on the child to eat it, make her feel guilty, or offer a reward if she eats it, such as dessert, Promising dessert as a reward just implies that the food really doesn't taste very good. And don't refuse to give her dessert if she hasn't eaten as well as you expected. In fact, child care specialists say you should never use food as a reward. Instead, make dessert something healthful, such as fruit, wholesome cookies, ice cream or yogurt, and make it a regular part of the meal. But don't make the mistake of always offering your child something different to eat if she doesn't like what you have put on the table. This can give her the idea that all she has to do to get something she likes is to refuse to eat what you are serving. It's better to offer her a choice of several nutritious foods and let her eat the ones she likes. Having your child help plan the menus and go shopping with you and choose nutritious foods she likes may also help her to be more interested in mealtimes.

REFUSING TO EAT OR NOT EATING ENOUGH

Parents sometimes worry that their child isn't eating enough. Child care specialists say parents shouldn't worry about this. Unless a child has something physically wrong, he will eat enough. A child's appetite normally decreases after infancy, but parents often don't know this. By becoming anxious and pressuring him to eat, parents will make the child tend to use food as a weapon for control and lay the groundwork for real eating problems.

Don't let mealtime become a battleground, experts warn. Parents who try to make their children eat a certain food or always clean their plate almost always lose because you can't really make a child eat. And if you make a big issue out of what they eat, children will see that all they have to do to win is refuse to eat what you want them to. This can lead to a continuing power struggle at mealtimes and some serious eating problems. So as soon as your child loses interest in eating his meal, just take his food away and send him on his way.

I know well from my own experience how mealtime can escalate into a power struggle with a child. One of my children had a poor appetite as an infant, and I, not knowing any better, did all the things I mentioned above that you shouldn't do. When he would fall asleep after taking half his bottle as a newborn, I'd tickle his feet and prod him to take more. When he started solid foods, he wouldn't eat much, and I would coax him and play all kinds of games to try to get him to eat. By the time he was three, the only foods he would eat in any quantity were noodles, black olives and grape juice. He would awaken us several times most nights because he was hungry and thirsty. It wasn't until he was four that he slept through the night.

Children usually refuse to eat either because they are not hungry or because they have been forced to eat, agrees Sue Marcio, director of R&K Tiny Tots Nursery School. She suggests giving a child who is a poor eater very small portions of food that he likes and that is nutritious. Although some child care experts advise not giving the child anything to eat between meals, Marcio recommends leaving nutritious food such as raisins or cheese and crackers in a dish somewhere that the child can reach. She suggests giving finicky eaters frozen milk bars to make sure they get enough milk. And if a child is not hungry, Marcio says parents should let the child go play, then when he comes back and is hungry, feed him.

Here is a summary of suggestions offered by several child care experts and pediatricians for preventing eating problems in small children or stopping them if they start:

1.   Serve the child only a small portion of food at a time, even of food the child likes. Let him ask for more.

2.   Give fruits instead of vegetables if the child won't eat vegetables.

3.   Give the child attention other ways if he seems to be trying to get it by refusing to eat.

4.   Don't serve the meal when the child is overtired or overexcited.

5.   Keep mealtimes pleasant. Avoid conflicts and argument at meals. Even a baby and toddler can sense anger between his family members and finds it upsetting.

6.   If you give between-meal snacks, use healthy, nutritious foods and serve them midway between meals, never within an hour of a meal.

7.   NEVER use food as a reward or punishment. Don't say, "If you don't eat your vegetables, you can't have dessert," or "If you eat some of this, you can have dessert." Using food as a reward or punishment connects food with love and approval, and the child may grow into an adult who turns to food for satisfaction when he lacks love and approval.

8.   Don't beg a child to eat just a little more. It's irritating to the child and may make him balk even more at eating at the next meal.

9.   Don't punish refusal to eat something—for instance, by saying "You're going to sit there until you clean your plate." This will upset your child, make a connection between anxiety and mealtime in his mind, and start a power struggle that he will most likely win. He probably won't clean his plate. Either you will get disgusted and send him on his way after a while, or you will make him sit there for hours, which is cruel.

10.   Don't MAKE your child eat a certain amount of food or a certain food.

11.   Don't keep junk food in easy reach.

12. Have good eating habits yourself so you can be a role model.

13. If a child doesn't like what you have given him and doesn't want to eat, don't hassle him. It's a good idea to check and make sure he isn't sick. But if he is all right, just calmly take his plate away, send him off to play, and tell him he can eat at the next meal.

PLAYING WITH FOOD

One thing you should do is insist that your child be polite and mannerly at the table. Don't allow your children to play with food or throw food around, even when they are preschoolers. Playing with food is normal for toddlers, but parents probably need to take action if children use their fingers to eat or to play with their food beyond age four or five. Ignoring the problem may not work, because if the child is doing this to gain attention, ignoring it may just cause the problem to escalate. If your child starts to throw his food, take the food away and tell him food is not for throwing. Distraction may also work with a toddler who wants to throw food. If he picks up his cup and looks ready to spill his milk out, for instance, hand him a cracker and take the cup, instead of yelling at him or saying "No." Don't tolerate a school-age child playing with his food with his fingers. Tell him firmly that playing with food is not allowed. If he persists, take his food away.

EATING TOO MUCH

What about children who overeat? Bickering, sibling rivalry, problems at school or at home may lead some children to develop a compulsion to overeat. Dr. Foster Cline has found that gorging on food may be one characteristic of children who never developed a secure, trusting relationship with at least one primary adult in the early years of their life. Parents who don't give their children much interest and attention, but instead offer them food when they are restless or bothersome may start an eating pattern that makes them turn to food when they want love and attention. The result is an obese adult.

You should never try to get a child to lose weight by shaming and making fun of the child. Instead, give her plenty of love and attention, and if she is bothered by her weight tell her you can help her lose weight by planning a menu with her and helping her choose low calorie foods and avoid foods that are fattening. Try not to keep fattening and junk foods around and plan lower calorie meals and snacks for the whole family. And urge her to start a regular exercise program.

Failures and Mistakes

Your child is going to fail many times when he tries to do something. He'll fail and fall down a lot before he learns to walk, he'll spill a lot of food before he learns to eat decently, and have many failures before he is toilet trained. When he is older he may fail to throw a ball as well as you think he should or he may fail tests in school. In dealing with a child's failures and mistakes it's important that parents do not get upset and ashamed because their child has failed to perform as expected. Instead of blaming the child or offering excuses, it's important for parents to encourage their child.

When your child does make mistakes, help him understand that mistakes are a natural and normal part of growing up, and not a sign that he is no good or a failure as a person. You need to praise him for trying and explain that failure is nothing to be ashamed of, that everyone makes mistakes and fails at things throughout life. Psychologist Loyd Rowland says that many times what people consider failure is not failure at all because the person has learned from the experience. He may have learned what he should not do or how he could do better the next time. It can help if you explain this to your child and encourage him that he probably will be able to do what he has failed to do if he keeps on trying.

Children who fail a lot get very discouraged, particularly if they feel they are failing to accomplish something their parents expect of them. So don't set such high standards or have such high expectations for your child that it is impossible for him to reach them. In a newsletter for the Mental Health Association of Connecticut Rowland stresses that " no child can keep on failing without being damaged by it." Repeated failures are likely to make him timid, particularly if parents nag or shame him when he fails. It is vital that parents handle their children's failures gently and with encouragement, says the psychologist. "Work it out somehow so that your child succeeds a good part of the time in what he tries to do. Children live up to our expectations for them," he observes. "If we expect them to fail or act stupid or clumsy or stubborn—and tell them so—they will live up to the *picture* adults paint of them."

Another important thing to keep in mind about failure is that children may fail at something because they have not matured enough to be able to do it well. Parents should not push their children to do something because Johnny or Joey, who is the same age, can do it. Children differ a lot in how fast they mature and what they can do at a certain age. Instead, Rowland advises parents to let children go along at their own pace in learning new things. He observes that parents will find it almost impossible to teach a child of 18 months to peddle a tricycle because his muscles and nerve and coordination are not developed enough. But by the time he is three "he has the *tools* inside his legs, and he can make a tricycle go all over the place, and learn quickly." So to avoid failures his advice is to teach a child something if he seems to have matured enough to learn it fairly easily. "If learning is too difficult, you had better wait."

Fears

It is natural for a child to have fears, and he should never be punished for them or made to feel guilty because of them. An infant, for instance, is naturally afraid of loud noises or of falling and may for a time be afraid of a bath. A baby also usually goes through a period where he is afraid of strangers. This fear is a good sign because it shows he has matured enough to tell the difference between his parents and other adults and is secure with his parents because they have cared for him well. An older child normally may be afraid when he encounters strange new experiences, when his parents leave him or if he thinks they may leave him. Preschoolers also may be afraid of certain things, of dogs, perhaps, or the dark, or of getting hurt. Sometimes a frightening television program may make a child afraid. Most of these fears generally are not serious and are outgrown.

If your child is afraid of something, first of all take his fear seriously and be sympathetic. Don't ignore it or dismiss it. Don't call him a baby or otherwise shame him for feeling afraid, and don't force him to stand up to his fear and then punish him if he doesn't, warns psychiatrist Albert Solnit, former director of the Yale Child Study Center. Shaming the child will just make him bury his fears and can make him more anxious and timid. Punishing the child for his fears will just give him the idea his parents don't understand him and again discourage him from communicating fears or possibly other things to them.

Some parents want their children, especially sons, to be braver than is usual for their age. For instance, they will call their son a sissy if he is afraid of the water or of a bigger boy who bullies him. "Bravery and courage come with solving problems step by step," says psychologist Loyd Rowland. "Nobody ever made a child braver by calling him 'sissy.' In fact, that is a term which I don't think fathers or mothers should ever use." But parents also should not go to the opposite extreme and create an environment where the child can avoid his fears, says Solnit. This will deny the child the opportunity to learn to deal with fears he is bound to have later in life.

Instead, what you should do if your child is afraid of something, Solnit says, is first find the basis for the child's fear. Ask the child what he is afraid of and why and listen carefully. Usually it's not a traumatic event, and often, he notes, the fear stems from the child's primary fear of being separated from his mother.

You also should be sympathetic towards the child and reassure him. This may mean holding a small child who is frightened to comfort him, putting your arm around an older child, and saying you can understand why he is afraid. This labels the emotion he is feeling and tells him it's all right to have such feelings. Child specialists say it also helps if parents admit they too had fears when they were a child and talk about some of the fears they had. They can also let the child know that adults are also afraid sometimes.

But showing you understand and sympathize with the child`s fear isn't enough. You have to help the child deal with it. Parents should actively try to do something to alleviate the child's fear. For instance, if a child is afraid of lights moving on his wall at night from cars passing in the street, as my daughter was, explain what is causing the lights and pull down her window shade. If your son is afraid of the dark, leave a night light on in his room. Don't just say "There is nothing to be afraid of" or tell him to "Be a big boy." This will only make him feel ashamed as well as afraid. Instead, encourage the child to talk about his fear and then help him get over it.

Sometimes you may be able to ease a child's fear by an explanation if he has been frightened by a new and unfamiliar situation. My daughter, for instance, became hysterical and clung to me terrified the first time she saw a train. She was three or four, and I had taken her down to the station to meet my mother who was coming for a visit. It's easy to understand how the size, the noise and the speed of a train would be terrifying to a young child. To my daughter the big, noisy train rushing towards her probably seemed like some monster that was going to destroy us all or sweep her away.

In such a situation, it's important to hold and comfort your child and find out exactly what about the situation frightened her. I said something like, "The train made a terribly loud noise. Did that scare you?" When she said "yes," we talked about what else was scary—how big the train was, how fast it went. In such a situation, agree that the things that frightened your child can be scary to a little one. But after you show you understand and sympathize with her fear, you may be able to explain it away. Showing my daughter the railroad tracks and explaining that the train could only go on the tracks helped her understand that it couldn't hurt her if she stood away from the tracks. Holding my daughter and explaining why the train wouldn't hurt her calmed her, and she soon got over her fear of trains.

However, I could have handled the situation better if I had realized the train might frighten her and prepared her in advance. Getting a children's book about trains that explained that they are big and noisy, but bring people many places and don't hurt them, might have prevented her hysterical outburst. If you are going to take your child someplace where he might be afraid, try to prepare him in advance by gradually making him familiar with the situation. If you are going to have to leave him at a day care center, for instance, it's wise to take him for a visit ahead of time, have him meet the teachers and some of the children, and talk about all the things he will do there and the fun he will have. Hospitals recognize the importance of preparing a child ahead of time for a situation that might be frightening, and they have books about children coming to the hospital and programs to show a child who must be hospitalized what the hospital is like before he is admitted.

Psychiatrists agree that it's very important for parents to find the cause of a child's fear and help him overcome it. If a child seems very fearful about something connected with school, Solnit suggests talking to his teacher to find out why and devising ways to help the child overcome the fear. Talking to the child's doctor or pediatrician may also be a good idea if the fear persists, he said. If parents do not help a child express and deal with his fears, he may become timid and withdrawn and not make friends easily. If they ignore their child's fears, and especially if they shame or punish him for being afraid, the child may suffer severe emotional damage.

This is because each time the child encounters a situation that frightens him, the stress causes changes in his body chemistry. Adrenaline, the hormone that causes your heart to pound and your palms to grow clammy when you're afraid, is secreted, as well as other hormones that affect many organs in the body and cause changes in brain chemistry. Each time the child encounters whatever he is afraid of, be it a parent, animal, or school buddy, the fear reaction is likely to be stronger unless he finds reassurance or learns to deal with the fear. If the fear and stress is experienced over and over, the hormonal changes that occur can be harmful to the person in many ways, says Dr. Mary F. Asterita, assistant professor of physiology and pharmacology at the Indiana University School of Medicine, reports Arthur Henley in his book *Phobias*. The chemical system in the brain may become so sensitive that intense feelings of fear are provoked not only by the object that originally frightened the child, but eventually even by things connected with it. A child frightened of dogs, for instance, may become frightened of all animals unless someone helps him deal with this fear. And if guilt is connected to a fear, the child may develop a real emotional problem. If a child dislikes and is afraid of his father, for example, Henley says he may feel so guilty and disturbed by feeling this way about someone he depends on and is supposed to love that his subconscious mind may shift the hatred and fear to something else, perhaps a dog or cat his father owns. The result can be a full-fledged phobia.

Dr. Rowland, in one of the *Pierre the Pelican* bulletins the Connecticut Mental Health Association sends to new parents, has some general advice about children's fears:

- Protect a baby from anything that might frighten him. Babies seem to forget fears unless they are exposed to the frightening situation again and again. If a little child is frightened hold him, comfort him and reassure him that everything is all right.

- Understand that fears can spread. If a child is frightened by a dog, for instance, he may also become frightened of other animals.

- Don't ever frighten a child, even in play. Don't hide in a closet or behind a door and then jump out and scare him. And especially don't scare him in the dark.

- Try not to pass on your fears to your child. A child can sense when his parent is afraid, even if the parent tries to hide it. If you are afraid, you may have to calm yourself down before picking up your child and trying to reassure him.

Here are some suggestions for dealing with specific fears children may have:

The vacuum cleaner - If this frightens your baby, don't use it close to him for weeks or even months. Instead, advises Dr. Rowland, wait until he is busy doing something in one room and vacuum in another room away from him. Don't get it close enough to him to frighten him and make him cry. After a while he will decide on his own that the vacuum cleaner won't hurt him. Once he starts getting used to it, you can explain how the button turns it on and off and let him do this if he wants.

The dark - Leave a night light on in his room or in a hall outside his room with his door open. If it is necessary, sit quietly with him for a time in his room until he feels safe. Show your child that the darkness of night can be interesting by taking him for a walk at night to look at the stars and moon and planets or the lights of the town from a hilltop.

Dogs or cats -Let the child watch a dog or cat through the window when the animal is romping or playing, advises Dr. Rowland. Gradually let him get acquainted with a friendly dog or cat, but don't let the animal get too close too soon. Teach him to talk softly to a dog, to pat a friendly dog slowly and gently, and to stand still and not run when a dog is near.

Thunder - Hold a small child and explain that it is just a loud noise in the sky and won't hurt her. If the child is old enough to understand, I think it helps to explain what thunder is in words the child can understand (perhaps something like clouds bumping into one another) and stress that it won't hurt the child.

Getting lost, losing a parent in a store, or some other frightening event that might happen - Plan ahead with your child about what he should do if the event should happen.

Monsters - Tell the child calmly that there are no such thing as monsters. If he thinks one is in the closet or under the bed, put the lights on and go look with him to show him nothing is there.

The water - Don't force a child who is afraid of the water to go in swimming or to put his face in the water. And don't make him feel guilty if he is afraid, as the mother in the Introduction to this book did. Recognize that it is frightening to many children to go into an ocean, lake or pool for the first time or to put their face under water. Let the child get used to the water at his own pace. If these fears occur in swimming lessons, reassure the child that it's all right and that he will get used to the water as he gets older, and he won't be afraid to swim and put his face in the water. When he finally does so, be sure to praise him for overcoming his fear.

Fear a parent won't return - Whenever you have to leave your child, reassure him that you will be back. Don't make fun of his fear and tell him to be a "big boy and stop crying." This will only make him feel guilty for a great fear that is natural in children—the fear of losing his parents. If your child is old enough to recognize numbers, show him a clock and tell him you will be back when the little hand is on a certain number or between two numbers.

If your child has severe or long-lasting fears which you can't help him conquer by the above methods, it would be wise to take him to a child psychologist or other mental health professional to find out what is causing his fears and to help him overcome them.

Fighting

FIGHTING IN PRESCHOOLERS

Most children will fight at some time or other in their life, but you can often prevent fights in preschoolers if you know what to say to children and how to defuse fight-provoking situations. Sue Marcio, a Connecticut nursery school director, believes fights can often be prevented if children are taught from the beginning by their parents and nursery school teachers that they are to keep their hands to themselves and treat people kindly. Parents can also help prevent fighting among siblings by treating their children the same and by treating them fairly. They should not, for instance, give one child a lot of chores and another, who is about the same age, very few. Nor should they let a preschooler get away with hitting an older sibling and then punish the older child for hitting back because he should "know better."

It also helps to have a watchful eye and step in when you see something happening that could start a fight, say child care experts. For instance, if Michael has just built a house of Lincoln logs, and you see David about to knock it down, step in and don't let him. Instead, take David by the hand and say something like, "Michael made that house and it's his. We don't break other people's things." Then lead him away into some other activity. If a younger child keeps destroying what an older one is building and a fight is looming, you sometimes can deflect a battle if you ask the older one to teach the younger how to build with the logs or blocks, or whatever.

A good general rule is if you see something that suggests a fight is imminent—for instance, if one child pushes or hits another —say firmly, "Tell him how you feel. Don't push (or hit)." It is also important to get right over to the children. Don't try to stop a fight by yelling at children from across the room. Squat down so you are at their level, ask what the argument is about, empathize with the children's feelings of anger or frustration, and help them work out a solution to the problem.

If a fight does occur among preschoolers, early childhood specialists say the parent or adult supervising the children should not let them fight it out, but should intervene as soon as possible. Nursery school director Dolores Andreucci says her teachers will separate the children and explain to them "We don't fight with our friends." If a child persists in starting fights, she will send him to a chair or a separate room for a time out period. As a last resort, he will be sent further away to the director's office. She will also explain why he is sitting apart from the other children, saying something like "Johnny is my friend like you are my friend. I won't allow Johnny to hit you, so I can't allow you to hit him." Then she tells the child to sit there "until he feels happy inside."

Laura Spencer of the Stork Club Child Care and Development Centers says the adult supervising the children should take the children aside, have them explain what happened "and then express to them the possible consequences that could occur if their fighting got out of control. Children often are unaware how their actions can affect others," she says. Once the situation is resolved, she has the children apologize to one another. She believes children sometimes fight because they are bored and want something to do. She has found that giving them some extra responsibility, such as making them safety monitors reminding their classmates to play safely, sometimes helps to correct the behavior of children who tend to get into fights.

Spring Glen Church Nursery School teachers advise trying to talk about the problem first and show children how they can resolve disagreements by taking turns and sharing. The teachers also suggest telling the children if they can settle the argument without fighting, that's fine, but otherwise the parent or adult in charge will settle it. If the children can't settle their argument and the fighting continues, they recommend sending each child to a different room for a time out period. The adult may set a timer and tell the children they can come out when the timer goes off.

Stork Club Child Care Centers teachers suggest stressing the positive, encouraging cooperation between children and pointing out those that are playing well together. They also say an adult who does not see how the fight started should not make a decision about who is to blame. If the fight is over a toy, it's wise to acknowledge the children's feelings first, by saying, for example, "I can see you both want the toy." Then you can suggest seeing if they can play with it together, if it is something suitable for this, such as a ball or truck. If not, you might say you will give it to one child for a time, and when he is finished with it, he will give it to the other child. To decide which child will get it first, you might put a marble or coin in one of your hands without letting them see which one, and have them choose which hand they want. Removing the toy and redirecting children to another activity is another solution. If your children are fighting over a toy, you can also tell them if they don't stop fighting and share it, the toy will be put away.

Disagreements between children can be an opportunity to teach them appropriate ways of handling situations and ways to solve problems on their own. As nursery school teachers and other child care experts advise, when children start fighting, tell them to stop and tell the other person how they feel instead of hitting him. Get them to talk about what happened and about their feelings. You can help develop empathy by explaining why what one child did made the other angry and asking the first child how he would feel if he were treated that way. You should also ask the children how they think the problem could be solved. Finally, you might even talk about what people should do and how they should act in different situations that could cause problems. In this way a fight between children may be made into a worthwhile learning experience.

If two children repeatedly seem to have difficulty getting along, separating them for a time and pairing them off with other children may help. Redirecting their attention and activity may be useful too. If one child seems to start fights with other children a lot, there may be something in the family situation at home that is making him angry and upset, and he may be taking this out on other children. In this case the family should seek help from a counselor or child guidance clinic.

One thing you should not do is tell children who are fighting that they are bad because this can damage their feelings of self worth. Lack of self esteem is a major cause of mental and emotional problems later in life. Marcio says, "Sometimes we tell children it's not nice or naughty to do something. We never tell them they're bad, but that their action was bad so we do not damage their self esteem."

Another thing you should not do is spank your children if they fight. The reason should be obvious. By spanking them you are sending the message that even though it's wrong to hit when you are a child, it's acceptable when you are an adult.

FIGHTING IN OLDER CHILDREN

Some child behavior specialists believe that parents should not intercede immediately when a fight begins between children because it can give the child the idea that he can't take care of himself, and he is more apt to be timid and fearful around rough and aggressive children. And once they are in school, children may have to learn to deal with a bully by hitting him back.

It makes sense to step in right away and stop a fight between two- and three-year-olds before they hurt one another or get in the habit of hitting and fighting to solve their problems. However, if you can, it's often better to let older children settle their quarrels themselves without getting involved. But there are times when you must step in, for instance, if a bigger child is beating up a smaller one, if a child is hitting another with something (stick, bat, etc.), if a child is getting hurt, or if several children have ganged up against one.

FIGHTING AMONG SIBLINGS

Fighting among siblings is common, and the best way to decrease it, say child behavior specialists, is not to get involved in their quarrels. Children often quarrel to get a parent's attention or to get back at a sibling who has angered them by getting mother or dad on their side. If your children quarrel a lot, take them aside for a few minutes and tell them you do not want to get involved in their fights from now on. You want them to settle their own arguments. If they try to drag you into one of their battles, calmly remind them that you are sure they can work out their disagreements themselves. Educator Jane Nelsen, who recommends this approach, says one mother who used it reported that fights between her children decreased 75 percent.

If you do get drawn into a fight between children, child specialists say don't get caught in the trap of trying to decide who is right and who is wrong, who started it and who did what. And don't punish one child and not the other because it will only make the punished child resentful and more apt to start another fight with the favored sibling. Treat both of the children the same. Send each to a separate area for a time out to cool off. Take away the same privilege from each for fighting. When they see they both get the same consequences for fighting, they are less likely to try to draw you into their arguments and try to get you to take sides.

Here are some suggestions psychologist Louise Bates Ames has for preventing and decreasing fighting among siblings:

To prevent fights:

- Praise your children whenever you can and give them attention when they behave well so they don't feel they have to misbehave to get it.
- Try to make each child feel special somehow.
- Don't favor one particular child.
- Don't compare a child with his sister or brother.
- Encourage your children to solve their disputes on their own.

To stop or decrease fighting:

- Remove anything fought over for a periods of time.
- Hold any child who is physically attacking a sibling.
- Isolate children if they are quarreling; have them play in separate rooms.
- Use time outs if children fight.
- Take away a privilege for breaking the rule of no fighting.
- Teach children to work out their disagreements with words.
- Give work assignments to angry siblings so they can put the energy of their anger into something worthwhile.
- Don't let yourself be dragged into the fight as judge.
- Don't show that their fighting annoys you or they are apt to do it more.
- Try to find the reasons behind a pattern of fighting.

(For further information, see Sibling Rivalry.)

Playing with Fire

It's normal for children to be fascinated by fire to some degree. It seems magical to see a flame suddenly appear when you light a match. But you need to talk about fire with your child and get the idea across to him that it is dangerous and why it is dangerous. Explain what fire is and how quickly it can spread and burn down trees and houses if people are not careful about how they handle it. Try to find a book about fire to read to him. Explain how smoke from a fire can keep people from getting air so they can't breathe, which is why we have smoke detectors. Explain why matches are dangerous. Train a small child to give any matches he sees to you immediately. It's not wise to forbid a preschool or school age child to ever light a match, however, child behavior specialists say, because it may provoke him to try it just once, and the consequences could be terrible. Instead, make it a rule that he can only light a match if an adult is supervising him. For instance, you might let him light the candles on a birthday cake.

If you do find your child playing with fire and violating your fire safety rules, you need to punish him immediately to show you mean business. Explain again why it is dangerous to play with fire. Then send him to his room for several hours, take away a special privilege, prohibit him from going to a game or party he is planning to attend, or give some other suitably serious punishment. Although some parents would spank a child for this, spanking can make a child, especially an older child, very angry and resentful, and he might just do what you have spanked him for out of spite. It is generally a very poor method of discipline.

If your child continues to play with fire, you should take him to a therapist because playing with fire can be a sign that something is severely upsetting the child and can be a cry for help.

Harassment by Other Children

How do you handle the situation when your child comes home and says that other kids have been picking on him or bullying him?

First of all, don't ignore the situation just because you're too busy or have problems of your own, or because you think children's squabbles are just minor difficulties you don't need to bother about. If the problem bothered your child enough so that he or she felt the need to tell you about it, it means the child can't handle the situation and needs some help from you.

Second, never tell your child he or she is too sensitive or "just a crybaby" if he complains that others have picked on him. Such comments will just make him feel guilty for feeling hurt and angry, and he will feel even more inadequate. Also, they will make him suppress his feelings of anger and resentment, instead of expressing them to you, because he'll be afraid of losing your acceptance and affection.

In any instance when your child is being picked on by other children, you need to do something. The first thing you should do is empathize with your child. Show you understand how he feels. You might say something like, "It makes you feel really sad and hurt that (whoever it was) said that to you, doesn't it? And you're angry too, I bet." Try to draw him out and have him express his feelings. You might also empathize by telling him of a similar situation that happened to you as a child and the way you felt. Try to find out why the children were picking on him, when it started, what they said. Then explore with him the possible courses of action he could take.

Helping your child express upsetting feelings like anger, fear, and sadness is very important, mental health specialists say. Expressing such feelings verbally helps get rid of them and helps the child learn to deal with them. But if you squelch these feelings in your child, make him feel it is unacceptable to express them, it can lead to mental and emotional problems later in his life. He may suffer from depression if he subconsciously turns his suppressed anger against himself because he feels inferior and unable to cope with life as others can. Or occasionally the feelings may explode in violent rage.

This happened with one high school student who was an Eagle Scout, but was not popular because he was thin, unathletic, and extremely intelligent. When he complained to his father, an ex-Marine, that some boys at school used to harass him and hit him, his father's only response was "Fight back." But he knew he couldn't fight the group of them. One day he decided to run away, but the car wouldn't start. Feeling trapped and helpless, he took a few of his father's guns, loaded them and walked into school to get his tormentors. Instead, he came upon the principal first, who told him to get rid of the guns. So he shot and killed the principal.

This is, of course, an extreme case, but if the Eagle Scout's father had taken the time to listen to his son, understand his problem, and go to school and give him some support against the boys bullying him, the tragedy might have been averted. It illustrates, however, the essential things parents must do when their child complains of being harassed by other children: listen and get all the details, help the child handle the situation, or take action yourself.

It is especially important for parents to come to their child's aid if his classmates or peer group call him derogatory names like "nerd" or "retard" and treat him like an outcast. "Even one year as the outcast or bad kid can really damage the child's future chances at school," says Dr. Sandra Sexson, psychiatrist and director of training in adolescent and child psychiatry at Emory University.

She says try to find out first why other children consider your child different and are making him a scapegoat. Ask your child what they say about him and why so you can help him solve the problem and get them to realize what a worthwhile person he is. If he is being ridiculed because of his clothing or unkempt appearance, you can help him improve that. If it is because he has some disability, you may have to talk with his teacher and have her help the class understand your child's problem. Perhaps he could even be encouraged to do a talk about his disability, what causes it, what famous people have had it and how they have overcome it. If you cannot get the help of your child's teacher, contact the school social worker or school psychologist, but don't give up until the cruelty is stopped.

Here is how one excellent father, who raised three good, responsible children, handled the situation when his high-school-age daughter complained that some boys in school, one of whom she had dated, were harassing her. Not only were they insulting her, but they also would hit and push her. Ed told his daughter not to worry, he would handle the situation. Then he took time off from work, went to school the next morning and asked to see the principal. He was told the principal was not in. He said he would wait. When the principal finally appeared, he told him what the boys were doing to his daughter and said he wanted them called down to the office immediately and was not leaving until he saw them.

When the boys came down, he told them who he was and said his daughter had told him they were insulting her, hitting her and pushing her. Ed told them in no uncertain terms he wanted it stopped immediately, using some strong language to make his point. "If it doesn't stop," he said, "I will call the police and have you arrested." Then he turned to the principal and said, "I'm holding you personally responsible for having this behavior stopped. If I hear that it isn't, I'll also file charges against you."

"Is that understood?" he asked the boys.

Cowed, they mumbled, "Yessir."

His daughter had no further trouble with them. But the incident did much more than save her from a few bruises. It showed her that she had a parent she could count on when she needed help, a parent who cared enough about her to take the time and effort to make sure his daughter was treated well.

Sometimes, however, the parent doesn't have to intercede, but can resolve the situation by telling the child an effective way of handling it. Ed's wife Joyce did this when their son was in grammar school and kept getting beaten and punched by the class bully. He was afraid to fight back because his parents had taught him not to fight, and he was afraid he would get in trouble with them and with his teacher. But when his mother found out about the situation, she told him in this case it was all right for him to defend himself. If the boy hit him, she told her son to haul off and give him a good hard punch in the nose or mouth. He came home the next day and said he had done what she said and gave the bully a nosebleed. He was afraid he would be punished by the teacher, but he wasn't, and the bully never bothered him again. The incident also illustrates that sometimes the quickest way a child can show he will not be a punching bag for a bully is to defend himself and hit back. (For further information, see Bad Children.)

Hitting

You shouldn't get too frazzled if your preschooler hits another because this happens often among children this age. With preschoolers try to prevent hitting before it occurs, if possible, by intervening if a fight is developing. You might do this by removing one child from the scene and giving him something interesting to do, or by distracting both of the children with a different toy or a new activity. If hitting does occur, however, most child care specialists believe you need to take action.

What you say is important because some parents say the wrong thing when one child hits another. You shouldn't tell the child he is a "bad boy" for hitting because telling a child he is bad can give him a poor idea of himself and his self esteem can be damaged, say child behavior specialists. Instead stress that what he did was bad and cannot be permitted. Also, do not imply that it's all right to hit some people and not others. Don't say things like "You shouldn't hit a girl" or "Don't hit your brother. He's only a baby." Also, don't give a long lecture about how we shouldn't hit and how we need to get along nicely with other children, etc., etc. Nor does it do much good if you just tell the child he SHOULDN'T hit. And trying to get a two- or three-year-old who hits to understand how the other child feels doesn't work yet because children's empathy with others isn't well developed yet at this age.

Some specialists in child behavior don't believe an adult should go running to intervene as soon as one child hits another. They say the children should be left to work out the problem themselves. The child who is hit is likely to hit back, and the first child will learn from this that hitting isn't a good way to settle things because he gets hit and hurt in return. If adults interfere and rescue the child who his hit immediately, they say it makes the incident more serious than it is, and the child may end up becoming a cry-baby and look for adult help when any child bothers her instead of learning to deal with children who are mean. Of course, if your child is really hurt or in danger of being hurt—for instance, if a bigger child attacks her or several children gang up on her, or a playmate hits her with a block or other object—you obviously need to step in and help her right away. And if one child hits your child often, you may have to forbid the child to come into your yard to play and explain why to her parents.

However, most child care experts believe adults generally should intervene if they see one child hit another. This is especially true if the adult is a parent supervising her child and others at play or a nursery school worker or a teacher because they are responsible for the safety of the children under their care. Parents also need to intervene when two or three year olds hit because this is the age when it is crucial to set limits on a child's behavior. If you wait longer, it gets harder.

A bulletin from the Early Childhood Education program at the former Fairfield University Teachers Center suggests the following when a child hits: Explain the reasons why this behavior has to be changed; Say "I want you to stop hitting Joey because it hurts him," instead of the vague "It's not nice to hit." Tell him also that if he hits other children, they won't want to play with him and they are more likely to hit him if they get mad at him. Children need clear cause and effect explanations. Value judgments from parents aren't clear to them and so often don't work.

Child behavior specialists say it is important to make it clear to a small child that you won't let him hit. You may even have to physically hold his arms and tell him "No hitting other people." But you also need to get to the reason why he is hitting and the feelings provoking this behavior. Try to get him to tell you how he feels. Then name the feeling he has and show you understand why he feels that way. If you can see the reasons for his actions, try to get him to see them. And do what you can to prevent a similar situation from occurring and provoking him to hit again.

For instance, if you see Mary getting ready to hit Andrew, you could say, "Mary, I know how angry you are because Andrew scribbled all over your drawing. But I cannot allow you to hit him and I can't allow any children to hit one another. I have to keep you all safe. Andrew has been sent for a time-out, and I will help you start another drawing." If a child who hits is still full of anger even after you stop him from hitting and defuse the situation, suggest that he go hit a pillow or bang a drum, run around the house several times or do something else physical to get rid of his anger.

Nursery school director Janet Verney of Children's Discovery Center in Branford, Conn., first tells a child who hits that hitting is not the kind of behavior that is permitted in a nursery school. If the child hits someone again, she will use a time out period, sitting him in a chair away from the other children for a few minutes. Dolores Andreucci of Cradles and Crayons Child Day Care Center in Guilford also uses a time out period for hitting, and she also may ask why the child hit another and if he is sorry.

Louise Miller of Spring Glen Church Nursery School says the parent should hold the child until he calms down, be calm and explain that hitting is not allowed. She suggests also saying "I am sorry you are angry. It makes me unhappy to see you like this. But I do love you." She also observes that if a child sees his parent hit "of course he feels it is the thing to do."

Jeannette Stone in a booklet published by The National Association for the Education of Young Children advises that when a child hits, the adult states the rule against hitting but empathize with the child's feelings at the same time. For instance, say "I cannot let you hit people....I know how you feel, but I cannot let you hurt people, and I cannot let them hurt you." You might also tell the child that if he has to hit, he can hit the floor, or a pillow or a lump of clay. And it is also a good idea to kneel down and talk to the child directly at his level, looking into his eyes, while giving him the rules about hitting, according to the Stone. Sometimes it may also be necessary to hold an angry child to calm him. Or, if he is very upset, you may have to carry him away from other children and let him howl and thrash around by himself. There is no point is scolding or trying to talk about the situation when the child is that upset. Just remain firm in your direction that hitting is not allowed.

When the child calms down, you can put your arm around him, tell him everything will be all right, and tell him you are willing to listen to what made him so angry that he hit someone. You might add that everyone gets angry sometimes and has a hard time. This shows him it's okay to be angry sometimes and helps him learn to acknowledge and deal with angry feelings, rather than suppress them, which can cause emotional difficulties later on. Also, after you have told the child "I cannot let you hit him—it hurts," Stone says direct him to tell the other child what's bothering him instead of hitting him. Say "Tell him with words."

Never allow a child to hit a parent or teacher, warn early childhood educators at the Stork Club Child Care Centers in Connecticut. If this happens, tell the child how you feel and let the child know hitting hurts. Explain that you realize that the child is angry, but make it clear what the child can and can't do if he is angry. Hurting others or himself is something that is not allowed. Child behavior specialists say if a parent allows his child to hit him when the child is angry, it can be psychologically damaging for the child. He will feel guilty at the same time, and this conflict between anger and guilt at hurting parents whom he depends on will lead to anxiety.

Spanking a child who hits doesn't work because you are just repeating the behavior you want him to stop. I found this out from my own experience with my son. When he hit me once, I spanked him. It gave him the message that Mommy hits too when she is mad and it's okay, so he hit me back. Then when I spanked him harder, he hit back harder. The behavior must be stopped by other means, and the most effective is probably sending the child immediately to his room or to a room away from other children and all activity.

What about a child who gets hit by another? Should you tell him that it isn't right to hit, but if someone hits him, he should hit back? If you are supervising a group of preschoolers, most early childhood specialists say this isn't wise. It's better to just have a rule against hitting at any time. But an older child may need to defend himself in some situations by hitting back.

Finally, if your child hits other children often, particularly if he is of school age, child specialists say it could indicate an emotional problem. It would be wise to meet with the school social worker or consult a therapist to find out the reason for his behavior. It might be caused by a problem in the home—perhaps too strict discipline and the use of physical punishment. He may be taking out the anger and resentment he feels about his treatment at home on his peers because he can't retaliate against his parents. If this is the case, it is important that you get some help and learn better methods of managing your child. (For further information see Fighting and Anger.)

Hyperactivity

The hyperactive child can drive even the most patient parents up the wall. Most children will be hyperactive once in a while, and run around, knock into things and climb on things. The first thing to do is to try to figure out why the child is acting that way. He may be hungry or frightened or excited by something, or he may just be full of high spirits. Many two and three-year olds seem hyperactive at times because they are so full of energy, get into all kinds of things, and have a short attention span. But this is normal behavior for that age level.

However, if your child can't seem to settle down and play with something for more than a minute or two by the time he is about four, if he runs around aimlessly, knocks things over, get into everything and seems always on the go, he is most likely hyperactive. In some cases the hyperactivity may be due to an oversensitive nervous system which makes it difficult for the child to deal with new situations or experiences or a lot of information and distractions. Sometimes stress in the home environment, conflict between parents, and poor parenting methods can lead to hyperactive behavior or inner conflicts in the child that he cannot deal with.

When a child acts hyperactive, child development specialists say don't get angry at him and yell at him because this will only make him more anxious and hyperactive. And don't spank because this also will just increase the tension he feels and teach him that when people get angry, they hit. Turning on the television also is not recommended because so many programs, including cartoons, have so much activity and violence they can make him more excitable and hyperactive.

Instead, a publication of the National Association for the Education of Young Children suggests that you speak calmly but firmly to the child and give him some direction about what to do. You might say "How about playing with your blocks now?" At the same time gently lead him over to them and start building something with him. If he resists even this much direction, try to let him choose between two activities you suggest, and then help him get started with the one he chooses. You may also have to tell him firmly, "No more running around now. I want you to play here for a while," and then lead him over to a quiet corner where there are some toys or games.

You might also be able to calm down a hyperactive two or three year old by just holding him on your lap or singing to him or rocking him in the rocking chair for a little while. Sitting with him with his favorite blanket or stuffed animal may also help calm him and show him that this is one way he can comfort himself and slow himself down when he feels he is getting out of control, says pediatrician T. Berry Brazelton.

Hyperactive children need a very structured day, according to child behavior specialists. They need lots of time for active outdoor play, planned activities for different parts of the day, and times for quiet play and for rest. It also helps if you don't have a lot of toys out for the child to play with because just the abundance and the necessity to choose may make him excitable. Instead, keep most toys put away and bring out just a few for him to play with. Put those away before bringing out others. Sometimes you can distract a hyperactive child by bringing out something that captures his attention. For instance, you might show him how a meat grinder works and have him turn the handle, or have him talk into a tape recorder and then play it back.

One of the most important things is to give a hyperactive child attention. Play with him, take him on walks, to the park or other places where you can show him interesting things. A child is more likely to become hyperactive when no one is paying attention to him and he is left to his own devices. When a hyperactive child does settle down and plays with one thing for a while or finishes a puzzle or something else he is doing, be sure to notice it and praise him.

Be careful not to get into a power struggle with a hyperactive child. If he won't settle down and keeps refusing to do what you ask, give him a time out. Don't yell or get upset at him. Just calmly send him to his room until he can settle down and play quietly. If he refuses to go, take his hand and lead him there. If he comes out of his room, just take him back. It won't hurt if there are some things in his room for quiet play, but it's important to insist that he stay apart from the other children or the rest of the family until he is ready to control himself.

It is very important for a parent to help a child learn to control hyperactivity when he is two or three or he may get set in a pattern of this kind of behavior, says Dr. Brazelton. If parents don't put a lid on hyperactive behavior, the child will become disliked by other children and by teachers who cannot control him. He will be looked on as a bad child, and his self esteem will suffer. He will feel hopeless, helpless and inadequate. Even if he outgrows his hyperactivity by adolescence, he may consider himself bad, inferior, a failure by then, and he may have serious personality problems, says Dr. Brazelton.

A parent who is with a hyperactive child all day needs relief because stress can build up so much that the parent can come to resent and dislike the child. She may try to avoid him more, and her attitude will be sensed by her child. It is likely to damage his self esteem and make him even more excitable and demanding in an attempt to gain his mother's attention. So if you are home all day with a hyperactive child, have a babysitter or grandparent come in once or twice a week so you can get away for a while. Send the child to a nursery school a few times a week as soon as he is old enough. Ask your husband to take over the care of the child in the evening. Try to find a parent support group to join.

If your child is frequently and extremely hyperactive despite your best efforts to control him, it may be wise to seek professional help. It could be that the way you are disciplining him is actually making the situation worse. This was the case with an eight-year-old boy who finally had to be admitted to the Yale New Haven Hospital's child psychiatric unit because of his out-of-control behavior. Dr. Joseph Woolston, director, found that the mother's method of handling the child was contributing to the problem. She wouldn't do anything about his behavior until it got so bad she would get very angry. Then she would yell and scream and overdo punishment. Then she'd feel guilty and apologize and kiss her son and undo the punishment (see p. 79-80).

Some physicians give hyperactive children Ritalin, a stimulant drug which oddly does help to control hyperactivity. However, there are side effects, and it is wise to have the child seen by a neurologist, psychiatrist, or pediatrician to see if he really needs medication for hyperactivity. It is better to try and control the child's hyperactivity by the methods mentioned above, if possible, or perhaps by getting help from a child guidance center or specialist in child behavior or family therapist. Getting the help of a child psychiatrist or therapist for continued, severe hyperactivity is also wise because there may be something in the family situation or at school which is upsetting your child of which you are not aware.

Imaginary Playmates

Some children have imaginary playmates. They are most common among three and four year olds. One of my children had one, someone called Eddie Car (I never knew if it was a person or a car), and my granddaughter has an imaginary friend named Pamela who lives behind the shed in her backyard. Some children make up imaginary playmates just because they have vivid imaginations. Sometimes they may invent imaginary playmates if they are lonely and don't have friends of their own to play with. In this case it's important to find some friends for the child. Sometimes a child might just want to make up a story about an imaginary character and pretend it really happened.

The imaginary friend sometimes is the perfect little girl or boy a child would like to be. Children also may find it convenient to blame an imaginary playmate for something they have done for which they think they might get punished.

Don't make fun of a child for having an imaginary playmate, but let her know in an offhand way you know that her friend is a make-believe playmate. Louise Miller, director of Spring Glen Church Nursery School in Hamden, says not to worry if your child has an imaginary playmate for a while, but don't encourage the practice. Nursery school director Sue Marcio believes the child must be made to realize the playmate is imaginary. And she urges parents of children with imaginary playmates to make efforts to get them real playmates, for instance by encouraging the child to bring a new friend home for lunch. Getting together with another mother who has a child the same age is another way.

Imaginary playmates are nothing to worry about unless a child often pins the blame on the imaginary character for things he has done. This may indicate that the parents are being too strict with the child, say child behavior specialists. They may have set standards too high for the child and have unrealistic ideas of how children should behave at a certain age. The child might also be afraid of losing the parent's love or of getting him angry if he admits that he, and not his imaginary friend, broke the cookie jar or dropped a toothbrush down the toilet.

If your child does seem to be using an imaginary playmate to take the blame for what he has done, try to ease up on him. Let him know that it's all right to make mistakes and do things wrong sometimes, and that he is not going to lose your affection or get severely punished for occasional misbehavior or for something that was an accident.

Interrupting

Children have to learn that they mustn't interrupt and break into conversations when someone else is talking. When young children are playing together, it is common for them to interrupt and talk whenever they want, but by the time he is four or five a child should have learned he is not to interrupt when others are speaking.

How do you teach him this? Tell him from the first time that he interrupts that he should wait until the other person is finished talking to speak. Explain that it isn't polite to break in and talk when someone else is talking. People don't like it because it makes them feel you think what they are saying isn't important. After all, he wouldn't like it if someone interrupted when he was telling Mommy or Daddy something. You might add that when two people are talking at the same time it is also hard to listen and understand what each is saying.

Most important, parents need to set a good example for the child. They should show him the same respect they want him to show other people and not interrupt when he is talking. And they shouldn't talk so much, especially when they have other adults around, that a child can't get a word in edgewise without interrupting. If you sense that your child has something to say, wind down what you are saying quickly, look at him, let him talk, and pay attention. If a visitor keeps talking on and on, and your child is trying to get your attention, stop her at the end of a sentence by saying something like, "Excuse me, but I think Johnny wants to say something."

There are some parents who let their children interrupt. The child is the center of their world and they dote on him so much that if he looks as if he wants to say something, or says "Mommy" or Daddy," they will stop whatever they are saying at once, or ignore the person talking to them, and let the child talk. This practice can tend to produce a child who seems spoiled. He will think he is the center of attention wherever he goes, and whenever he wants to say something, he will expect everyone else to stop talking immediately and listen to him. So give your child attention and encourage him to talk, but make sure he also respects the right of other people to talk and finish what they are saying.

Kicking

If a child kicks you, don't respond with the comment many parents would make, "Don't you ever do that again, you bad boy!" This is a negative message that damages a child's sense of self worth because it labels him *bad*. And because it is an order, it is likely to make him defiant and provoke him to more misbehavior. And do not spank him, for that only shows him that although kicking may not be allowed, hitting is acceptable—at least when a person is big enough or powerful enough to get away with it.

Instead, give an "I" message. Tell the child how his kicking makes you feel. For instance, suggests psychologist Thomas Gordon, say "Ouch, That really hurt me—I don't like to be kicked." Such "I"-messages, he says get better results because they put the responsibility on the child for changing his behavior.

If the kicking is repeated, or if a child is kicking another child, parents need to make it clear that kicking is not allowed. Move the kicking child away from the other child, hold him, look directly into his eyes and say firmly, "Kicking is not allowed." Tell the child that if he is angry or upset about something, to say it in words instead of kicking. If he has to kick, tell him to kick a ball or a pillow, not people. If he still is all riled up and continues to kick, send him for a time out to another room away from everyone until he is sure he can get along with everyone without kicking.

Lack of Communication

Most parents have probably had the experience of asking their child "What did you do in school today?" and having the child answer, "Nothing." If it happens occasionally, it probably doesn't mean much. Maybe the child did have a boring day, or he's tired and doesn't feel like talking, or he's asserting a little independence. Or it's possible something happened that did bother him and he doesn't want to talk about it.

So how do you get your child to talk about what's been going on in his life? According to *Hartford Courant* Family Affairs columnist Mary Jo Kochakian, one thing you don't do is force the issue or get exasperated. Harriet Wetstone, a psychologist at the Institute of Living in Hartford, says this will only make your child clam up even more. The first thing you have to do is create an atmosphere in your home that is relaxed and accepting, say Adele Faber and Elaine Mazlish in the book *How To Talk So Kids Will Listen, and Listen So Kids Will Talk*. When a child feels that you will listen to him and that it is safe to tell you his feelings, he will usually confide in you.

To build an atmosphere that will encourage communication from your child, child behavior specialists say you need to start in infancy. You need to show your child from the time he is born that he can trust you and express his feelings to you. In infancy you do this by responding to the baby's cries and doing what needs to be done to make him comfortable, whether it be feeding him, changing him, holding him and cuddling him. Through this interaction he learns there is someone who will take care of him, someone he can rely on, and he learns to love and trust. When your child is a toddler you encourage open communication by comforting him and helping him to deal with disturbing feelings like fear and anger and by talking with him and taking an interest in what he does. When he is a preschooler and older, you encourage communication by stopping what you are doing to listen to what his has to say, by valuing and respecting his ideas and opinions, by not appearing bored or distracted when he is talking, and by being willing to listen to his problems, sympathize with his feelings, and help him to deal with his difficulties.

Many parents unintentionally turn off communication with their children by being too authoritarian and judgmental. If you always boss your child , direct him, correct him, tell him what to do and what not to do, and don't give him a chance to express his opinions or feelings about things, he will figure you don't really care what he thinks or feels. So he won't bother communicating much with you. Also, say child behavior specialists, if you respond when he does confide in you with judgmental or negative comments, you will turn off communication.

For instance, if he comes home from school upset and says the teacher yelled at him, don't respond with a comment like "What did you do to deserve that?" It immediately gives him the idea you are judging and condemning him without even hearing his side of the story. He will probably answer "Nothing," and communication will stop right there.

Instead, just ask a nonjudgmental question like, "What happened?" You may find that the teacher really was not justified in yelling at him at all. Even if she yelled at him because he did something wrong, like talk out in class, don't criticize and say "You should have known better" or "You shouldn't have done that." Again, this will discourage him from communicating to you things that are bothering him in the future. Instead, reflect and sympathize with his feelings by your facial expressions and with comments like "That must have embarrassed you." Take the time to sit down, look directly at him, and let him talk out his feelings, and then help him decide what he can do to prevent a disturbing incident like that from happening again.

Some children also may not want to tell parents about a problem at school because they are afraid they will lose their parents' approval. Or they may be afraid their parents will be worried or may embarrass them by going to the school to try to straighten out the problem. If you think something is bothering your child, Wetstone suggests you invite the child to talk about it. But don't say, "What's the matter with you?" Instead, she recommends saying, "You've been looking worried. I'd be glad to talk about it if you'd like to."

One way to get children to open up and talk about their day's experiences is to have everyone in the family at dinner talk about the best and worst things that happened to them that day, suggest Faber and Mazlish.

To encourage communication psychologists and counselors also suggest using open-ended questions, rather than questions that can be answered by one word like "Yes," or "No," Instead of asking "How was school?" when your child comes home, which will probably just produce the answer "Okay," ask "What good things happened to you in school today?" or "What did you learn that was interesting in school today?"

Dialogue between parents and children is extremely important, and you should do everything you can to encourage open communication between your children and you. Many studies have shown that when children feel they can't communicate with their parents, they are more likely to turn to drugs, abuse alcohol, and get into trouble. Psychologist H. Stephen Glenn and educator Jane Nelson report that research shows children in families who find time for activities that increase dialogue by only 30 minutes per week have a 32 percent lower rate of delinquency, a 27 percent lower rate of drug and alcohol problems and a 21 percent lower rate of truancy and underachievement.

Lying

Young children sometimes lie because they still don't quite know the difference between what is true and untrue. When you read stories to a small child, he will think they are things that really happened. If you tell him the events in the story didn't really happen, that there are no such things as giants or ducks that talk, you help him understand the difference between what is real and what is made up. If he then makes up stories himself, you certainly don't consider it lying.

Hamden nursery school director Louise Miller observes that a young child doesn't even understand the concept of lying. If an incident of lying occurs, she says to talk about it but don't label it lying. Instead, you might ask if what the child said is "true" or "pretend."

Dolores Andreucci, nursery school director, also thinks it's important to ask questions of a child who is lying. If a small child, for instance, claims another's toy is his, she would ask "Are you sure that's yours?" and often this is enough to get the child to admit that it isn't.

A teacher at the Stork CLub Child Care Centers says how lying is handled depends on the situation, but a parent or adult should not call a child a liar. Instead, she will ask the child if he is telling her a story and try to talk about what's happening and about the child's feelings. "Do not back a child up against the wall just to get the truth. This could be more damaging," she says. "You want to build a trusting relationship with the child so that he will come to you with a problem or concern."

Once a child is six or seven, however, he knows the difference between the truth and a lie. When children this age lie, it is important, first of all, to find out the reason. One reason children this age lie is because they know they have done something they shouldn't, and they are afraid of getting punished for it or afraid of their parents' disapproval, says psychologist Loyd Rowland in a bulletin distributed by the Mental Health Association of Connecticut. Sometimes they may lie and exaggerate to impress their friends. Children may also begin to tell lies because they notice their parents and other adults telling lies. You may tell your child it won't hurt when you put antiseptic on a cut, but it does. Or you may tell someone you don't care much about that you can't go to their party Saturday because you have made plans with friends. Then you stay home. Or you may promise to do something with your child, and then not keep your promise. If parents want their children to be honest, it is important that they model honesty, that they be truthful with the child and with other people and keep promises they have made, for a broken promise is like a lie to a child.

Children are apt to lie, says Rowland, if their parents are very strict and they are afraid of what will happen to them if they tell the truth. If their parents use physical punishment or harsh criticism or shame and humiliate them if they do wrong, children are apt to lie rather than risk such punishment. Also, if parents expect too much of their children and have too high standards, the children may lie because they are so afraid of disappointing them. So if you find your child beginning to lie, think about whether you are putting too much pressure on him to excel or be good or punishing him too harshly when he does wrong. If so, your child needs to talk out his feelings and get more assurances of parental love and acceptance. He does not need harsher punishment.

If you do find your child lying, child behavior specialists say don't confront him and accuse him of lying, especially not in front of others. He will probably just deny it in that case out of embarrassment. Don't say, for instance, "Did you break that cellar window?" when you know he was throwing the ball against the wall next to it. Instead, take him aside and tell him you have noticed the window is broken and would like to know how it happened. If he hesitates or lies, tell him he should never be afraid to tell you the truth. If he does own up to what he did when you take this approach, don't go punishing him harshly then, or he'll figure it's not very smart to tell you the truth from then on. Instead, try to find out the reason why he felt he had to lie. Get at his feelings. Then ask him what he thinks a fair punishment for what he did would be. You both might decide that having him do a certain chore for several months to earn money to pay for the window would be fair. Remember, your aim is not to punish lying but to find out what prompted it and solve the problem so you can get your children to communicate openly and honestly with you.

Children who lie habitually after age five or six, when they should know the difference between what is true and untrue, are likely to have a major psychological problem or have a lot of stress in their lives, say child behavior specialists. They need professional help. The lying may be especially serious with children who are also destructive and who never had at least one important adult caretaker who stayed with them through infancy and answered their needs. Such children may not have developed a conscience and the ability to love and trust others. They usually require extensive therapy.

Masturbation

Years ago people used to believe masturbation was harmful to a child, and parents would punish their children if they caught them masturbating or make them feel guilty about it. Now we know that masturbation is normal in young children. It is one way in which they explore and learn about their body. Babies play with their fingers and toes and like to touch parts of their bodies that feel good, so it is natural that sooner or later they would discover their sex organs and enjoy the sensation of touching them.

Some teachers at the Stork Club Child Care Centers in Connecticut even say although seeing a child masturbating often disturbs adults, it may be healthy for the child occasionally. "I wouldn't discourage children that it is a 'No, no'," says one teacher. "Children are curious about their bodies. Masturbation helps them understand a boy is different from a girl. It is pleasurable for them." And she adds, "It may alleviate any pressure, stress or pain they are experiencing at a particular time."

Although most parents now know that masturbation is not harmful, some still worry if they see their child masturbating. Louise Miller, director of Spring Glen Church Nursery School in Hamden assures such parents that the masturbation phase soon passes and is nothing to worry about. But she says parents should try to minimize the situations in which they find their child is likely to do it. Sue Marcio, another nursery school director, notes that a child who masturbates could be doing it because he is lonesome. The best remedy, she finds, is friends. She also recommends distracting the child with an activity. Child development specialists say it also helps if you make sure the child has a lot of things he can play with that keep his hands busy, like crayons and playdough, etc.

Children need to be taught, however, that masturbation is not something one does in public. Nursery school teacher Sue Marcio suggests telling a child who is masturbating that he doesn't see grown-ups doing that kind of thing. He should try not to do it, but if he wants to do it, he should do it in private.

However, a child should never be told that masturbating is bad and should never be made to feel guilty about it because mental health experts have found this can result in sexual problems, phobias, or other emotional problems that can persist throughout life.

Misbehavior

You can prevent a lot of misbehavior if you are clear and firm about the kind of behavior you expect from your child from the time he is a toddler. Child behavior specialists say if you don't set limits for your child when he is two, it becomes increasingly difficult to do so as he gets older. You need to teach your two-year-old that he doesn't throw things, hit or bite people, write on walls, etc. Parents need to stop such misbehavior calmly but firmly whenever it occurs. The preschool child also needs to be trained early to be helpful and polite—to pick up his toys, help with little chores, say please and thank you, and in general behave the way he needs to get along with people.

But even with your best intentions, your child is going to misbehave sometimes. What can you do about it?

One of the first things to do is to avoid the word "you" when you are trying to get your child to behave. Reprimands that use the word "you", like "You had better behave yourself," "You put that down right now," "Stop making so much noise," (you implied) are ineffective because they are just likely to make your child more defiant and hostile. Instead, says psychologist Thomas Gordon, send an "I" message. Tell your child how his actions are making you feel. For instance, instead of saying "You left the bathroom a mess," say, "I get very discouraged when I have just finished cleaning the bathroom and you come in and leave mud all over the floor and sink." Instead of saying to a preschooler who throws a block, "Don't you dare do that again," say "I am really frightened that a block will hit someone if you throw it and it will hurt them." Then you can redirect the child and say "Blocks are things we build with. They are not for throwing," as you show him how to build with them.

Be careful when you send an "I" message that you don't start it with "I am angry," says Gordon, because that implies "I am angry at you." Instead figure out why you are angry. Was it because your child embarrassed you, disappointed you, worried or frightened you (perhaps by coming home late). Then convey the emotion that is behind the anger in your "I" message.

"I" messages are less threatening than "you" messages to a child and less likely to cause resistance. They don't accuse the child of being bad or inadequate, but they put responsibility on the child for changing his behavior. Thus, says the psychologist, they promote the child's growth. Also, because they are honest expressions of feeling, they influence a child to express feelings that he has, and so they promote communication between a child and his parents and bring them closer.

Educator Jane Nelsen uses a four-step method for winning cooperation from children:

1. Guess how your child feels in the situation and tell him how you think he feels.

2. If possible, share a similar situation that happened to you in which you felt the same.

3. Ask the child if he will try to work out a solution with you.

4. Discuss with him what ideas he has to avoid the problem in the future. If he doesn't offer any, give some suggestions and see if he agrees.

For instance, suppose you took your eight-year-old daughter Susan shopping for clothes, but left your five-year-old daughter Mary home with her father because you knew she would be restless and bored in the stores. After you got home, Mary picked a fight with Susan and wrote with black crayon all over a shirt you had just bought Susan.

Guessing Mary's feelings, you might say to her, "Did you write all over Susan's shirt because you were angry that I didn't take you shopping too? Did you think I took her because I like her better than you?"

To this, your daughter would probably answer yes. Then you might say, "I can understand how you felt," and give an example of when your parents took a sibling somewhere and didn't take you, or when you were left out of something. Explain how you felt. Then explain why you didn't take her shopping. And put your arms around her and give her a hug, or hold her to show her you love her. "I didn't leave you home because I love Susan more than you. I love you just as much. But I knew I would have to spend a long time shopping for clothes for Susan, and I knew you would be restless and bored. I thought you would be happier staying home with Daddy and playing."

Then ask her finally, "What do you think we can do about Susan's shirt?" She might suggest washing it, and you could give her some liquid detergent and a brush and have her try to get the crayon off. If the shirt could not be salvaged, talk about how she might contribute some of her allowance each week to buy a new shirt for Susan. Also talk about how such a situation could be avoided in the future. You might agree to give her a choice about whether she wanted to go if you had to take Susan somewhere, and explain how long you would be and what you would be doing. You both might also agree to have her father do something special with her or take her somewhere if she were left home with him. You might also bring home some new article of clothing for Mary the next time you need to shop with Susan.

Why does a child misbehave in the first place? A child misbehaves because he basically wants to belong and be significant, but has mistaken ideas about how to achieve this, says Nelson. According to the theories of Rudoph Dreikurs, she says a child usually misbehaves for one of four reasons: (1) he wants attention; (2) he wants power; (3) he wants revenge; (4) he assumes he is inadequate. To get children to stop misbehaving Nelsen says it is important to identify the mistaken goal so you can figure out the most effective action to take. Examine your feelings first. If you are irritated or annoyed, the child is likely to be misbehaving for attention. If you feel threatened, and feel he is getting to be the boss instead of you, it's a power struggle. If you feel hurt by the child's misbehavior, his goal probably is revenge. If you feel inadequate to help the child, it is likely the child feels inadequate.

Another clue to the child's goal is his response when you tell him to stop misbehaving. If he wants attention, he will stop his misbehavior for a while, but resume it to get your attention. If he wants power, he is likely to defy you verbally or will just resist your attempt to stop him. If he wants revenge, he is likely to retaliate by saying or doing something that hurts you. If he feels inadequate, he is likely to be passive, hoping you will just leave him alone.

For a child who is misbehaving to get attention, Nelsen says you could ignore the misbehavior and give attention when he behaves well; redirect the child to a better behavior; give the child a choice of another behavior;impose a logical consequence; set up a regular schedule for spending more time with the child.

If a child is misbehaving because he wants power, Nelson says withdraw, cool off and wait until you don't feel the urge to make the child do what you want. Then you can have a discussion with him. Admit you have been engaged in a power struggle with him and that you want to change things and work together with him on solutions to behavior problems with understanding and mutual respect.

When the child's goal is revenge, do not retaliate, but remain calm and friendly. Tell the child, "I can see that you are upset, so we can't discuss this now, but I would like to talk to you later," Nelsen suggests. Then when you have both cooled off, try to find out what he feels hurt about, listen with understanding and without being judgmental, and try to remedy the situation.

When a child's goal is assumed inadequacy, you need to take time to explain carefully to your child what needs to be done and to train him so that he can do the job successfully. Don't give him the idea you pity him. Tell him you feel discouraged yourself sometimes. You might also try to find something for him to do in which he does feel adequate. It's important to spend special time with such a child and not give up on him. Express faith in his ability to succeed, and work on a plan with him so he can succeed.

There is no one way to handle behavior problems, but in general, child behavior specialists say the best way to deal with misbehavior is to give your child positive attention and encouragement. For instance, if your preschooler is following you around, pestering you, and getting into things when you are trying to cook or do housework, take some time out, take her on your lap, give her a hug and kiss, and tell her you love her. Then you might suggest that she go in the playroom and play with her toys while Mommy finishes her work, and then Mommy will come play with her. Ask her to decide while playing what she would like Mommy to play with her. If a child irritably grabs another's toy, if you go over, kneel and put your arm around the child as you explain about asking permission to play with someone else's toy, the encouragement and attention can often squelch the misbehavior.

Redirecting misbehavior into behavior that contributes to the family or group is also a good method to use. Teachers use this method when they take a child who cuts up a lot and make him the hall monitor. If your preschooler is taking silverware out of the dishwasher as you are unloading it, you can redirect her by showing here where the silver goes and having her put the pieces in the drawer where they belong.

Remember that when a child misbehaves it may very well be because of your attitude. If you have been too lenient or uncaring to set limits on his behavior from the time he was one or two, he is likely to keep misbehaving in an attempt to get you to notice him and give him some attention. And negative attention is preferable to a child than no attention from parents at all. On the other hand, overly harsh discipline can also provoke misbehavior. Although your child may behave when you are around, he is likely to take out his resentment on others, perhaps by bullying other children or getting into trouble at school. If you are bossy to your child and are always telling him what to do, you are apt to provoke misbehavior because the child will try to counter you at some time to get some power. If you often speak irritably and impatiently to your child, don't consider his feelings, or criticize and belittle him, he is likely to misbehave out of resentment and revenge. Thus, the key to preventing a lot of misbehavior is to treat the child with respect for his feelings and ideas, but to make it clear in a friendly but firm way the kind of behavior you expect.

CHRONIC MISBEHAVIOR

If a child repeatedly misbehaves, it is probably a sign that there is stress in the family or at school which has become too much for the child. Arguments between their parents, abusive parents, alcoholism in a parent, money pressure in the family, separation of parents, parental favoring of a sibling, overly harsh discipline, or problems with peers or schoolwork are some of the stresses that may prove too much for a child and cause him to misbehave, child specialists say. Parents then often punish the child for the misbehavior, but don't look for the cause of it. When your child misbehaves, find out why. If the misbehavior is severe or chronic, ask the child what is bothering him. Be understanding, and try to get him to express his worries and his feelings.

Mental health specialists say when misbehavior is chronic and severe, the child is likely to have an emotional or psychological problem. If the misbehaving child also exhibits destructive behavior, violent anger, or signs of depression, such as sleep or appetite disturbances, lack of concentration, withdrawal and apparent lack of interest in friends or activities, or unusual fears and anxieties, you should get help for the child right away from a child psychiatrist or other mental health professional.

New Baby

Having a new baby in the house is wonderful, but it is also an exhausting experience for many first-time parents. The baby demands a tremendous amount of time and energy from his parents, who rarely get a full night's sleep. All day long, and for much of the night, it's feed, burp, change the baby, figure out why he is crying, comfort him, give the daily bath, wash his clothes, etc. The new parent finds her whole life now revolves around the new baby. And babies cry a lot during the first few months of their life, which can be nerve-wracking for tired, inexperienced parents who don't really know what to do about it. New mothers may also suffer from postpartum depression because of hormone changes, exhaustion, and the stress of coping with this demanding new family member. If it is severe or doesn't lift in a few weeks, the new mother should consult her physician or a psychiatrist because help is available.

But these difficult first few months of the baby's life are of tremendous importance in cementing the bond between parents and child, says pediatrician T. Berry Brazelton. It is by struggling through this period, by learning what works and what doesn't work in dealing with the baby, that they learn to care for the child and develop confidence in their ability as a parent. "When new parents do not have the time and freedom to face this process and live through it successfully, they may indeed escape emotionally. In running away, they may miss the opportunity to develop a secure attachment to their baby—and never get to know themselves as real parents," Brazelton comments. For this reason he believes it is essential that all working mothers be guaranteed at least a four-month parental leave after childbirth.

Many of the sections of this book are designed to help parents, especially first-time parents, care for a new baby. See especially Chapters 3, 4, 5, 6, and the sections on Crying, Eating Problems, Sleep Problems. A new baby can also cause problems with other siblings, who may be jealous and act up, or may treat the baby roughly or regress in their behavior. For information on handling problems with other children when a new baby arrives, see Sibling Rivalry.

New Experiences

Toddlers and preschoolers often have trouble handling new experiences. Going swimming for the first time, having a birthday party with a lot of people, going to the dentist or for a haircut for the first time, riding on a train or just seeing one, and many other things that we take for granted can be upsetting or frightening to a young child.

If you are going to take your child someplace new or are planning something that will be a new experience for him, try to imagine first how he might feel. If it's a birthday party with a lot of noise and commotion, he may get confused and overwhelmed and not know what to do. If it's a train or plane ride, the size and noise of the train or plane may frighten him. You have to expect some of these feelings and if they occur be patient, reassure him, hold him and comfort him.

To make things easier for your child, prepare him ahead of time for new experiences. If he is going to start nursery school, for instance, take him there a few times, let him get to know the teachers and the place, and talk about all the things he will do there. If he is going to have a haircut, take him to the barber ahead of time just to let him see what the barber does. If you are going to travel by train with him, get a book about trains, talk about the trip, what it will be like, and how trains are big and make a lot of noise, but are fun to ride on. If it's a trip to the doctor, dentist or hospital, there are books about this you can get to read with your child to prepare him for the visit. To prepare him for his birthday party, talk about all the people that will come, the presents they will bring, and what will happen. Give him some guidance in how he should behave by explaining that you expect him to unwrap each present and show everyone, and then say thank you to the person who gave it.

Most important, go slowly. Don't force your child into the new situation or punish him if he acts up and doesn't behave as you want. Empathize with his feelings and encourage him that he will be able to handle the situation. Reassure him you will be there with him to help him, and stay right by him at least until you see he has adjusted to the new situation.

Noisiness and Yelling

All children make too much noise at times. The first way to handle it is with a polite request that they be more quiet. Try to give a reason. You might say, "I cannot hear Daddy on the phone." "All that noise hurts my ears," or "Cowboys and Indians isn't good to play in the house. It's too noisy and there is too much running around. Why don't you go outside to play it?" Or if one child is crying and making a lot of noise, Jeannette Stone, in a publication of the National Association for the Education of Young Children suggests saying something like, "Alicia, your loud crying makes it hard for us to hear each other," and then you might say to the other children, "When she can tell me with words what's the matter, she will."

Have toys and games around that children can play with quietly, and if too much noise and activity is going on, try to distract the children to some quieter games. Or you could ask them to play in another room if they are right in the midst of the family and the noise is bothersome.

If a child is yelling, figure out why. If he is yelling to his brother in another room, just ask him to go up and talk to him so he doesn't have to yell. If he is yelling in anger, label the feeling. Tell him you know he is angry, put your arm around him and tell him to talk about what made him so mad instead of just yelling.

Above all, if children are yelling, don't shout at them to stop because children imitate parents. "You do not yell at children to get them to stop yelling," says Stone, And don't hit a child who is yelling. Obviously it's only going to make him yell more, and it may also teach him that instead of yelling when he gets mad, it's better to hit.

It's Not Fair

Most children at one time or another will complain that something is "not fair." Perhaps Joan thinks it's not fair that her brother can stay up later than she can. Or perhaps Ann thinks it's not fair that her sister got a new dress and she didn't. What you don't do in these cases is bend over backwards to try to treat each of your children exactly the same. You don't run out and buy a dress for Ann also, or let Joan stay up as late as her brother even though he is four years older. This will only make things worse because your children will get the idea that all they have to do is complain something is "not fair" and they will get what they want. This obviously puts the kids in the driver's seat.

Instead, explain your reason for treating one child differently than the other. When Joan is as old as her brother, she will be able to stay up until 10 also, you might say. Or you might tell Ann that her sister needed a new dress for a school concert because her dresses are all getting too small. "When your dresses get too small and you need a new dress, you will get one," you could tell her.

If your children keep complaining that things are "not fair," just tell them life is not fair, say child behavior experts. Everyone doesn't get treated the same as everyone else. As a parent you try to treat all your children fairly, you might say, but there are bound to be times when one child will have some privilege or get something that the others don't. But sometimes they will get something their sister or brother doesn't, so it pretty much balances out in the long run. Assure them that you love them all very much, and your aim is to provide them with the things they need when they need them and to treat them the way you think best.

Obstinacy and Stubborness

Obstinacy and stubbornness can occur anytime in young children but are likely to start around age two. During the terrible twos the child is trying to assert his independence and his identity. He is likely to balk when you tell him to pick up his toys, eat his carrots, sit on the potty, come along with you during a walk, or do other things you want him to do. And stubbornness can continue through preschool years and even be found in school age children.

Children are more likely to become obstinate and stubborn if they are dominated and directed too much by their parents in their early childhood, say child behavior specialists, and if they are disciplined too much or too harshly whenever they don't do just what mother or father says. Eventually they are going to reach a point where they rebel, where they stand their ground and refuse to do what you want because they want you to know they are individuals too, with their own wants and needs and feelings.

The best way to handle stubbornness is to treat it calmly and casually, say child development experts. Avoid confrontations. If your child obstinately refuses to pick up his toys, you might use the "As soon as" approach and say, "As soon as you pick up your toys we will take a walk to the brook and see the frogs." If he refuses to eat his carrots or to eat his meal at all, don't try to force him. Just take his dish away and let him go play. He will eat more at the next meal. If he is hungry before that, you might have some nutritious snacks like cheese and raisins available. If you are out for a walk and your three-year-old daughter stops and refuses to move, psychologist Louis Bates Ames suggests saying "okay" and walking away. She says the child will probably follow you. If not, you will probably have to just go back and carry her. In general, she advises a "light touch and seeming indifference" in handling stubbornness in preschoolers. (For further information see Disobeying and Saying No.)

Pestering

If your child is pestering you, following you around and trying to get your attention when you are busy doing housework or something, don't call her a pest or tell her to leave you alone. That can make her think she isn't very important to you and will affect her sense of self worth. If she is pestering you, it means she needs and wants your attention, so stop what you are doing for a minute, give her a hug or take her on your lap. Tell her how you feel. Tell her you love her, but you get bothered when she keeps calling "Mommy" and wanting you to do things now because you have to cook dinner (or finish cleaning the living room for company, or whatever). Promise that you will play with her as soon as you finish. Ask her what she would like you to play with her, and then ask her to play by herself until you finish what you are doing. If she can tell time, tell her you will be finished and will play with her at a certain time, or else when the clock chimes, or in a little while. And keep your promise.

If your child tends to pester you to buy things for him when you take him shopping, tell him ahead of time that he can choose one thing he wants. If you are going shopping in the supermarket, perhaps he can choose some cookies or cereal he would like. If it is a department store, that can be more difficult. If the child is old enough to understand the value of money, you might have him choose something for $1 or whatever you think you can afford. Or, if he gets an allowance, tell him he can bring along money he has saved and buy what he wants with it. With a younger child who can't understand costs of things and wants the electric train or the $50 truck as soon as he sees them, it's best to just avoid temptation. Don't take him shopping, or at least not into a toy store until he is old enough to understand what he can choose and why he can't have any toy he wants.

Some children become real pests as soon as their parent, usually their mother, starts talking on the phone. Preschoolers especially seem to resent that someone on the phone is taking their mother's attention away from them. If this happens, take the child on your lap, give her a kiss, and tell her you can't hear Mrs. Jones talking when she is talking. Suggest she bring some quiet play toys like crayons and a coloring book over and color next to you while you finish talking. She might even do this sitting on your lap at the table while you are talking. Another thing that works, if she is old enough and the caller is a grandparent or favorite aunt, is to ask her if she wants to talk to the person. Usually after a child has done so, she will be satisfied for a while and go off and play. But don't carry on long conversations when you are alone with a toddler or preschooler and expect her to just play quietly and behave. It isn't fair to her because unless she is all involved in some game or television program, she will want and need your attention in a short time.

Picking Things Up

Getting a child to pick up his toys or his things is a problem for just about every parent at some time or other. Preschoolers can scatter their toys all over a room in no time flat, but picking them up is never something they want to do. And the situation often gets no better when children reach school age or adolescence. They leave a trail of books, clothes, and sports equipment after them as they come into the house, and sometimes their room may look like the city dump. In fact, one way my husband used to get our children to clean up their rooms when they were in grammar school was to tell them he was going to get the town's sanitation inspector after them if they didn't. I don't recommend this. It left my youngest with a fear of sanitation inspectors for a while. However, there are methods that work so that a parent doesn't have to keep nagging, reminding, scolding, and getting increasingly frustrated about the situation.

It is a good idea to establish orderly habits when the child is young, for there is a good chance then that they will last through his life. When a baby first starts walking around and getting into things is the time to start getting him into the habit of putting things back. For instance, if your toddler has pulled your pots and pans out of your cabinet, you might suggest, "See if you can put the little ones in the big ones and put them back," and show him how to do it. If he pulls his clothes out of his drawer, say, "Now let's see if we can get them all back in."

Nursery school teachers and child behavior specialists have the following suggestions for getting your child to pick up his toys and belongings:

- Make it easy for the child to put things away by having easy places within reach for his things. Have a toy chest with a lid that doesn't slam down on fingers in the room where he plays, low shelves for his toys, games, stuffed animals, etc., and dresser drawers he can reach for his clothes. Show him where articles of clothing should go. Have some hooks he can reach in closets or in an entry hall where he can hang his coat and hat. Explain that dirty clothes go in the hamper, and when he takes off his underwear, shirt and socks at night, he should put them in the hamper.

- Be neat yourself. If you leave things scattered all around he will pick up your habits.

- Get a young child in the habit of picking up toys and putting them away when he is finished playing. Help him do this at first. You might say, for instance, "Before we go to bed, we put our toys away," and work with him to do this. My daughter has trained her child to do this, and it became part of her three-year-old's pre-bedtime ritual to put her toys in the toy chest at night before going up to bed.

- Don't expect your children to pick up after themselves all the time. Kids are just not like that. There are times when you are going to have to remind them and times when you will end up doing it.

- Always stress the positive. For instance, if other children are present and are picking up their things, say, "I like the way Susie's cleaning up," or "Look how nicely Jimmy is putting away all the blocks."

- Expect that you often will have to help a preschool child pick up his things.

- If other children have been playing with your child, have them help pick up the toys when they finish playing. Sue Marcio, director of R and K Nursery School in Hamden, says if a child refuses to pick up toys because he says he wasn't playing with them, she says, "I wasn't either but I'm helping to clean them up. If we all help to clean up, then we can go outside" (or do something else that's fun).

- With small children, make a game of picking up, perhaps suggesting a race to see who can pick up his corner of the room first.

- Don't order your child to pick up his things. If someone keeps ordering you to do things, you are going to resent it and eventually you just won't obey. Your child will feel the same way if you are too directive. If you keep ordering him to pick up his toys, clean his room, etc., he is likely to defy you by ignoring your command and provoke a power struggle.

- Use an 'I"-message. Tell the child how you feel about all his things lying around, such as, "I'm afraid I will fall over these toys you have scattered all over the kitchen." This puts the responsibility on him to change his behavior if he cares about how you feel.

- Mention something pleasant that will follow picking up his things, such as "When you put away the toys we can read a story," or "After you help put the toys away, you can be the leader." or "As soon as you put your books away, we'll have lunch."

This technique is similar to a technique I have used which I call the "stop his world technique." I found this very effective in getting my son to pick up after himself. Tell your child once what you would like him to pick up, and go about your business. Act unconcerned and say nothing else to him. Eventually he will come and ask you a question, or ask you for something. Say, "As soon as you pick up your things, I will answer," or "As soon as you pick up your things I will give it to you." Don't argue or hassle. Just stop his world and keep replying like this until he does what he has been asked.

If you find your children are leaving their things around a lot, there are other things you can do, especially with older children:

- Tell them that you will pick up things left around, but will put them away and they won't get them back for a week or two.

- Have children pay a nickel or dime (or some other amount depending on their age and allowance) to get back things you have picked up.

- Get the children together and tell them that it bothers you to have all their things left scattered around the house. It looks messy and not very nice if someone should drop in and it doesn't look very inviting to Dad when he gets home from work. Ask them how you all can solve the problem. Work on a solution with them, which might be one of the above. Children are more likely to go along with something if they have had some say in it.

Putting Things in the Mouth

All babies put things in their mouth because it's their way of learning about the world around them. They have been used to getting pleasure through their mouth from the breast or bottle, so it's perfectly natural if a new thing comes along to put it in their mouth also to see what it tastes like and feels like. You worry, of course, about the baby picking up germs, especially if what they put in their mouth has been on the floor, but if you can't get there quickly enough to get the object away from your baby, don't worry. He'll survive. Your baby's immune system will probably be able to fight off the germs he picks up.

When you want to get something away from a baby or small child that he shouldn't put in his mouth, such as candy or a coin that's fallen on the floor, don't yell at the child or order him to give it to you. That's likely to make him hold on to it all the more, and your angry or irritated tone will just upset him. Instead, early childhood educators suggest just putting out your hand to him and saying "Thank you." The child may very well give you the object. If not, just take it. You can also distract him by holding out something he can put in his mouth, such as a teething ring, or something safe that will catch his interest, perhaps one of his toys. Then quickly take the candy or penny or whatever it is he shouldn't have. When a child is old enough to understand, of course, you should explain why we don't eat things that have fallen on the floor or why it's not good to put coins in one's mouth. But until then it's important to be watchful of your baby at all times and do your best to keep things he shouldn't have out of his reach.

Quarreling

It's normal for children to quarrel amongst themselves. Don't feel that you have to step in as soon as your child gets into a quarrel with another. Child behavior specialists say it's often best to let children work out their quarrels themselves unless they start fighting or one child is being cruel to another and upsetting him a lot. In fact, brothers and sisters will often quarrel to try to get their parent's attention and to try to get the parent to take sides and favor them. In these cases it's definitely best not to get sucked into the argument. Instead, tell the children you are sure they can work out their quarrels themselves. When they find out they can't get your attention and provoke you by quarreling, they will realize they have to settle their own arguments, and quarreling will most likely lessen.

Of course, there are times when you do have to step in and settle a quarrel—if the children are little, or if things are starting to get out of hand with shouting, hitting, or fighting. In this case, child development specialists suggest:

- With preschoolers you need to tell them firmly that hitting is not allowed. Hold the arms of the hitter and physically separate the children, if necessary, to make your point.

- You can sometimes stop a quarrel before it becomes a fight by distraction. With young children, for instance, you might take them by the hand and say "Let's go in the kitchen and make some cookies," or "Let's go play with the new play dough."

- Acknowledge the feelings of the children who are quarreling. Tell them you realize they are angry, but they are not to hit and yell at one another.

- Give them a time out. Put each child in a separate room until they calm down and can play peacefully together.

- Don't take sides. You were not there to see the whole situation, most likely, so don't let them try to get you to be the judge. You can't win that way. If you favor one, the other is sure to resent it and probably will misbehave again to get revenge.

- If your children seem to quarrel a lot, think about whether you may be contributing to it by favoring one over another.

For instance, if you let the youngest get away with things because he is just a baby, and punish the older child for the same thing (such as hitting or taking the other's things), you are setting the stage for quarrels. The non-favored child is going to try and get back at the one you favor, and a continuing cycle of quarrels can begin. So try to treat each child fairly and as equally as you can, and give plenty of love to both.

If children don't seem able to resolve a quarrel, you may have to sit down with them and help them find the solution. Sometimes you may be able to find the cause of a quarrel fairly easily and work with the children on finding a solution that is fair and just to both. If the quarrel was caused by one child taking a toy belonging to the other, for instance, you may have to explain to the child who took it some basic principles of private property—that certain things belong to certain people, and you need to ask permission before taking them or using them. Give examples of things that belong to each child, to you, to your spouse. "Sometimes people will lend their property to others if they are asked, which is a kind and generous thing to do," you might say. Then tell them,"Sometimes you want to play with your sister's toy, and sometimes she might want to play with yours, just as happened today," and ask, "How can you solve this problem?"

See if the children can work out a system in which each will ask the other at times for permission to use her toy or borrow a possession. Stress that if the person does not want to lend the item at the time, he or she may have reasons, and it might help to talk about them. But the child should not just take the other's possession if refused permission to borrow it. He should find something else to do and ask again later. You might also point out that if someone is generous and does lend his possessions, other people are more likely to be generous to him. (For further information, see sections on Fighting and Hitting.)

Threats to Run Away

There may come a time when your child is so angry at something you or someone in the family has done that he threatens to run away. Most likely it will happen after you have punished him for some misbehavior. But educator Barbara Brenner says his threat may in a perverse way be a compliment to the way you are bringing him up. It means he knows he's important to you, and the worst punishment he can threaten you with is what he fears the most—abandonment. But she warns that parents should not handle such a threat with angry or mean words of their own, such as "Good, I'll even help you pack," or "Fine, and don't come back." They hurt the child and don't solve the problem. They may even spur him on to actually run away.

What should you do? She suggests saying something like "What's making you so angry?" or "Let's talk about what's bothering you...Maybe you'll change your mind." Another good idea is to give the child the reassurance he is really looking for by saying "I won't let you run away. I love you and need you." Or, she adds, you might say, "Maybe you need some time to yourself. How about running away to the backyard until lunchtime?"

School Problems

PREVENTING PROBLEMS BY
PREPARING YOUR CHILD FOR SCHOOL

To help your child do well in school and avoid problems, it is important to prepare him at home before he begins school. The child's first teachers are his parents, and how he does in school depends to a large extent on what they have taught him and how well they have taught him in the first five years of his life. The child must be taught many things as a preschooler—to take responsibility for his actions, to respect other people and be polite to them, to follow directions, to be truthful, to finish what he starts, and much more. Parents also need to help children learn to solve problems they encounter in life, to get along with other people, to be kind and considerate. It's a big job, but the way you train your child, the limits you set on his behavior, and the love, attention, and encouragement you give him in those crucial first five years are the foundation for his whole future life.

It's also important to create an atmosphere in the home that shows that learning and study is important. If your child often sees you reading books and newspapers and sees that you consider learning valuable, he will pick up such values. But if you spend most of your time watching television, it's not likely he will have the idea that learning anything from books is very important in life.

Parents should encourage reading by reading to the child and choosing books designed for the child's age level which he will enjoy—books about children, animals, adventure, etc. Try to read to your child every day, perhaps just before you put him to bed for the night. Ideally a parent or someone should spend at least 20 minutes a day reading to a preschool child, says Dr. Wood Smethurst, director of the Reading Center at Emory University. Parents should also hang up posters and signs, encourage children to write, and hold the book close to the child when they read to the child so he can associate the book with a certain story and printed words with spoken words. But parents should not pressure a child to read, he warns, or they may turn their child off to reading.

When your child starts school, take an interest in what he is doing there and let him know school is important. Encourage his efforts and praise his accomplishments. Put the papers he brings home up on the refrigerator. Don't say things that might undermine the authority of the teacher or make him lose respect for her. For instance, if the teacher has given him an assignment to do at home, don't tell him he doesn't have to do it. Back up the teacher. And make sure he has the equipment he needs to do his schoolwork and a place away from the distraction of television where he can work.

PROBLEMS WHEN YOUR CHILD BEGINS SCHOOL

The first few weeks of school can be a difficult time for many children. Your child may be nervous and have stomach aches or headaches and not want to go to school. Or she may have nightmares, or be easily angered or upset. Don't punish her, but be understanding and encouraging. Don't dismiss her fears and anxieties. Instead, try to get her to talk about them, reassure her and help her deal with them. Some children are upset when they begin school or nursery school because of separation anxiety. They fear something might happen to their parent while they are away, and being left alone is the greatest fear a child has. If there is tension in the family, this is all the more likely to happen. So you may have to talk this out with your child. It may help to let her know where you will be when she is at school and where the teacher can reach you, if necessary. Let your child know that she has to go to school because the law requires it, but that you and her teachers will work together to see that she enjoys school and learns the things she needs to know as she grows up.

One of the best ways you can help your child succeed in school is to take an interest in what he is learning. Praise his efforts and the work he brings home. Don't criticize if he didn't cross a *T* or made a *B* backwards. Also, use whatever chance you can get in your everyday routine to help him learn. If you have two pennies in your pocket and there are three on the table, ask him to count with you how many that makes. When he is learning his letters, buy AlphaBits cereal or alphabet soup so he can have fun finding different letters for you. Buy toys that promote learning. There are lots of them, such as flash cards, quiz games, jigsaw puzzles of the United States. As he progresses in school, buy a globe to show him what the earth and different countries look like. Take him to museums, zoos, aquariums, on nature walks, and give him other experiences that make him realize learning can be exciting and fun.

It's very important not to be critical of a young child and not to make him feel ashamed of his mistakes when he is beginning to learn things. If you point out all the errors in his paper, or if you correct him every time he hits a wrong note when he is beginning piano lessons, you can make him so nervous and anxious that he won't want to learn. He will be afraid to try because he will fear he'll make a mistake and you will pounce on him for it. And be very careful not to emphasize achievement too much. Don't give your child the idea that he must bring home all A's and be at the top of the class. This makes him feel he is only a worthwhile person to you if he does better than everyone else, not worthwhile for the person he is himself. This can cause emotional problems later in life. The child is likely to become a perfectionist who will grow up with anxiety about making a mistake, and who may well develop feelings of inferiority and depression when he finds he can't be the perfect individual you want.

Early childhood educators also warn that you should not compare your child and his achievements in school with other children or with his sister's or brother's accomplishments. This only builds inferiority feelings in the child. Instead, encourage and support his efforts. Check with him at night to see if he has any homework and needs any help with it. If he does, help him. Go to meetings his teacher schedules and PTA meetings to learn how he is doing and how you can help him.

Finally, a stable family life is important for your child's success and accomplishment in school. A child can't concentrate on studying if he's upset about things at home. In fact, some educators believe emotional problems are the biggest cause of school failure.

If school problems do occur, the first thing to do is to listen to your child's complaints. Don't immediately assume he was in the wrong if the teacher punished him or yelled at him, but don't go to the other extreme and rush to defend him if you get a complaint from his teacher about his behavior. Get the whole story. Ask your child open-ended questions like "What happened?" "How did this problem start?" Acknowledge the emotions he is feeling, avoid blaming or shaming him, and ask him if he can think of any solution to the problem, or if he could do something differently so it would not occur again. But if your child is really upset about something in school, perhaps a child who is bullying him or a teacher who is overly critical, call his teacher and arrange for a meeting with her. Talk over the problem and see if the two of you working together can make school a more pleasant and successful experience for your child.

REFUSAL TO GO TO SCHOOL

This is a problem that practically every parent will encounter at some time. On the first day of school or nursery school it is common because the child naturally is afraid of being left in a strange place by his parent and left among a group of strangers.

Child care specialists have some of the following suggestions to make the transition to school easier:

- Before your child's first day at school or nursery school visit the school with him to have him meet the teacher and see his classroom. Many schools have a day when parents can bring incoming kindergarteners to school for a visit. If your child's school doesn't, make it a point to call the school and make an appointment for a visit. Your child is much less likely to refuse to go to school if he is going to a place which is familiar and to a teacher he has met.
- On the first day of school have your child bring along a favorite toy or book.
- Put a piece of paper in his school bag with his name, address and phone number.
- Walk with the child to school or to the bus stop and wait with him for the bus.
- Be enthusiastic about school and talk about things he will do and learn that are fun and interesting.
- Be firm that the child has to go. Don't change your mind if he cries, says he has a stomach ache, or tries to convince you to let him stay home as long as you are sure he is well.
- Be around after school so your child can tell you about it and discuss any problems. If he is reluctant to talk, you might ask him what the most exciting thing was that happened that day.

Leaving a child at nursery school can be even more difficult than leaving a child in kindergarten. Many nursery school teachers believe the parent should leave quickly after bringing the child to the school. Teachers at Spring Glen Church Nursery School in Hamden encourage parents to have a casual attitude and not show distress. They say the parent should say calmly "This is the day you go to school," then bring the child to school, interest him in something, say goodbye and leave. Sometimes it will help the child if he brings something that he can show to others or share with others, they add.

I disagree about the wisdom of leaving a child so abruptly at nursery school, however, because of my own experience with one of my children (see Crying When Left section). If a mother thinks her child is going to be very upset when she leaves him at nursery school, she should find a nursery school that will agree to let her stay with the child at first, if necessary, leaving for longer and longer periods, until he is able to accept her absence. She should also make sure to ask if she and her son can come and visit for a little while before his first day. If she can find out the names of other children who will be in his class and provide opportunities for her child to get to know one or two, it will also make the transition a lot easier for him. Also, you should always assure your child when you leave that you will be back to get him at a certain time, perhaps when the hands of the clock are on particular numbers.

SCHOOL PHOBIA

If a child continues to become upset about going to school and develops a school phobia, it needs to be dealt with because it is not likely to go away by itself, says Dr. Joseph Zanga, pediatrician. Sometimes a child will express the phobia explicitly, saying he's afraid of going to school or that he doesn't want to go. But often school phobia takes the form of various symptoms, such as a stomach ache, headache, or even vomiting. Asking the child what upsets him about school is important because if it is a teacher or some children who are making him fearful, a talk with the teacher may help. But sometimes school phobia develops when a child begins school because the mother subconsciously doesn't want to let go of the child, says Zanga. She has smothered him with so much attention that the child is very dependent and can't separate from her. In such cases counseling may be needed for both the child and the parents.

If an older child develops school phobia, however, it is more likely that some problem at school has caused it. Ridicule from peers for his appearance or behavior, lack of academic success, lack of ability in physical education classes, or a demanding or insensitive teacher can be some of the causes. Or the child might feel he can't do the work, or that his parents are expecting too much of him. Again, it's important for parents to talk with the child to try to find out what is bothering him about school. If he feels overwhelmed by the work or by pressure from his parents, it's important for the parents to get help for him so that he can succeed and to assure him he doesn't have to be perfect. Sometimes if the child and parents discuss the problem together with the teacher and principal, and perhaps the school social worker, some solutions may be found to make school more comfortable for the child. If the problem persists for months, however, Zanga says the child may need counseling from a psychologist or psychiatrist.

Sex Play

Children begin to be curious about their bodies when they are as young as three and four. They also may be curious about the bodies of other children. So you might have the unsettling experience of coming upon your child and a playmate naked and examining one another's bodies or "playing doctor." What should you do?

First of all, don't overreact or tell the children they are bad, or punish them. By doing this you will just make them think there is something shameful about their bodies or their sexual organs. This could have serious consequences, say mental health experts. It could make them feel guilty about their normal sexual urges as they get older and cause some psychological problems. Or it might have the opposite effect. The children might increase sexual activity, but in secret, because what is forbidden is often most enticing.

Instead, with preschoolers you might casually comment that yes, Johnny has a belly button and penis just as your son does. But explain that people don't go around taking off their clothes and examining one another's body. Tell them to get dressed and suggest something else they might do.

To discourage sex play try to make sure young children play in areas where you can supervise them, not in closed rooms or off in the woods. And let your children know that any time they have questions about their bodies, they can ask you.

By the time children are in elementary school some sexual activity is fairly common. They may masturbate, examine each other's bodies, perhaps kiss a person of the opposite sex. What do you do about all this? First of all, don't get up tight. If you punish the child or make him feel really guilty about this behavior, you probably won't stop it. You will just make it seem more exciting to him, and he'll be more careful that he doesn't get caught next time. Also, as noted above, connecting excessive guilt or severe punishment with normal sexual urges could lead to psychological problems when he is an adult.

However, parents do have to restrict the sexual behavior of young children. If you see your child masturbate, for instance, don't make him feel guilty, shame him or make him think what he is doing is disgusting. Instead, get the idea across that this is something people do privately, not when there are other people around. If you find your child indulging in sex play with children of the same or opposite sex, don't get angry or punish him. Sit down and have a serious talk with him about sexual behavior. Explain that sex is pleasurable, and was meant to be pleasurable so people would want to do it and have children. But it is not appropriate behavior for a child. Explain that this type of activity is meant for adults because they are mature enough to handle it. Be understanding and sensitive to his feelings, and answer his questions honestly. If necessary, get him a book that explains anatomy and reproduction. It's better that he gets accurate information from you than if he picks up misleading information about sex on the streets.

In elementary school it's also a good idea to tell children that they should not let other people touch the private parts of their bodies. Explain to them that if someone tries to do this, or if some boy or man exposes his penis to them, they should tell you about it and tell their teacher if it happens in school.

Also, be aware of the influences in society that encourage sexual activity among young people—sexually explicit records and movies, enticing clothing, the frequency of people living together without being married, soap operas in which the characters' main activities seem to be jumping into bed with one another, etc. Do your best to counter these influences. Make sure your children dress modestly and appropriately. During their elementary school and early teen years monitor what they watch and listen to, and if you hear them playing records or seeing a program that promotes promiscuous sexual behavior, tell them you don't want them to listen to it or watch it. Explain why. Talk about a boy's strong urge for sex, and the difficulties that a young girl can get in if she allows him to have sex with her and gets pregnant. Explain that part of growing up is learning to take responsibility for one's behavior, and that includes sexual behavior. Young people need to be responsible about this because they are not ready emotionally to have sexually intense relationships and not able yet to provide a secure and loving home for a baby, should they get pregnant. In the teen years it makes sense to explain to your children the diseases, including AIDS, that a person can get from promiscuous sexual activity.

If your child's sexual behavior seems excessive or compulsive, you should consult a therapist because the child may have an emotional problem or be under some severe stress.

Sex Questions

The time will come when your child will ask questions about the facts of life. It begins at a younger age than you might expect, often during preschool years, and one of the first questions is likely to be "Where did I come from?" You don't need to go into an explanation of sexual intercourse at this time. The child is not ready for that, and it's important to answer just the questions he asks and give him the type of information he is old enough to handle. But don't give him the old story about the stork. It's important to answer your children's questions about sex truthfully from the time they are very small so that they will trust and believe in what you say, child specialists stress.

What do you say when a child asks where he came from? Explain that he grew from an egg inside his mother's body, in a part of her body called the uterus. A seed from his father's body joined the egg and made it start growing, and when he was big enough, he came out. If he wants to know how he got out, explain that there is an opening at the bottom of a woman's body through which the baby comes out.

The coming of a new baby is sometimes a good time to explain to your preschooler where he came from. He will notice that his mother's stomach is getting bigger, and it's a good time to tell him that there is a baby growing inside there, just as he grew inside his mother. Then follow up with an explanation.

At some time the child may ask how his father's seed got into his mother's body. Be honest and use correct terms, advises psychologist Jonas Salk. Explain that when a man and woman love one another, they hug and get very close, and the man wants to place his penis in an opening in her body called the vagina. When he does this, fluid comes out that contains the seed, which moves up in her body until it joins the egg. It's probably a good idea though to tell your children that not all parents tell their children about sex when they are young, so they should not tell all this to their friends. Instead they should wait until their friends' parents want to tell them.

It's important also to tell your daughter about menstruation and your son about wet dreams when they are 10 or 11 so they are not shocked by these things. Explain what menstruation is, and how the blood is not anything to be alarmed about, but fluid that was needed in the uterus to prepare for a baby. If no egg and sperm have joined to form a baby that month, the body gets rid of the fluid. Make sure you also tell your son that wet dreams are perfectly normal and do not mean he is wetting himself or that there is something wrong with him. Explain that they are a way of releasing some of the sperm and seminal fluid that is building up in his testicles now that he is becoming a man.

Child development specialists stress that you should tell your children the truth about sexual matters when they ask because if you evade their questions, you will make them think sex is something secretive or shameful. Then they will probably become more curious, seek information about sex from their peers, and maybe get wrong information. Making sex seem a taboo subject may also encourage a child to experiment with it secretly with his friends. In fact, some child behavior specialists say children are not as likely to experiment with sex as much when they get older if they have been given correct information about it calmly by their parents as children.

Sharing

Don't expect that sharing is going to come naturally to kids. It doesn't. If a child is playing with a toy and is happy with it, he is not going to want to share it with another. Children under three, in fact, don't understand sharing and are not really capable of it, so it's unrealistic to expect them to willingly share a toy, say child development specialists. Children this age play alongside one another and have not matured to the point where they really play with one another. Forcing a young child to share may even disturb the child emotionally because expecting behavior from a child that he is not capable of at his stage of development can be psychologically harmful. Even a three-year-old is not likely to share his possessions willingly with another child, especially a younger sibling whom he feels is taking some of his parents' love and attention away from him.

Don't punish a child who won't share or tell him he is a bad boy or make him feel ashamed. Nor should you force children to share or make fun of a child who won't share, child specialists say. You need to use gentle suggestions, explanations, and sometimes distraction, and then reward the child who shares with praise. For instance, you might say, "Michael, you have three trucks. Will you give one to Daniel so he can play trucks too?" It's also a good idea to get across the concept of taking turns with things. For instance, you could suggest, "Michael, Daniel would like to play with that truck. Would you let him play with it for five minutes, and then you can have a turn with it again.?" If the child is is too young to understand what five minutes means, tell him when the big hand of the clock is on the next number.

If Susan takes a toy from Mary, explain that it isn't polite to grab something away from someone else. Tell Susan to ask politely if she can play with the toy. If she does, and Mary agrees, both children have learned about sharing and the value of politeness. If Susan won't share, distract one child or the other. You might say, "Mary, how about coming to color with me with my new crayons while Susan plays with the doll for a little while." Or you could say, "Susan, come on with me and we will read a new storybook, and you can play with the doll later." It also helps to explain to children that if they share their toys with other children, then other children are more likely to let them play with their toys. And you also need to teach them that if they borrow something, they need to return it in good condition to the owner, or people are not going to want to share things with them.

Children also learn sharing by seeing parents and others in their family share things willingly with one another. They learn the value and joy of sharing and giving by giving gifts to others at birthdays and at Christmas. And as they grow older, if they are guided gently into sharing with others, they will learn that sharing is a nice thing to do, it makes other people like them more, and it makes them feel good.

Children who are raised by loving and affectionate parents will learn to share more easily than children whose parents have not been warm and loving, according to child behavior specialists. This is why a child who won't share with a younger sibling needs not punishment or shame, but more assurance from his parents that he is as important to them and is loved as much as his younger sister or brother. It's a signal to parents that they need to spend more time with the older child and do something special just with him. If parents are nurturing and sensitive to all their children's feelings, and model caring and generosity, it's a good bet their children will grow up to be caring, generous people also.

Shyness

It is common for a baby at a certain stage of development to be shy with strangers. For the first few months of his life the infant will usually be content to be held by anyone, but when he begins to differentiate his parents from other adults, he may cry if stranger picks him up or shy away if someone other than his parent holds out his arms to him. Parents shouldn't give the baby to the other person in this situation or let him keep on crying in a stranger's arms because it will only upset the child more. Instead they need to hold and comfort the infant and be content that this is just a normal phase their child is going through. In fact, shyness with strangers is a good sign at six months to a year, say child development experts, because it shows the baby has come to associate his parents with love and security and wants to be with them rather than with people he doesn't know. If some friend or relative who is strange to the baby insists on talking to him or wants to hold him even though you can see the baby is frightened and shy, just explain that the infant needs some time to get to know them and warm up to them. Then either visit with the guest while you hold the baby or put the baby down in the crib or playpen with a comforting toy or blanket and go visit with your guest in another room.

This infantile shyness usually disappears in the second year, but some children remain shy throughout their preschool and school years. If you have a child like this, don't pressure him to speak up to people or join in when a group of children his age are playing. If he hangs his head and won't talk to someone you meet, don't embarrass him by saying in front of the child that he's shy. That only makes him feel that you think he is inadequate as a person, and it will affect his self esteem. If you see your child or any child standing around on the sidelines while a group of children are playing, he isn't going to get the courage to join in if you embarrass him by asking what's wrong with him that he is not playing with the others. Instead take a little time to talk to him or play with him so he won't feel so lonely and left out.

It's also important to praise a shy child for things he does well and to try to arrange situations with a few people where he feels enough at ease to take part. Perhaps getting him used to playing with one or two cousins he knows well can help him gain confidence to play with other children.

If your child is shy, it is also important to find the reasons for the child's shyness so that you might change anything that could be contributing to it. If a child is smaller or younger than other children in his neighborhood, or if he hasn't been around other children much, he is likely to be shy. If he has some impediment, such as a hearing difficulty, poor eyesight, mental retardation, it can also make a child feel different from other children and shy. In this case he needs plenty of love and reassurance from you that he is a worthwhile person anyway, as well as help for his disability. There are some children who are by temperament quieter and slower to warm up to new people and new situations, notes psychologist Edward Zigler. Be sure not to force such a child to join in the group's activities right away because you want him to be extroverted and popular. And don't make him feel guilty for remaining on the sidelines. Let him join in when he feels comfortable in the situation.

Sometimes children are shy because they have been disciplined too strictly at home, say child psychologists. If parents are too strict and authoritarian and don't allow the child to express his feelings and ideas openly at home, he is likely to be afraid to express them in front of other people. A child who is often told to be quiet, who is put down, ridiculed or often criticized by his parents or siblings is bound to feel inferior and is likely to be shy around other people. If you show your child you have time for him and listen respectfully to his ideas, and accept him the way he is, you give him the idea he is important and worthwhile, and he is more likely to have the courage to express his opinions to others and be outgoing and friendly.

One way that may help prevent children from being shy is to hold weekly family meetings in which you encourage each child to participate. Problems that come up and family plans can be discussed in these meetings. By calling on each child to express his ideas and by listening respectfully to them, you build the child's self esteem. You make him feel that what he thinks and says is of value and he is of value as a person. He is much more likely then to feel secure and free to express himself around other people.

A child who is very shy and withdrawn, who is docile and obedient, and doesn't smile much or seem to have fun may have a serious emotional problem. Such children have a lot of pentup anger, according to psychologist Lee Salk. They were given the idea by their parents that anger was bad, but they were not shown how to deal with their negative feelings. Such children he says, "are apt to come apart later in life particularly during adolescence when the pressure of life may seem overwhelming." There are other reasons that can cause a child to withdraw, according to Dr. Salk, such as severe family problems, traumatic events, a child who bullies him at school, or parents who set too high expectations which the child feels he cannot meet. But whatever the cause, it's important to get professional help for a child who is extremely withdrawn.

Sibling Rivalry

WAYS TO HELP PREVENT IT

How you handle the arrival of a new baby can have a big influence on how much sibling rivalry develops between your children. It's normal for a child to be jealous of a new baby in the family, but parents can take steps before the baby is born to minimize jealousy and make the baby's arrival less of a difficult time for the older child, according psychologist Loyd Rowland, author of new parent bulletins distributed by the Mental Health Association of Connecticut.

First, try not to have another child until the youngest is about three. Children under three are extremely demanding of a parent's time and attention and are bound to be resentful of another baby. Prepare your child ahead of time for the arrival of the baby. It's best if the mother explains how the baby is growing inside her and when it is ready she will go to the hospital so the doctor can help get the baby out. Have your child put his hand on his mother's abdomen and feel the baby kicking. Buy a child's book about how babies are born and read it to him. Have the child help you pick out clothes for the new baby and help you arrange the baby's things. But don't make the mistake of moving him out of his crib so the baby can have it. Move him to a big bed well ahead of time, or if he is too young, buy another crib.

A week or two before the baby is due the mother should explain that she will have to go to the hospital soon so the doctor can help her have the baby, and she will be there a few days. You might even take your child to see the hospital. Let the child know who will be taking care of him, and make sure it's someone he knows well and trusts, or better yet, a grandparent or aunt whom he loves. It will be difficult for the child when his mother is away, so it's important for a mother to keep in touch with him by phone and let him come to see the new baby so he doesn't think she has gone and forgotten about him because of his new brother or sister. She might also send home a gift or two for him from the gift shop.

The way parents act when they return from the hospital with the new baby is crucial in determining how their child will react to the new member of the family, say child behavior specialists. Your older child will have mixed feelings about the new arrival. He is bound to feel jealous and left out when he sees his parents holding and feeding the new baby and spending so much time with the infant. Because of this, it's important to pay a lot of attention to the older child. Never tell your older child you don't have as much time for him now because of the baby. This will certainly make him very jealous of his younger brother or sister and can lead to trouble throughout their childhood.

Don't tell your older child not to touch the baby. Show him how and where to touch the baby and explain that babies need to be touched gently. If he wants to hold the baby, tell him to always tell you, and you will help him hold her. Let him help you hold the bottle to feed her sometimes. Make him feel that it is "our baby" and encourage him to sing to her, shake a rattle for her, rub her gently, etc. to help make her happy.

Sometimes giving older children a baby doll with a toy bottle can help them adjust to the new baby because then they can identify with their mother and be a mommy or daddy, too. They can care for their baby while you are taking care of their new brother or sister. Also, since visitors will be coming with gifts for the baby, keep some new books or little toys in your drawer to give the older child if they should neglect to bring something too. Most important, though, is finding time each day to spend alone with your older child, playing with her, taking her out somewhere, or just holding her on your lap and cuddling and talking to her. Remember that if the older child acts jealous, it's a sign she feels left out and needs more attention.

DEALING WITH JEALOUSY OF A NEW BABY

If your older child becomes demanding or acts jealous when you have to take care of the baby, find ways the older child can help you. You might have him get get a clean diaper or tissue when you're changing the baby, help you put the infant's clothes away, or, when the baby starts eating baby food, help you choose his menu for the day.

To make it easier for the older child to accept the newcomer, you might show him pictures of himself when he was as little as the new baby and say just as he grew, so the baby will grow big enough after a while to be someone he can play with. And now that he's the big brother (or she's the big sister) you might buy your older child some grown-up item or article of clothing the child has been wanting or give the child some special privileges—perhaps staying up later or watching an extra television program.

Don't expect your older child to love the baby right away. Don't tell him he should love his new brother or sister. Understand that he will be jealous of the new arrival, and don't be upset if he wants to send the baby back to the hospital. Tell him it's all right if he doesn't like the new baby, but he must not hurt him. Parents should NOT say "you shouldn't be jealous of your brother (or sister)" because it doesn't do any good and will only make the child feel guilty about feelings which are normal in this situation. Nor should parents punish the child for jealousy. This only makes the situation worse. But because jealousy is very common at this time, parents should be watchful when the two children are together in the same room.

Dr. Richard A. Oberfield, associate clinical professor of psychiatry at New York University Medical Center, says that parents often need to actively intervene to help their children deal with their angry feelings about the new baby. Having the child help care for the baby is often not enough to dispel such feelings, and if angry outbursts against the baby occur, parents need to talk with the child about this. If the older child pulls out the baby's pacifier, for instance, or shows anger in some other way, parents should not give him a lecture about how he should love his baby brother or sister more. "The child needs to explore the angry or hurt feelings behind the deed rather than cover them up. Children need a vent for those feelings," he says.

If a child is acting jealous, child specialists say it is helpful for parents to label the emotion and show they understand why the child is feeling that way. "Parents should help the child find words for his feelings," says Oberfield. For instance, a mother might say "I know you feel jealous sometimes because Mommy has to spend so much time with the baby. But as soon as I feed her (or diaper her or whatever) I'll put her to bed and we will do something together." Or she might say, "Even though you love your new sister, I bet you were pretty mad when I had to stop playing to feed the baby." Another way to get your child to talk about the way he feels is for you to reveal your struggle with similar feelings as a child towards your brothers and sisters and how they were resolved. By showing children we understand and empathize with their disturbing feelings, child specialists say we help dispel such feelings. Oberfield also stresses the importance of spending time alone with the older child. "Individual attention without the new baby—even for a walk to the store—can do wonders," he says.

If your older child seems to be getting into a pattern of hurting the younger one, you have to take action. This most commonly happens when children are less than three years apart. It may not happen when the baby is tiny and can't get around, but once he starts crawling and getting into the older child's things, his resentment may well up, and he may hurt the baby. If this starts to happen, you may have to forbid him to touch the baby and tell him he has to stay away from the baby for a week or so, advises psychologist John Rosemond. Then gradually allow him increasing contact, and praise him for being loving and gentle with the baby.

Even if your child acts friendly to the new baby, he may still be jealous, but may hide his feelings. Sometimes this jealousy may take the form of regressive behavior. My daughter, for instance, who was two and a half when her sister was born, wanted a bottle again, something which is quite common at such a time. Don't make a big deal of it, say child care experts. Give the older child the bottle. I did, and she decided in a day or two it wasn't much fun and drinking from a cup was much better. Sometimes the child may begin wetting his bed again. If so, don't punish him, but reassure him that you love him and everything will be all right. You might also voice the feelings he is repressing by saying something like, "Even if you don't like the new baby now at times, when he is bigger you will. You will have a brother (or sister) who will be fun to play with." Generally though, if you give the older child hugs, time on your lap and enough attention and ignore the babyish behavior, it usually goes away fairly soon.

SIBLING RIVALRY AMONG OLDER CHILDREN

Specialists in child behavior have a number of suggestions for preventing sibling rivalry among older children and dealing with if if it occurs.

- Don't favor one child over the other. Don't let the youngest get away with things that the others would be punished for, for instance, because he is still your baby.

- Don't let your older child boss around the younger or tease or ridicule him.

- Don't expect an older child to do a lot of chores or be responsible often for care of the younger children, and then allow the other children to spend most of their time playing.

- Don't get involved in your children's quarrels unless there is hitting or fighting or cruelty involved. Children often quarrel to get attention from their parents. If the attention isn't forthcoming, the quarreling often stops. Instead, tell them you are sure they can figure out a solution.

- If your children really can't settle a quarrel on their own, sit down with them and get them to brainstorm for possible solutions, then choose the one they think best.

- Distract children who are arguing by getting them involved in some activity.

- If children start fighting, give them a time out. Send each to a different room.

- Avoid making comparisons between your children. Don't say, for instance, "Joseph always has brought home good report cards. Why can't you?" This will just make one child resent the other, and the other feel that he is better than his brother or sister.

- Don't rush in and always punish an older child who hits or aggravates a younger one and defend the younger because of his age. Realize this has probably happened because the older one needs more of your attention. Explain that you don't want him to hit, but you want to know why he is doing so. Get him to talk about his feelings. Then do something special with him, and reassure him that he is loved as much as the younger. Just punishing a child in such a case can make sibling rivalry worse.

Sleep Problems

Sometimes parents have problems trying to get their child to go to sleep or to sleep through the night. If you're one of them, you have a lot of company. Ninety-five percent of the children in one study went through a period in which they cried or called for their parents at night at least once a week, according to Joan Cuthbertson and Susie Schevill, authors of *Helping Your Child Sleep Through the Night*.

SLEEP PROBLEMS IN INFANCY

During the first few months of your baby's life you can expect that he will be awake and crying once or twice during the night when you would like to sleep. In such cases it's usually because he needs to be fed, but if he won't settle down after he's been fed, burped and changed, you may have a baby with colic (See Crying). Usually by three to six months a baby will sleep through the night.

It will help an infant get to sleep if you wrap him snugly in a receiving blanket. A newborn also seems to sleep better when positioned on his side with his back against the crib padding. Rocking the baby in your arms or in a rocking chair, holding the baby up on your shoulder and walking with the infant are also ways that will sometimes help get baby to sleep. It also helps to do the same things in the same order just before putting the baby down to sleep. For instance, you might rock him a little and then sing the same lullaby, and then put him in his crib with his teddy bear or special blanket. However, pediatrician T. Berry Brazelton warns that you should not get a baby in the habit of falling asleep in your arms because then you, the parent, become part of the baby's sleep routine.

Some babies go through a period during their first or second year when they resist going to sleep at night and cry when you put them in their crib. It sometimes happens when a baby is teething, but sometimes just occurs because the baby doesn't went to be left alone and away from his parents. If you have this problem with your baby, make sure first that your baby is fed, changed, cuddled and not sick or in pain. There are medications you can rub on his gums if you think teething is the problem. Giving a bedtime bottle with milk, water, or juice also helps soothe a baby and get him ready for sleep. Giving a small baby a pacifier can help. So can giving him a soft baby blanket or putting a favorite stuffed animal in his crib each night. Timing is important too. Watch to see when your child starts to look sleepy. My grandchild, for instance, lies on the floor and starts to suck her thumb when she's getting tired. This is the time to scoop her up and put her in her crib, and she will usually settle, her parents have found.

Dr. Richard Ferber, director of the Center for Pediatric Sleep Disorders at Children's Hospital in Boston and author of the excellent book, *Solve Your Child's Sleep Problems,* notes that sleep problems sometimes occur because parents have inadvertently caused the wrong things to be associated with sleep in their child's mind. For instance, if you rub your child's back to put him to sleep every night or give him a bottle or something to drink as part of his bedtime routine, if he awakens during the night, he may need the back rub or the bottle to get back to sleep again. It's better to get him used to taking something comforting to bed, such as a favorite blanket or stuffed animal, so that if he awakens at night, he can find it and comfort himself with it, and get himself back to sleep. Babies need to learn to get themselves to sleep, and they sometimes do this by rubbing the binding of their blanket or a part of their stuffed animal, or by thumb sucking. Leaving a night light on can also help a baby see he is in the same familiar surroundings if he awakens at night and help him get back to sleep.

If your baby keeps on crying because of inappropriate sleep associations when you put her in the crib at night or during the night, Dr. Ferber suggests going to her at increasing intervals, after five minutes at first, then 10, then at 15 minute intervals if she is still crying. He says to talk soothingly to her, pat her, but don't pick her up. The next night increase the time before going in to her to 10 minutes, and work up to 20. Within a week night time crying should stop.

SLEEP PROBLEMS IN TODDLERS AND PRESCHOOLERS

Child care experts say preparation for sleep is most important in avoiding or solving sleep problems after infancy. Parents should not expect that they can just tell their child to go to bed and he will go. Children need a quiet, pleasant time with their parents for an hour or so before their bedtime. This means avoiding exciting, violent television programs or a lot of physical activity. Singing to a child, reading a child's book to him, rocking him, saying prayers with him and talking about his day are all good ways of preparing a child for sleep.

It's very important that one or both parents share this quiet time before sleep with the child. Teachers at the Stork Club Child Centers in Connecticut say this special quiet period alone with your child before bedtime is a time when you can really communicate with him and get him to express his feelings. It's important for both sound sleep and emotional stability that parents give their child a chance to express feelings he had about things during the day, and show by careful listening and empathetic comments that they understand his feelings. It is also a time to talk about any worries or problems he may have had during the day and help ease his mind.

Keeping the same bedtime every night helps avoid sleep problems. And it's important that parents be firm about bedtime and not let the child keep procrastinating, say child behavior specialists. Nor should they keep running in when the child calls and keeps asking for things or asking questions. If they do, the child will soon see he's controlling things.

For some children a warm bath before bedtime helps to relax them. A snack before bedtime and keeping a night light on his room may also help a child get to sleep. Having a favorite blanket or animal to take to bed with him may also make a preschooler feel more secure and better able to get to sleep. And of course a hug and snuggle with mother and/or dad helps a child feel secure and relaxed.

Talking about the importance of sleep and the special things the child will be doing the next day also helps get children to sleep, say the Stork Club teachers. Laura Spencer of The Stork Club stresses that nap time should be used as a positive experience, not as a punishment, because this creates confusion for the child. This also applies to bedtime. "Go to bed" should not be the order given to a child who has misbehaved. By making naptime (and bedtime) a time to cuddle with a favorite toy, look at interesting books, listen to soft music, a parent can make it a time to enjoy.

A regular routine before bedtime every night helps older children as well as babies get to sleep. My daughter Carolyn, who always had a knack for handling children and did a lot of babysitting, used to go through a special routine with one rather difficult child , having him say goodnight to his stuffed animals one after another in the same order, and then ending with a goodnight to her and a hug and kiss. He looked forward to the little ritual, and it had a calming effect on him. Sometimes she would tease him and skip the last goodnight, and the little boy would say indignantly, "You forgot to have me say goodnight to you."

"Oh, that's right, I did," she'd say, and he would give her a big hug and kiss and then settle contentedly to sleep.

If your child is rebelling at the idea of going to sleep, it may help if instead of saying "Go to bed," you just tell him to get into his pajamas and to rest in his room. Nursery school director Dolores Andreucci of Guilford, Conn. tells children at her school who don't want to take their nap to rest. Let your child take some favorite books in with him or a favorite toy or two, or play the radio softly in his room. Just insist that he stay in his room. Eventually he should get tired enough to go to sleep.

There are certain ways you should never handle a child's refusal to go to sleep, child specialists say. Don't threaten your child or punish him if he is afraid of the dark or if he can't get to sleep. The child needs comfort and understanding in such situations. You don't help a child get over one fear, such as fear of the dark or of separation from his parents, by adding another fear— fear of punishment, says public health specialist Dorothy Noyes Sproul. Nor do you help him conquer his fear by making fun of him or by telling him to act like a big boy or to stop acting like a baby. Denying the existence of the child's fear, just saying there is nothing to be afraid of, also does no good and can do harm because such an attitude can make the child feel guilty and inadequate as well as fearful.

Parents also should NOT take the child into their bed if he won't go to sleep. This is a big mistake, say child care experts, because if you allow it at first, you may not be able to get your child out of the habit. "Never get into bed with children or allow them in your bed. Once you do that, they'll want it all the time," warns Sue Marcio, a nursery school director who has a degree in early childhood education. Instead, tell your child she has her own bed just like you do, and then give her a hug and kiss when the bedtime routine is finished, and leave the room. Telling her you will be nearby and leaving the door open a little may make her feel more at ease. If she really seems upset because of anxieties, nightmares, or whatever, you may have to sit beside her bed for a while until she relaxes and goes to sleep.

What causes problems in getting a child to go to sleep? Sometimes errors in child rearing that cause anxieties and fears in the child, or concern about failure to meet parents' expectations, Sproul says. Concern or anxiety about what the child's parents are doing, especially if the child senses discord between them, can keep a child awake. If a child has had some bad dreams, this may also make him afraid to go to sleep. Fears of monsters, thunder, shadows, the dark, being alone, and many other things can also make a preschooler resist bedtime. If you sense fears are keeping your child awake at bedtime, it's important to talk about these fears with your child and to show him there is nothing to fear. For instance, you can explain to a child who is afraid of shadows moving on his wall that it is just the shadow of a tree outside his window. If nightmares bother him, you need to assure him they aren't real, explaining in simple terms that they are just pictures people get in their minds when they sleep.

Another reason many children give their parents trouble at bedtime is that they feel their parents are trying to get rid of them when they tell them to go to bed, says educator Jane Nelsen. Naturally parents are often tired after a long, hard day, especially today with both parents often working, and they want time to themselves to relax at night. But when children sense their parents want to get away from them, they feel discouraged, hurt and unwanted, and so they will do whatever they can think of just to keep their attention. By spending a quiet time before bedtime with your child in which you both share your feelings you can often avoid bedtime problems, says Nelsen, because this gives the child a sense of belonging and security. She says sharing the happiest and saddest event of the day is a good way to settle your child for the night.

WAKING EARLY IN THE MORNING

If you have a child who goes to the other extreme and wakes you early in the morning, you need to get across to the child as soon as he is old enough to understand that it's all right for him to be awake, but he should play quietly or look at picture books in his room if he's awake when people are supposed to be asleep. Having interesting toys in his room, and perhaps some crackers and juice may let you get a few more winks. For a child who always wakes early, you might set an alarm or a clock radio and tell him he may get up when the alarm rings or the radio goes on.

WAKING DURING THE NIGHT

For some parents the problem is not getting the child to sleep but keeping him asleep. What do you do about a child that habitually wakes up at night and wakes up his parents? For an infant a diaper change, a bottle, and some rocking and cuddling will usually get him back to sleep. For an older child, sometimes just holding and calming the child may be enough. Leaving a night light on may also help because your child may be afraid of the dark when he awakens.

But sometimes parents have a big problem with an older baby or toddler who has already given up night feedings, but suddenly begins to wake again at night. Sometimes he wants a bottle again. Child specialists say this sometimes happens because of separation anxiety after the child has been separated from his parents for a short time, perhaps when they went on a weekend trip. It can also happen after a baby has been sick and wakeful for several nights, and his parents gave him a bottle at night to soothe him and get him back to sleep. Or parents might bring on this night wakefulness by running in and picking up the child as soon as he cries or whimpers during the night, instead of letting him learn how to get himself back to sleep. To break the habit, first make sure your child is dry and comfortable, hold him a little, offer him a drink of water and perhaps a cracker, reassure him that you are nearby and everything is okay, then put him in his crib. You may have to sit with him in his room a little while until he gets back to sleep. But if this goes on night after night, you may have to let him cry himself back to sleep a few nights, pediatricians say, or he is likely to get in the habit of waking you up every night.

Once your child can get out of his crib or is sleeping in a bed, if he wakes up and wanders around at night, make sure your outside doors are locked. Don't lock his door, however, for that can frighten a child and is dangerous in case of fire. If he wanders a lot, you might get a gate to put across his door. It helps too if you leave some books and toys around in his room at night and tell him to keep himself busy with them if he awakens instead of waking you up.

Some children not only wake at night but insist on getting into their parents' bed and sleeping with them. Don't allow it, child specialists warn. Louise Miller of Spring Glen Nursery School suggests taking the child by the hand and calmly leading him back to his own bed, saying "This is where you sleep." She also advises giving the child a special toy for comfort. Mrs. Marcio says most of the time when a child wakes up at night and wants to come into his parents' bed, it's because he's had a bad dream. If this happens, you should never punish the child or laugh at his fears. Instead, Marcio advises comforting the child and sitting in a chair in his room for a while to calm him and get him back to sleep. If your child continues to want to sleep with you at night, you might need to put a cot or recliner chair in your child's room for a while where you can doze until your child gets back to sleep. In such cases, something is apparently frightening or bothering your child, and it's important that you get him to talk about it and then reassure him that you love him and are there to make sure he is safe.

To get children age one and a half to three to sleep through the night Cuthbertson and Schevill suggest putting a clock radio near your child's bed, setting it for about the time you have to get up, and telling him that he can only come into your bed when the music comes on in the morning. The first time the child wakes and calls you, go to him once and repeat the instructions about waiting until the music comes on. If he keeps waking you and wanting to come into your bed, you will have to calmly take him back and keep repeating the instructions if he's in a regular bed, or finally put a baby gate across his doorway. When the child does stay in his room all night without bothering you, they say be sure to praise him a lot.

If none of these methods solve the problem, there may be a physical or psychological problem causing the child to wake. Even young children are very sensitive to upset and discord in the family and to a disturbed emotional state in a parent. It raises the frightening possibility in the child's mind that the disturbed parent or parents may leave the child. A physical problem such as an ear infection or allergies can also cause a child to wake at night. It's a good idea to have your pediatrician check your child if she suddenly starts waking up at night, especially if you see her touching her ear at times.

I know from personal experience how exhausting and frustrating it can be to have a child who wakes you up every night. My son woke us up one to three times a night until he was four years old. When he was two, our pediatrician prescribed a small dose of Benadryl, an antihistamine, to calm him. It helped a little, but he still woke us most nights. He would always be hungry and thirsty, and we found he would have to have milk or something to drink before he would get back to sleep. Since he was a poor eater, we attributed his wakefulness to hunger, but didn't know what to do about it. Finally, when he was four, we solved the problem on our own. We left three glasses of grape juice beside his bed every night. From then on he didn't wake us, and the grape juice was gone every morning. The floor in his bedroom got pretty sticky, but at that point a good night's sleep was more important to us than a hardwood floor. It wasn't until he was in grammar school and developed a chronic sniffle and cough and occasional wheeze that we took him to an allergist and found he was allergic to practically everything that grows, as well as to our cats. It occurred to us then that he was probably waking up and wanting something to drink because he couldn't breathe through his nose and his mouth got dry. Years of allergy shots followed, but fortunately no more sleep problems.

HANDLING BEDTIME IN OLDER CHILDREN

Many of the suggestions for helping preschoolers get to sleep and sleep through the night also work with elementary school children, such as spending a quiet time with them before bedtime and a having a pleasant pre-bedtime routine. Don't get into a power struggle over insisting that your child go to sleep at a certain time. But child behavior specialists say you should have a set time when he is expected to go to his room and get ready for bed. He can read in bed, play with toys there for a while, and before long he is likely to get tired enough to go to sleep. Just make sure there is no television set in his room.

Sleep problems that are severe and persistent in a child of any age, and problems such as continuing nightmares or sleepwalking, may require the help of a mental health professional because at the root of them may be some anxiety, fear, or frustration that needs to be diagnosed and then treated appropriately.

Spitting

A child may occasionally spit at another child in an outburst of anger. Handle this the way you would hitting or fighting. Label the child's feeling to show you understand why he is behaving this way, but make it clear this type of behavior is not allowed. For instance, tell the child, "I understand you are angry, but I cannot allow you to spit at other people. We do not do this. It is not a polite way to act toward other people." Explain that if he does need to spit anytime, for instance, if he has a cold and coughs up mucus from his chest, he should spit in a sink or in a Kleenex. If he repeats the behavior, use a time-out. Remove him from the group or from the rest of the family and send him to another room alone or to his room until he feels he can behave and will not spit.

Spoiled Children

When children misbehave or make a fuss when they can't have what they want, people often say they are spoiled. This isn't always the case because such behaviors are often normal for the child's age or are the result of some stress in his life. For instance, if your baby seems to cry a lot, it isn't because you pick him up and comfort him when he cries. Babies normally cry a lot, and you're not going to spoil your child if you pick him up when he cries and comfort him when he is a baby, says Dr. Bruce McIntosh in an article in *Pediatrics* magazine. Toddlers who get into everything are not spoiled, he adds, but merely acting normally. Nor are two-year-olds who are negative and resist parents' attempts to control them. They are just going through a normal phase of discovering they have a mind of their own.

Family problems, such as divorce, frequent arguments between parents, spouse or child abuse, alcoholism and drug abuse can produce behaviors in a child that might make him seem "spoiled" to the untrained observer, says the pediatrician. In a divorce, for instance, parents might be hesitant about setting the limits the child needs because of their own guilt.

Indulging children by giving them too much attention or too many things does not result in spoiled children as long as their parents have been clear about the type of behavior that is expected and have set limits on their behavior, says McIntosh. But indulgence can cause spoiling, he says when the parent tries to meet the child's needs by giving him material gifts and unqualified acceptance, but does not set guidelines for what is acceptable behavior. (See Permissive Discipline in Chapter Four.) A truly spoiled child is self-centered, immature, has no consideration for others, wants his own way all the time, must have gratification of his wishes immediately, and is likely to throw temper tantrums.

Some examples of "spoiled" child behavior that McIntosh cites are demands for middle of the night feedings by older babies; frequent crying at night because the child gets attention from it; and frequent temper tantrums. In the first case, he recommends increasing the time between daytime feedings and not feeding the baby every time he is held. In the second situation, he said parents should not respond right away to crying in the middle of the night. He notes it is normal for a baby to cry for 10 to 15 minutes before settling down to sleep. As for temper tantrums, he says to ignore them. And if punishment is needed, he says the use of a time out invoked without hesitation and consistently for misbehavior is usually successful.

Some children act spoiled and put up a big fuss if they can't have some toy or food they see when they are in a store with their parents. To prevent this kind of behavior parents and grandparents must make sure they do not get in the habit of buying their child something every time they take her shopping. If parents find they have to take a young child grocery shopping regularly, it can help to tell her she can choose one thing she would like to eat, such as the cereal she would like. Occasionally on a trip to a department store, you may let her choose some toy under a certain price. Avoid toy stores, in general, if you are not prepared to do this. But on many shopping trips, just explain to her beforehand that you are going with her to buy clothes or food or whatever, and you do not have the money to buy her any toys at this time. If she sees something she wants and acts up because you won't buy it for her, sympathize with her feelings. Tell her yes, you know that is a great truck or a beautiful doll, but you don't have money to buy it now. Maybe she will get it for her birthday, or maybe Santa will bring it at Christmas. And then ignore the cries and move on to another part of the store. If you prevent such demanding behavior when your child is young, she is less likely to grow into a spoiled adult who thinks she needs a lot of material possessions to make her happy.

Stealing

It is natural for toddlers to take toys that don't belong to them or pick up anything that interests them without being concerned about who owns it. This can't be considered stealing because children don't usually have a sense of personal property until age three or four. Even three and four year olds often take other children's toys because they still don't have a strongly developed conscience, and what they want is of most importance to them.

To help prevent children from taking things that belong to others when they get older, begin teaching your child about personal property as soon as he is old enough to understand the difference between what is his and what is yours. Point out, for instance, that this is his hat, that is Daddy's hat, that this is his dish, that is your dish, etc. If a neighbor's child comes over on his tricycle and your child wants to ride it, stress that it is "Johnny's tricycle" and he can only ride it if Johnny gives permission. You might suggest that he let Johnny ride in HIS little car if Johnny lets him ride on his tricycle. In this way you teach about both personal property and sharing.

If your young child takes something that doesn't belong to him, you should not make a big thing of it or shame the child. Nor should you spank him or punish him harshly. Instead, explain that the item is not his and he needs permission from the person who owns it or else he cannot take it. Then go with him and have him return it to the owner at once. In this way he learns it is not right to take things belonging to other people unless they say he can do so, and you will help him develop a conscience. If he has taken something in a store, have him return it to the store owner or checkout girl and say he is sorry. Punishing a young child severely for stealing is not kind or wise say child behavior experts, because the child is just learning moral behavior. Insisting that he return what he has taken is enough of a punishment.

Children in the early grades of grammar school sometimes steal things from their friends, or from stores or school. Sometimes it's because they want to impress other children, or they may just see something they want very much and they don't have a very strong sense of right and wrong. However, it may be because the child is unhappy because of problems in the home or at school.If you suspect a school-age child has stolen something, don't immediately accuse him of stealing. For instance, if your child suddenly comes home with a new toy or jacket you've never seen before, confront him and ask him where he got it. If he says his friend gave it to him, check with the friend. Find out what really happened before you accuse him or do anything.

If you find he did steal something, you shouldn't punish a child this age severely either. This can just make him angry and resentful, and instead of stopping the behavior he may just learn to be sneakier and more successful at it. But don't go to the other extreme and protect or excuse your child or insist he did not steal something if someone accuses him of taking something. This will just produce a spoiled child who thinks he can get away with taking what he wants and who develops no sense of responsibility for his actions. Talk to your child and to others involved until you find out the whole story.

If you find that your grammar school age child has stolen something, you should make the child immediately return what he has taken and tell the person he is sorry, say child behavior specialists. Go with him when he does this. Explain that it is not fair to take something that belongs to someone else, and ask how he would feel if someone took his bike, or some other valued possession. Then take the time to sit down with him alone and ask about why he took the item. Find out about his feelings and if there is something at home or at school that's bothering him.

If stealing continues after the child is of school age or is chronic, professional help may be needed. Stealing in a school-age child can be a sign of a need for love, attention and affection. It can be the signal of some problem in the family and an unconscious cry for help. It can also be a sign that something happened to break or interrupt the important emotional bond that must be established between the child and its parent in the first few years of the child's life. Mental health professionals have found that children who never established a strong bond of love and trust with a parent or significant adult in the first few years of their life often grow up without a conscience and without the ability to love. They may lie, steal, vandalize, assault, and be violent children and adults (see pp. 15-17).

Here is how psychiatrist Foster Cline found out what was causing the problem in the case of an eight-year-old boy referred to him because of chronic stealing at school. He sat Ed on his lap, and with pencil and paper in front of him, said "Well, you see, Ed, there was this little chap who sometimes felt quite lonely. Sometimes he felt like he didn't have enough friends, and sometimes he didn't feel like he got all the attention he needed." He drew a picture of this little boy. "Now, Ed, do you suppose that someone who feels a bit lonely and needing some attention feels full or empty? Right! Quite empty. It's like he has a little hole in him." He drew a hole in the boy he had drawn, and tears in his eyes.

The therapist explained that nothing feels worse than a hole, so the little boy tried to fill up the hole with things like food, and sometimes with pencils, combs, erasers. "He would take all of these things to try to fill up the emptiness. But how do you suppose it felt? Right! It is really not perfectly wonderful to fill an empty spot with combs and pencils. They cause a bit of irritation." He drew pencils and combs in the hole in the boy he has drawn, and the word "Ouch" coming from the boy's mouth. Then hugging the child a little, he said "What do you think this little kid really wants instead of poky pencils and hard old combs? ...Right. He wants a few hugs and kisses. He wants love. Does he want an arm around the shoulder?...Does he want a friendly pat here and there? Right! But does he ask for them?... No."

After Ed admitted he would rather have hugs and kisses, the therapist talked with Ed's parents in front of him and explained how Ed had been trying to fill his emptiness. Ed's father was the kind of parent who did not believe in holding, hugging or physically expressing affection to his son. The therapist talked with Ed's parents about the importance of touches and hugs. He modeled such demonstrations of affection and then had Ed's father do the same thing. Even though the father felt uncomfortable at first, with further family therapy Cline hoped that Ed's father would learn to express the affection his son son badly craved, and Ed would no longer feel a need to steal.

Swearing, Name Calling and Bad Language

At some time or other your child will probably startle you by using a swear word or some kind of foul language. If the child is only about two or so, ignore it because at this age he is still just learning a lot of new words and repeating them without knowing what they really mean. However, take it as a warning to be careful of your own language because he may well be copying words he has heard his parents use.

When a child gets to be three or four he may use bad language if he gets angry with another child or with you. Don't get upset because it's better that he is expressing his anger with words instead of by hitting or having a temper tantrum. However, child development specialists say it's wise to step in and stop it before it becomes a habit. When something your child says makes your ears burn, first of all, don't act shocked or the child is likely to use bad language all the more to provoke you. And don't get angry or punish the child because this could make him want to get back at you by using bad language around others even if he doesn't use it around you. A good way of handling it is to just tell him calmly that people don't like to hear such words.

Here's how some nursery school teachers handle the problem: Janet Verney first will try to replace the word, telling the child to say another word instead. For instance, you might tell your son to call a friend he's mad at a "snake" or "worm" instead of the foul word he has used. Ms. Verney also might say, "I know you have nice words. Please use them." If the bad language persists, she will tell the child he may go into the bathroom and say those words as much as he wants in there, and when he is finished, he may come out. Telling the child if he wants to use such language to go say those words in his room where no one can hear him is a good idea. This allows him to express his anger, but sends the message that we don't use swear words or smutty language around people.

Josee M. Bancroft, who has been a day-care center director, says parents may just ignore bad language if the child is alone at home. This is okay if the child is quite young or if he is not calling his parent a bad name. However, if the child uses bad language in a group situation, action must be taken. What she does is to say to the child "Many people don't like those words, and so we don't want to start using them here." Teachers at Hamden's Spring Glen Nursery School use the same approach, saying something like "No one likes to hear that."

Nursery school teacher Sue Marcio tells children who swear that they are using mean words. She blocks her ears and tells the children she doesn't want to hear mean words. If some child should say his Daddy uses those words, her response would be "I will have to talk to Daddy and tell him not to use those words."

Nursery school teachers also suggest that parents praise their child for speaking well because if a child receives attention for good language hopefully he will be less likely to use bad language.

Teasing

Teasing is upsetting to a child and should be stopped whether the teaser is a child or an adult. It is a way of belittling a child, and it can hurt his feelings and make him feel inadequate. If a child teases another child in your presence, make it clear to the teaser that it is unkind to tease and make fun of someone and you want it stopped immediately. If the child continues to tease, send him for a time out or, if necessary, send him home.

When your child goes to nursery school and then to regular school, however, he is going to be on his own and will have to learn to handle teasing. Children tease other children sometimes if they are different—for instance, if they are handicapped. They will also tease if they feel insecure or jealous of another child. By ridiculing someone else, they make themselves feel more confident and superior. Also, they may tease because it gets them attention and admiration from other children.

What do you do when your child comes homes and complains that other kids are teasing him? Don't tell him to forget about it or belittle him. Find out what the teasing was about. Empathize with his feelings. Tell him you know he felt hurt by what the person said. If he was teased because he is fat, or is small for his age, or didn't know something in school, reassure him that he is just great in your eyes even if Johnny called him "Fatso" or "Shrimp" or "Dimwit." If he is being teased because he can't keep up with others in class, see his teacher and get him some extra help because a child needs successes in school. In other words, listen, find the reason, and then do something to help if he has some problem that is making other children tease him. If one child seems to tease him a lot, you might tell him to try teasing the child back. That sometimes stops it.

If it is an adult doing the teasing, it may be necessary to tell the adult that you don't like her teasing your child about his shyness, clumsiness, or whatever, that it is not kind or considerate, and that the person would not like it if she were kidded about her size or about some habit or facial feature she had.

Too Much Television

If you think your youngster watches too much television, he's not unusual. The average American child spends four hours a day watching television, according to statistics. This is time when he could be doing something much more worthwhile, such as studying, reading, exercising, learning a musical instrument, helping around the house, or just talking with other family members. It is essential that parents limit the amount of television and child can watch and be firm about it, child educators say. How do you go about doing this?

First of all, don't be glued to the television set yourself. If you have become a TV addict and watch whatever soap opera, game show or sitcom is on, no matter what the quality, your child will soon pick up the habit. He will figure television is considered much more important in your family than reading, learning, talking, or doing something useful.

Second, limit the amount of time your children can watch television each day. Don't get in the habit of using television as a babysitter for your young children. They need to spend that time learning about things by looking at books, building, playing, developing their language skills by talking with people, getting fresh air and exercise to build a healthy body. One or two programs a day on weekdays should usually be enough for children of any age. For school age children it's a good idea to make sure their homework is done first unless there is some special educational show on in the afternoon or early evening. And don't let them spend hours a day on weekends watching the tube. Send them out to play, take them to the library to get some good books or to a museum, have them help you with work around the house, play games with them, have them bake cookies or make a model car with you, or whatever, but find something more useful for them to do. Most important, encourage reading instead of television watching. Many educators today believe the reason Scholastic Aptitude Test scores have declined so much over the years is that children are spending so much time watching television instead of reading.

Third, monitor the programs your children watch. Look over the *TV Guide* with them and decide what programs they will watch each day. Most programs in the afternoon and early evening are for adults and cannot be understood fully by a young child. Also, many programs today are full of sex and violence. If some parents knew the ideas their children were being exposed to on MTV, for instance, they would probably be shocked. Don't be afraid to forbid your children to watch programs that emphasize violence, drinking and sexuality because they may give your children the idea this is the adult way to behave. Help your child choose good programs as you look over the television listing with him. For instance, if you see that the movie *Star Wars* is on, or perhaps a good program about animals, you might tell him and suggest he might want to give up watching Saturday cartoons so he could watch that.

Saturday cartoons, by the way, are not harmless. They are full of violence, and many mental health experts say watching violence on television can frighten children and can also make them more violent and aggressive. Educator Barbara Brenner says her son was a perfect illustration of this. He used to watch Popeye just before her husband came home from work, and started greeting him with the socks and punches he had just seen in the cartoon. When they switched his programs, the punching stopped.

It's important for parents and children to watch television together so that parents can see what their children are watching and the ideas they are getting from programs today. They also need to talk about the programs together so parents can point out actions that are not approved by the family, discuss good values illustrated in programs, help their children to learn to judge the value of programs, and teach them not to believe everything they see in commercials.

Temper Tantrums

Probably one of the most embarrassing and frustrating things that can happen to a mother is to have her child go into a full-fledged temper tantrum in the middle of a supermarket. I've seen it happen a few times, and the mothers were at such a loss they did exactly what they shouldn't do. One spanked the child, which just got him more upset and made him cry louder. That made her even more embarrassed and other people in the store more uncomfortable. Another mother threatened to leave her child right there if he didn't stop. This only made the child frightened as well as angry because the idea of being abandoned by his parents is terrifying to a child. The result was that he too just screamed louder.

Before talking about how to handle temper tantrums, it's important to understand why children have them. Usually it is because the child can't do something he wants to do, or someone stops him from doing what he wants. When you stop a baby or toddler from doing something he wants to do, it's natural for him to kick and scream because he can't express his frustration with words. Temper tantrums are normal in two and three year olds for the same reasons. They get frustrated because they still don't have the skills to do some of the things they want, or because adults won't let them do do all the things they want. Sometimes something as minor as not being able to fit a piece in a puzzle or put on a doll's dress can cause a small child to explode with frustration and have a tantrum. Or sometimes a child may not be able to choose between two things he wants, for instance going out to the store with Daddy or playing with new blocks Aunt Susie just brought. Because he can't decide, he goes into a tantrum. Tantrums are also more likely to occur when a child is hungry or overtired. A child may also have a tantrum if he has found he can get what he wants by throwing a tantrum.

An occasional tantrum is nothing to worry about, but if tantrums occur frequently or if they occur in an older child, they can be a sign of trouble. In a child over three a tantrum may mean he is overtired, but it may also mean parents are too strict and dictatorial or else they go to the other extreme and don't exert enough control over the child. Psychologist Loyd Rowland says one of of two things is wrong if a child is having a tantrum or more a week: he is meeting up with too many "No's" and "Dont's" whenever he tries to do something; or he has learned he can manipulate his parents by having a tantrum.

The best way to handle tantrums is to try to prevent them before they occur. To prevent tantrums child behavior specialists suggest:

- Make sure your child is fed or gets a rest before he becomes cranky and irritable.

- Don't take your child shopping or visiting if he's tired or hungry.
- Don't take your toddler or preschooler grocery shopping because children that young are likely to get tired and bad-tempered during a long shopping trip.
- Help a child if he is having a problem with something.
- Step in to prevent any situation which is upsetting your child from developing into a tantrum.
- Think about whether you are being too strict with the child and preventing him from doing too many things. If so, stop using "No" and "Don't" so much.
- Make sure you are giving the child enough love and attention.

But what do you do if a temper tantrum does occur? There are certain things, first of all, that you should NOT do, say child care experts:

- Don't spank your child. This just shows him that when you get mad at someone, it's all right to hit.
- Don't threaten punishment and tell him he's going to get it when he gets home. It won't help him regain control, will just make him angrier and he'll probably scream all the louder.
- Don't holler at him. It just shows him you yell and scream too when you get mad, so why should he stop it?
- Don't threaten to leave him. This just forces him to cope with a terrible fear as well as the anger he can't control, and it will make him even more upset.
- Don't reward a temper tantrum. Don't give your child candy or cookies or some goodie to get him to calm down or buy the toy he is screaming for in the store. This will just give him the idea he can get whatever he wants by throwing a tantrum, and it will produce more of this kind of behavior.

What should you do? Some experts suggest just ignoring the tantrum, which is all right if you are alone at home, but difficult to do if you are in the middle of a store. Ignoring the tantrum and letting the child just scream can provide a release for his anger and frustration, but most child behavior experts believe you need to step in and do something immediately when a child gets out of control. It can be frightening to a small child when he loses control of himself, and he needs you to step in and show him you can get him under control. Nursery school teachers I have consulted take some action when a child has a temper tantrum, especially if the child is hurting himself, for instance, by banging his head, or hurting another child. This is what they and other child behavior specialists recommend:

- Stay calm. Don't get angry at the child.

- Hold a small child having a tantrum, or a child hurting himself or others, and try to soothe and reassure him.

- Explain that you know the child is angry and you are sorry because but it doesn't feel very good. But you cannot let him go on acting like that.

- Remove the child quietly to his room or to another room where he can be alone. Tell him that people don't like to hear his screaming, and he will have to stay in the room until he stops acting that way. When he has calmed down, he can come out. Stay with a small child who is having a tantrum. Don't ever lock the child in a room because this is frightening to a child.

- When he calms down, find out what made him so upset, and try to solve the problem so it won't happen again. Explain that other people don't like to be around children who throw tantrums because it hurts their ears and disturbs them, so if he gets angry about something, he should try to say it in words and not yell and scream.

A teacher at the Stork Club Child Care Centers in Connecticut usually moves the child to an area where he is by himself and tells the child when he is feeling better he can join the group. She may also try to calm the child by telling him to take deep breaths or by rubbing his back. Some pediatricians suggest splashing cold water in the face of a child having a tantrum, and this does sometimes work.

Occasionally distraction can quiet a child having a tantrum. My husband, who has a natural knack for handling kids, used distraction beautifully when our grandchild had a temper tantrum in the public library. He had picked out some books for her to take home when she suddenly went into a tantrum. He had no idea why. As he led her yelling and screaming out of the library, he whispered, "When you get to the car, you can only blow the horn once." Katie, who loves blowing the car horn, stopped the tantrum immediately, rushed with him to the car, and when he opened the door, scrambled in, blew the horn a couple of times and gave him a big grin. Her mother discovered the reason for the tantrum when they got home. Katie had wanted to take some of the Berenstain Bears books home, but couldn't remember the name, so she went into a tantrum out of frustration. It's a good illustration that tantrums are sometimes the result of a frustrated preschooler's inability to communicate his ideas or feelings about something.

When your child has a tantrum, the most important thing is to figure out why the child had it and if you could have done something differently and prevented it. Perhaps there is something happening at home that is upsetting him, such as the arrival of a new baby, and he needs more of your attention. Could you have used distraction or diversion to prevent the tantrum? Were you too busy with your own activities to give him the loving and cuddling he wanted? Were you trying to get him to do something that was beyond his ability? Remember, if you see your child beginning to be frustrated about something, step in and help him, distract him, hug him, and do what needs to be done to prevent his frustration from erupting into a tantrum.

But what if a tantrum occurs in the supermarket or another public place? If it is necessary to take your child with you when you grocery shop, let him have a snack, such as a little box of raisins or a cookie, while you shop if you think he may become hungry and irritable. Or it may help to prevent a tantrum if you promise him he can pick out one thing to eat as you go through the store, such as a box of cookies or a bag of potato chips.

If your child does have a tantrum, do something about it at once. Try the techniques above. But if they don't work quickly, child care experts say take the child to a rest room or out of the store until the tantrum subsides. "Put your groceries aside, ask a clerk to watch your groceries, and take him out in the car until he calms down," recommends Sue Marcio, director of a Hamden nursery school. Tell your child he can't act that way in a store, it bothers people, so you have to take him out of the store.

After he calms down and you get home, talk with him about what made him act that way. Get him to express his feelings and let him know it's all right to feel angry, but not good to express it by yelling and screaming in a store. Talk about what you can both do to help him from having temper tantrums in the future and discuss other ways he can act if he gets angry (see Anger chapter). Encourage him to talk about it when he starts to feel angry instead of just screaming. Most important, don't forget to praise your child when he behaves well on a shopping trip. Praising good behavior gets better results in the long run than punishing bad behavior.

Thumbsucking

It's perfectly natural and instinctive for a baby to suck his thumb. There have even been X-Rays of babies still in the womb that show the unborn child sucking his thumb. The baby has a strong sucking reflex, which nature provided to make sure he would eat, and if he doesn't get enough sucking through feeding, he'll suck whatever else is around and enjoy it. Usually his thumb is the most convenient thing he finds.

Although pacifiers were frowned on years ago, the general opinion today is that they are useful for soothing a baby who is restless and needs to suck. An infant who is given a pacifier is less likely to start sucking his thumb. Allowing a baby to suck more at the breast or bottle can also make him less apt to suck his thumb. Giving him some water between feedings if he is wakeful can help satisfy his sucking need.

Once a child gets in the habit of sucking his thumb, it may continue through his preschool years and even longer. Thumbsucking makes a tired or unhappy child feel better and gives him a feeling of comfort and security. Parents should not get too concerned about it even if the practice continues into his school years. They should NEVER shame or ridicule a child for sucking his thumb, child specialists say. Nor should they try to stop a young child from sucking his thumb. All this will only make a young child feel guilty and ashamed for comforting himself the best way he knows.

Also, forcing a child who sucks his thumb to stop the habit or pulling his thumb out of his mouth will only make him suck his thumb more, says Sue Marcio of R&K Tiny Tots Nursery School. Marcio instead recommends distracting the child when he starts sucking his thumb with activities that keep his hands busy, such as coloring or painting. Louise Miller of Spring Glen Church Nursery School says instead of criticizing a youngster for thumb sucking, parents should praise and reward him when he remembers not to do it.

The American Academy of Pediatrics says that parents should not use any treatment to stop thumb sucking in children under four because making the child feel guilty about it can harm his self-esteem. After age four, however, orthodontic problems such as an overbite are possible, and some pediatricians suggest treatment.

If a child continues to suck his thumb as he nears school age and parents are upset about it, teachers at the Stork Club Child Care Center suggest putting a bandage or unpleasant tasting substance on the thumb. One such substance is something called Stop-Zit. In a research study parents were instructed to coat their child's thumb with the substance after each incident of thumb sucking and in the morning and at bedtime. In 17 days all the children in the study had stopped sucking their thumbs. When the treatment was gradually discontinued, the children still did not suck their thumbs when checked three and six months later, reports Dr. Peter Gott.

This method does work, according to the American Academy of Pediatrics. However, some child specialists don't advise putting anything on the thumb to prevent thumbsucking unless the child himself asks for help in stopping the practice. Psychologist Louise Bates Ames says that children who are prevented from sucking their thumb by application of a bitter substance or any other method may masturbate instead. She would not advise using a bitter substance unless the child were seven or older and wanted help to stop the habit. Psychologist Jonas Salk also believes using this method to stop thumb sucking is humiliating to the child and can cause psychological problems.

If an older child continues to suck his thumb, you can explain that it isn't a good habit because there are often germs on our hands that can sometimes make us sick if they get into our body. Also, adults and other children his age might make fun of him for doing it. Suggest that if he feels he has to suck his thumb, to do it when he is in his room or alone somewhere. And encourage him that he will outgrow the habit eventually.

Toilet Training

Child development experts agree that parents should not pressure a child to become toilet trained. A child cannot be trained until he is physically ready and develops control of the muscles needed for bowel movements and urination. Every child develops at a different pace. It is not unusual for a child to be three years old before he is trained. Many parents put too much emphasis on toilet training, and the result is that the child balks and resists using the potty. A power struggle develops which the child will win because she knows one thing her parents can't do is make her have a bowel movement or urinate. But a big battle over the potty will upset her, may cause her to have negative feelings connected with urination and defecation, and may even lead to emotional problems. So be casual about toilet training, but let her know this is a skill she is expected to learn.

When do you start training? A generation ago parents plopped their little one on the potty when he was about a year old and because they could often judge when he was going to go, they thought he was trained this early. Today pediatricians generally recommend starting between two and two and a half years. If you wait too long, however, your child can get so used to messy diapers that he may not want to bother with the potty, says psychologist Loyd Rowland. Begin training when the child can understand what you tell him, has one or two bowel movements a day at fairly regular times, and starts to imitate things Mom and Dad do. At any rate, don't begin before 18 months. Once you start, have the child sit on the potty seat once a day at first, then several times a day at about the same time. Be pleasant and casual about it, but make it a regular routine. Being half-hearted and hesitant about toilet training may prolong it and frustrate parents, says Dr. Spock.

Children generally can control bowel movements before they can control urination, so it's a good idea to work on bowel training first, child development specialists advise. To start, get a small potty chair that goes on the floor, not on the toilet seat, because it is easier for the child to get into and makes him feel more secure than being in a seat high up on the toilet. Tell your child the chair is a present for him, and just leave it in the bathroom for a while for him to get used to. After he has sat on it a few times, explain that he can make his BMs in it. When you see signs that a bowel movement is coming, such as a red face and some noises, take your child's diaper off and suggest he make his BM in the potty seat. But don't make him sit on it. Pediatrician T. Berry Brazelton found that when parents used this method and did not put pressure on their child to become toilet trained, their children generally trained themselves completely by the age of two and a half and seldom even wet the bed.

However, if your child resists sitting on the potty seat and doesn't seem to understand, wait a few weeks. If he resists again, try to soothe him by giving him a favorite toy or a book to read on the potty, You also should sit quietly with the child and encourage him while he is on the potty or perhaps sit with him and read to him. But child specialists warn that you should not use any physical or verbal pressure, such as threatening the child with something if he does not sit in the potty seat or making him stay there until he has a movement.

When your child does go in the potty, be sure and praise him and tell him he's getting to be a big boy (or she's getting to be a big girl) learning to do BM's in the potty. If he fails to have a movement, say nothing, or just say, "We'll try again another time."

Sometimes a child will have his bowel movement after you take him off the potty chair. In such cases NEVER punish the child. Nor should parents say a child who has wet or soiled himself is a bad boy or a bad girl, warns nursery school teacher Sue Marcio. Connecting punishment and feelings of guilt with the bathroom can have harmful psychological repercussions and may even make the child constipated, say Marcio and other child care experts. If your child has a movement after you remove him from the potty, it can be exasperating. But remain calm, don't scold, and say "Tomorrow let's do it in the potty like a big boy." If the child tells you after he has had a bowel movement, don't get discouraged and don't scold him because he at least is getting the idea of this bodily function. Encourage him by saying maybe next time he can tell you sooner so you get him him to the potty and he can do it there like big boys do.

It's likely that your baby will urinate sometimes when he is on the potty to have a bowel movement. In this case, praise him for doing "piddle" or urinating in the potty, or whatever word you use. Then, when you find he is dry for several hours, take off his diaper and ask him to see if he can piddle in the potty again. I found it sometimes helped with my children if I turned on the water faucet. If he does urinate, be sure to praise him. If he doesn't, just say "We'll try again later" and wait for another time when he has been dry for a few hours. And don't scold or punish if he wets after you get him off the potty. Just remind him that sometime he will be a big boy and be able to urinate in the potty. Sometimes it helps a child become trained if he watches a parent or a big brother or sister going to the toilet.

When your child begins to get some control of his bowel movements and urination, it's a good idea to get training pants. This makes it more likely to realize when he is starting to urinate or have a bowel movement and makes it easier for him to go on the potty because he can quickly pull down his pants. This also makes him feel he's getting to be like a big boy because he can wear big boy clothes. Getting training pants before some control is established isn't a good idea because too many accidents are possible that may embarrass or upset your child.

Eventually your child will outgrow the little potty seat and will want to go on the big potty. You can get a seat that fits on the toilet then, or some parents just teach their children to sit backwards on the toilet for better balance. Boys, as they get bigger, will easily learn to urinate standing just by watching their fathers.

Even when your child can stay dry during the day, you will probably have to keep diapers on at night because it takes time to develop nighttime control. If you leave the diapers off before he has control, your child may feel ashamed if he wakes up and he and the bed are all wet. To help him get nighttime control, make sure he goes to the bathroom right before he goes to bed. If it keeps on being difficult for him to stay dry at night, limit liquids in the evening and perhaps wake him and take him to the bathroom when you go to bed (see Bedwetting).

Be patient and calm through the toilet training process. Realize that it takes a lot of time for a child to learn voluntary control of his bowel and urinary muscles. Don't treat potty training differently from other stages of a child's development or emphasize it too much, warns Brazelton, or the child will use it "for rebellion, for negativism, to tease those around him." Children will become trained, he says, "when it's their achievement, not their parents'." Eventually your child will get the idea that he should use the toilet the way older people do. And since children usually want to be like bigger boys and girls, your child will want to copy older children's toilet habits once he is in nursery school. "When a child is ready, he will do it easily," says Louise Miller, director of Spring Glen Church Nursery School in Hamden.

Marcio finds little rewards useful in toilet training a child. She gives a child she is trying to train a calendar and tells him "When you are a big boy, you can go potty for me and I'll give you a star." She too connects using the toilet or potty with the idea of being a "big" boy or girl, rather than a "good" child. She may also suggest that when the child goes potty he will have "big boy" underwear.

Teachers at the Stork Club Child Care Center in Connecticut say it can also help in toilet training if parents try to make it fun. You might decorate the bathroom walls with colorful pictures and talk about the pictures with your child while he is on the potty, or give him a child's book to look at. This will make him feel more content and relaxed in the bathroom. Holding the child's hand can also help relax and comfort him. They also recommend avoiding words like "poo poo" and "wee wee" because they segregate children from adults. Instead they advise using the regular terms bowel movement and urination and treating toilet training from a mature standpoint.

Touching Things and Getting Into Things

Parents should not get all uptight if their toddler or preschooler wants to touch and handle a lot of things. It's perfectly normal because one of the ways children learn is by touching things. But what if the toddler tries to touch things you value that are breakable or things that are dangerous? Some parents think the way to discipline a child who does this is to spank him or slap his hands and say "No!" This will probably succeed in stopping him from touching the object, but it also is likely to make him cry and be unhappy and angry. Too much of this kind of discipline can also hinder a child's natural tendency to explore and learn new things and produce a fearful, timid child. After all, would you want to examine something new and interesting or venture forth into new situations if you repeatedly got slapped for such behavior?

A better way of handling the situation is to take things you don't want the baby to touch and put them out of his reach, advises nursery school director Sue Marcio. It's a good idea to do this and childproof your house before your baby begins crawling around. If he does get his little hands on something he shouldn't have in your house or someone else's, don't grab it away from him and scold him. This is only likely to produce tears, anger and rebellion. Try distraction or substitution instead. Give the child something else of interest he can have. Or sometimes, if you just hold out your hand and say "Thank you," the child will hand over the object. One mother I know uses this method quite successfully. If neither of these techniques work, you may have to move the child. Step in as you see him reaching for a forbidden object, or even after he has taken it, take his hand and suggest pleasantly that you both go play ball, color, or do something he would enjoy. Then, if he has picked up the object, you can suggest, "Let's leave this here while we play."

Don't expect a child to learn not to touch certain things if told once or twice. Parents will probably have to tell the child over and over. But they should not get angry because it takes a child time to learn what is his to explore and what shouldn't be touched because it is dangerous, breakable, or belongs to someone else. One thing you should be very firm about, however, is that the child is not to touch dangerous things like the stove or knives. Explain not just once, but a number of times, that these things can hurt him.

Marcio also recommends that if a child takes another child's toy or touches something in another person's house he should be told he must not touch "because these are not our things, they don't belong to us." He should also be taught that he must ask permission first from the owner if he wants to play with someone else's things. Such early lessons about private property can be tremendously important in character development. Unfortunately many children never are taught them and even in elementary school think nothing about taking another child's toy, riding his bike or using his possessions. They could very well grow into adults who are careless of others' property and possessions or who may casually take things belonging to others.

Whining

A whiny child can be especially irritating. Some preschoolers go through a period when they are whiny. Don't ignore a whiny child. Handle the whining right away. How you handle it, however, depends on the cause, so you have to figure that out first. There can be a number of causes. Sometimes a child is tired or hungry, and you stop the whining by getting him to rest or feeding him. Sometimes whining can indicate a child isn't feeling well. When parents say no to a child's request at first and then give in after repeated pleas, it may get the child in the habit of whining to get what he wants. In this case, parents need to stick to rules they make and mean it when they say no. Whining can also mean the child isn't getting enough attention from a parent.

If your whiny child isn't hungry, tired, or sick, psychologist Louis Bates Ames has a few suggestions about how to handle it:

1. Stop what you are doing and spend some time doing something with the child. Play with her or read to her, for instance. After that, if the child begins whining again, you can tell her you spent some time with her, and now you have things to do and she must play by herself. Suggest something specific she can do.

2. Leave the room when the child whines.

3. Send the child to her room and tell her she can come out when she thinks she can talk in a normal voice.

4. Say calmly, "I can't hear you when you whine. It hurts my ears. Just talk to me in a nice voice and then I'll see if I can help you."

Saying firmly, "No whining. Talk to me normally and then I'll listen" as soon as the child starts whining is usually enough to stop it, our family has found.

Ames says most parents find that the sooner you deal with whining, the less apt it is to become a habit.

Conclusion

Don't expect that you are going to be the perfect parent now that you have read this book. Learning to be a good parent takes practice. However, I hope this book has given you some sound general principles to follow. Much of this basic information should, I believe, be required for the young people graduating from high school who will be tomorrow's parents. It will give them the tools to raise responsible, loving and well-adjusted children. It will also give them the confidence of knowing they can handle some of the difficult situations that will come up when they are raising their children.

Many leading psychiatrists and psychologists today are advocating parenting education in the high schools. Psychiatrist Foster Cline comments that the first year of life is more important than any other. During this year the infant learns half of all the knowledge he will gain in a lifetime and becomes more intelligent than any creature on earth except for older humans. During this time also the foundations of his personality are laid. "All through life, long after the early years have disappeared in wisps of memories, the way we express our love and the way our personality sparkles are largely based on our experiences in the first year and one-half of life," he says. Cline calls it "heart-breaking that the essential qualities necessary for a solid infancy are not touched upon by school systems emphasizing American history and foreign relations." Cline says in his opinion many parenting concepts should be taught as early as junior high school.

Columnist William Raspberry advocates a mandatory course in parenting in schools for boys as well as girls. He points out that the young people who will be the next generation of parents in today's society are growing up in a culture very different from their mother's and father's. There is an emphasis on sex, drugs, drinking and materialism. Many of the children are growing up in broken families. A sixth of all children and more than half of all black children are born to single mothers, who are often young and inexperienced and have no one to turn to for help in the difficult job of parenting.

The fact that we have more than one million runaway children in this country is startling evidence that many parents don't know how to parent and don't care about being good parents. Most of these children, whose median age is 15, are from middle and upper class homes. About a third run away because of incest or physical abuse, but most are kicked out of their homes, according to the National Network of Runaway and Youth Services. Their parents have not wanted to put forth the time, love and effort needed to raise them, perhaps, in some cases, because it was too much for them. They just didn't know how to manage their children—no one had ever given them the tools, the knowledge and skills they needed, for the job. The first thing we must teach the parents of tomorrow is that children are important in our society, that they deserve love and care from their parents and the kind of upbringing that helps them grow into responsible, well-adjusted adults, and that those parents that neglect or harm their children are criminals who can be arrested and imprisoned.

"We spend a lot of time on the subject of sex education in the schools. Maybe it's time to introduce mandatory courses in parenting—for boys as well as girls. Parenting skills, difficult enough for the lucky half of us to acquire, are all but impossible for the unlucky half to come by," says Raspberry.

"And yet nearly all of them will become parents. We'd better start doing what we can to help them do it right."

Appendix A

A CHILD'S PATTERN OF DEVELOPMENT

It's important to know how a child develops and when on the average he will do certain things. If you have some knowledge of child development, you are less likely to make the mistake of pushing your child to do something before he is developmentally ready to do it. This can be psychologically damaging to the child because it can make him feel inadequate and inferior when he really isn't so at all. Such feelings can remain with him through childhood and adulthood and hamper him in developing friendships and achieving success.

The following list is just a guideline, an average. Some material in it is adapted in part from W.K. Frankenberg, et. al., Denver II, Revision of the Denver Developmental Screening Test, some comes from *Love and Discipline* by educator Barbara Brenner in the Bank Street College of Education's Child Development Series, and from other sources.

Many children will achieve some of these things before the age under which they are listed. Other children will accomplish them later. If this is the case, don't worry because children are different. Some begin to talk at 10 months, and others don't start until after two years. If a baby is very delayed in achieving some of the accomplishments listed, however, it's a good idea to consult a physician.

ONE MONTH:
Regards people's faces
Lifts head slightly when lying on stomach
Responds to bell

TWO MONTHS:
Looks at mother's face while nursing
Holds up head a little while when put to your shoulder
Notices patterns and movement
Follows you with his eyes
Smiles

THREE MONTHS:
Laughs and squeals
Grasps rattle
Turns his eyes toward a sound
Begins to bite on things

FOUR MONTHS:
Can be held in a sitting position for a short time
Head is steady when sitting
When put on his stomach, holds his head up and pushes up with his arms

FIVE MONTHS:
Turns to the sound of voices
Can tell the difference between his parents and strangers and may cry when a stranger approaches him
Reaches for an object
Rolls over
Moves arms and legs and lifts fanny when put on stomach on floor in preparation for crawling
May get first tooth
Bears some weight on legs when held in a standing position

SIX MONTHS:

 Sits without support
 Starts to make speech sounds
 Watches you when you talk
 Can hold his bottle with his hands
 May say Mama or Dada after parent has said it
 Feeds self crackers

EIGHT MONTHS:

 Shy with strangers at first
 Plays peek-a-boo
 Can crawl
 Stands holding on
 May take hold of spoon when being fed
 Babbles, imitates speech sounds

TEN MONTHS:

 Pulls self up to a standing position
 Gets to sitting position
 Is interested in other babies
 Plays pat-a-cake
 Says Mama, Dada, other simple words without knowing meaning
 Responds to own name
 Has thumbfinger grasp
 May walk holding on to furniture

ONE YEAR:

 Indicates wants without crying
 Begins to learn to feed himself
 Knows meaning of Dada and Mama
 May say one or two other words also
 Stands well momentarily

FOURTEEN MONTHS:

 Drinks from a cup
 Begins walking
 Imitates housework
 Gets into everything and must be taught not to do dangerous things (touch the stove; run into the street)
 Starts to handle spoon and feed self
 Learns to say more words, including "No"
 May have temper tantrums when frustrated

SIXTEEN MONTHS:

 Plays on his own more and likes to push and pull toys
 Climbs on things
 Is full of energy
 Scribbles spontaneously
 Uses spoon
 Says three words other than Mama, Dada
 Runs

EIGHTEEN MONTHS:

    Combines two different words
    Says short sentences
    May try to climb out of bed
    Can sing
    Can understand speech
    Starts to do things when asked
    Can identify nose, eyes, mouth, etc.
    Removes garment

ONE YEAR AND EIGHT MONTHS

    Tries to dress himself
    Is speaking in sentences
    May try to help mother
    Likes to be read to, but attention span is short
    Imitates what parents do
    Likes to make big lines on paper
    Walks up steps
    Kicks ball forward

ONE YEAR AND TEN MONTHS

    Throws ball overhand
    Enjoys playing with blocks, sand, mud, clay
    Names one picture
    Follows two of three directions

TWO YEARS

    Puts on clothing
    Washes and dries hands
    Plays interactive games, such as tag, hide'n seek
    Asks questions
    Enjoys looking at picture books
    Is seeking autonomy, trying to discover how far he can go and all the things he can do without getting hurt or in trouble
    Starts to use plurals

TWO YEARS, FOUR MONTHS

    May be toilet trained
    Likes to say "No"
    Asks a lot of questions
    Begins to make up stories
    Imitates other people
    Wants to eat by himself and stops when he has had enough
    Likes to open and close doors
    May recite a nursery rhyme or sing a song
    Imitates vertical line

TWO YEARS, EIGHT MONTHS

    May be able to undress himself, but not dress himself completely yet
    Enjoys playing alone with toys, pots, etc.
    Gives first and last name
    Balances on one foot
    Jumps in place

THREE YEARS

Dresses with supervision
Can separate from mother easily
Copies letter O
Can play alone
Also enjoys playing with others
Shares more with other children
Understands almost all you say
Enjoys books more
Has discovered sex organs by now and may masturbate
Understands and follows certain routines, such as washing up, brushing teeth, going to sleep at a certain time
Is able to remember to do some things without your telling her
Wants to please and conform most of the time
Loves new words
Generally has trouble with new experiences, such as haircuts, trains, or nursery school
Has an idea what's allowed and not allowed (for instance, hitting the baby is not allowed), and is beginning to develop a conscience

THREE YEARS, EIGHT MONTHS

Dresses without supervision
Buttons up
Understands cold, tired, hungry (at least two of three)
Helps around the house
Can ride a tricycle or bike with training wheels
May have fears (water, loud noises)
May be somewhat uncoordinated
Plays in groups with other children

FOUR YEARS

Expresses himself easily and freely
May be boisterous and break things
May be difficult, run away, lie, swear
May still have trouble handling new experiences
Has a sense of good and bad, right and wrong
Is learning the difference between lying and telling the truth
Understands the difference between today, tomorrow, yesterday
Will share and take turns
Understands at least three of four prepositions
Recognizes colors
Can give opposites to some words
Catches bounced ball
Draws a man in three parts

FIVE YEARS

Shows signs of internal government and self control developing
Enjoys doing what pleases you
Calm and friendly
May try to do more than he can or should
May take risks
May resent it if you try to help him

May still have some trouble with new experiences
Copies
Draws a man in six parts
Defines six out of nine words

Notes

INTRODUCTION

p. 2. Glenn and Nelsen's statistics are from their book *Raising Children for Success*.

CHAPTER ONE

p. 7, Answer 2 (3), Jane Nelsen in her book *Positive Discipline* and others suggest this approach.

p. 7, Answer 3 (4), This suggestion comes from Glenn and Nelsen's book *Raising Children for Success*.

CHAPTER TWO

p. 12, Information from the International Congress of Pediatrics comes from a press release from the American Academy of Pediatrics, "Pediatrics in the Future—The Child of the 21st Century," July 8, 1986.

p. 12, Information on mental illness in children is from National Mental Health Association publications, from a press release "Study Finds Mental Disorders Strike Youngsters Earlier Than Thought," from the National Advisory Mental Health Council, Oct. 9, 1990, and from a telephone conversation with National Institute of Mental Health spokesperson.

p. 12, Statistics on the number of people who took parenting classes or joined parenting support groups in Connecticut sponsored by DCYS came from a *Hartford Courant* article, "Courses help parents cope," by Valerie Finholm, April, 1989.

pp. 12-13, Cline's comments are from his book *Parent Education Text*.

p. 13, The quotes by Gordon are from his book *P.E.T. Parent Effectiveness Training*, pp. 2-3.

pp. 13-14, The quotes from the National Association for the Education of Young Children publication are from its publication *A Guide to Discipline* by Jeannette Stone, pp. 10-11.

CHAPTER THREE

p. 15, Information about the National PTA report came from an article "Self esteem, key to kid's well-being," in the *New Haven Register* in the 1980s.

pp. 15-17, Cline's explanation of the "soul cycle" and the "rage reaction" can be found in his book *Understanding and Treating the Severely Disturbed Child*.

p. 16, Brazelton's ideas on the importance of parent-child bonding in the early months of life are from a chapter by Brazelton entitled "Issues for Working Parents," in *The Parental Leave Crisis*, ed. Zigler and Frank.

p. 17, Kagan's views on the resiliency of children are from a NIMH pamphlet on Dr. Jerome Kagan by Herbert Yahraes, "Childhood Environment and Mental Health," 1978.

p. 18 Spitz's studies are reported in "Hospitalism: An Inquiry into the Genesis of Psychiatric Conditions in Early Childhood," in *Psychoanalytical Study of the Child*.

p. 18, The study of how cuddling and holding rats in infancy affected brain chemistry was reported by Michael J. Meany et al. in "Effect of Neonatal Handling on Age-Related Impairments Associated with the Hippocampus." *Science*, vol. 239, February, 1988.

p. 19, Donald and Eleanor Laird's study of school children was reported by Dorothy Noyes Sproul in her book *Your Child Step by Step Toward Maturity*.

p. 20, Glenn and Nelsen's comments about the effects of parental activity with children come from their book *Raising Children for Success.*

p. 20. The study on depression in children by Thomas and Lynette Long was reported in a United Press International story, "Many latchkey teens found to be depressed," in August, 1986.

p. 21-22, The information about White-Bowden is from Sifford's story "Tell Kids They're Loved While There's Still Time," that appeared in *The Journal Courier,* June 4, 1986.

p. 22, The University of Maryland study was reported in *Your Child Step by Step Toward Maturity,* by Sproul.

p. 24, How to listen to a child's behavior is from Sproul, *Your Child Step by Step Toward Maturity.*

p. 25, Information on the results of using open-ended questions with inner-city children is from Glenn and Nelsen's book *Raising Children for Success.*

p. 26, Results of the study on divorce by Papadatos came from an American Academy of Pediatrics press release on his speech before the International Congress of Pediatrics, July 8, 1985.

p. 26, Information from Jacobs is from a personal interview.

p. 26, "Studies have also found that...outbursts of anger." is a summary of an article"Parental Arguing," in *American Family Physician,* Oct. 1985.

p. 26, Results of the study by Mindy Rosenberg came from a press release from Yale University, Feb. 10, 1987.

pp. 26-27, Kovac's comments are from an article by Kochakian, "Spousal abuse also affects youngsters," in *The Hartford Courant,* May 16, 1989.

p. 27, The summary of Long's study came from a press release from *SELF* magazine, April, 1980s.

p. 27, Mellin's study on obesity was reported in a UPI story by Rob Stein, Oct. 16, 1984, in the *New Haven Register.*

p. 28, Spock's opinions on the effects of divorce are found in his book *Raising Children in a Difficult Time.*

CHAPTER FOUR

p. 31, The 22-year study on the effect of authoritarian discipline on children was done by Dubow, Huesmann, and Eron, and reported in *Child Development,* June, 1987.

p. 31, The study that found a link between harsh discipline and the development of depression and/or alcoholism was done by Holmes and Robins.

pp. 33-34, Streit's research is described in detail in Glenn and Nelsen, *Raising Children for Success,* pp. 177-183.

pp. 34-35, Comments here on negative control and positive control are from "Let's Think about Discipline," Bulletin 9 of the *Pierre the Pelican* newsletters by Rowland, distributed by the Mental Health Association of Connecticut.

CHAPTER FIVE

p. 38, Salk's comments on meeting the needs of children come from the newsletter "A Letter from Dr. Lee Salk," August, 1982.

p. 39, Lowery's quote is from "A Time for Affirmation" in the newsletter *Advent and You.*

p. 39, Glenn and Nelson's sentence "I feel...about...because" is from *Raising Children for Success,* p. 100.

p. 41, Spock expresses this opinion in his book *Raising Children in a Difficult Time.*

p. 41, The quote from Brazelton is from his book *Toddlers and Parents*, p. 223.

p. 43, The comments by Lewis are from a personal interview.

p. 44, For studies showing effects of severe punishment on children see Dubow et al.; Holmes and Robins, Lewis, D.O., and Henley in bibliography.

p. 45, Information on Wexler's experiment on the subconscious effect of words was obtained in an interview and written in the article "Sad words make sad people, Yale study shows," by Barbuto in *New Haven Register*, April 5, 1987.

p. 46, Glenn and Nelsen's views on locus of control are from *Raising Children for Success*.

p. 47, Cline's discussion of whether a problem is the child's problem or the parent's comes from his book *Parent Education Text*.

pp. 48-49, Information on studies on temperament of children by Thomas and Chess was obtained from a National Institute of Mental Health Pamphlet, "Styles in Temperament and their Effect on Behavior," by Herbert Yahraes, and from "On Being a Parent" by Zigler and Cascione.

p. 49, Ames' comments on rewards and bribes were taken from her book *Questions Parents Ask*.

p. 49, Smith's comments are from her "Learning Together" column, "No need to equate rewards with bribes," which ran in the *New Haven Register*, Oct. 20, 1985.

p. 51, Title XX program teachers' advice on managing preschoolers is from the bulletin "Building Trust and Guiding Behavior" by Dixler, et. al.

CHAPTER SIX

p. 54, Solnit's comment is from a personal interview.

p. 54, Lewis's study of 97 jailed male juvenile delinquents in Connecticut was reported at a Yale conference on child abuse on April 14, 1984. Articles on her other studies are in the bibliography.

p. 55, The findings and quote by Holmes and Robins are from "The Influences of Childhood Disciplinary Experiences in the Development of Alcoholism and Depression" in *Child Psychology and Psychiatry*.

p. 57, Rowland's comments are from Bulletin 9 of the *Pierre the Pelican* newsletters.

p. 57, The National Association for the Education of Young Children's views on spanking are from Stone, *A Guide to Discipline*, published by the association.

p. 58, The summary of Huesmann and Eron's study and Miller's comments are from an Associated Press article, "School bullies fail to make the grade in life, study shows," that ran in the *New Haven Register*, Feb. 24, 1987.

p. 60, Information on the results of shaking a baby are from a study by Laura Ment et. al. reported in *Connecticut Medicine*, June, 1982.

p. 61, Cline's comments on yelling are from *Understanding and Treating the Difficult Child*.

pp. 61-63, Information from Solnit on the results of shaming a child and extended silence were obtained in a personal interview.

p. 64, Ames' list of putdowns comes from her column "Treat anger toward child creatively" that ran in the *New Haven Register*, June 23, 1985.

p. 68, Information from Grinder on the effect of double binds and threatening were obtained during an interview.

CHAPTER SEVEN

pp. 71, 75, Rosalyn's story was told at a conference at Yale Medical School by Dr. Ira Levine and reported in a *New Haven Register* article, "Cure for causes of suicide far from being discovered" by Barbuto, Oct. 20, 1985 (a pseudonym has been used).

pp. 71, 79-80, George's case was discussed at an interview with Dr. Joseph Woolston and reported in a *New Haven Register* article "Little boy, family find solutions at Yale clinic" by Barbuto, July 14, 1986 (a pseudonym has been used). Woolston's comments also come from this interview.

p. 71, The statistics on the prevalence of mental illness in this country are from a fact sheet obtained from the National Institute of Mental Health, "U.S. Adults (in millions) by Selected Mental Disorder," March, 1990, and are based on the Epidemiologic Catchment Area Program conducted in five cities, the largest survey of mental disorders ever done in this country.

p. 71, The statistic that 15% of Americans need regular psychiatric care is from a press release by the Upjohn Science Information Center, "Can Mental Illness be Prevented?" by Dr. Joachim Puig-Antioch.

p. 73, The quotes from Cline are from his book *Understanding and Treating the Difficult Child*, p. 10.

p. 73-74, The studies by Mandel were reported in the article by Jon Franklin, "Criminality is Linked to Brain Chemical Imbalances" in *The Mind Fixers*, a supplement to the *Baltimore Evening Sun*, July 30, 1984.

p. 74ff, Information from Jacobs in this chapter came from a personal interview.

pp. 74-75, LaCamera's comments were reported in the article "Doctor claims emotional abuse damaging to children," by Barbuto in the *New Haven Register*, March 29, 1985.

p. 75, The story of the boy who stabbed his mother was reported in an Associated Press article, "Former altar boy charged in stabbing death of mom," in *The Journal Courier*, Feb. 26, 1986.

p. 76, Beck's theories are summarized in "Three Cognitive Theories of Depression," by Bebbington in *Psychological Medicine*.

p. 76, Comments by Woods are from a short personal interview.

pp. 76-77, Hoehn-Saric's and McLeod's comments are quoted from the article "Generalized Anxiety Disorder" in *Psychiatric Clinics of North America*, March, 1985.

p. 77, The study that found why behavior problems occur more often in children of adolescent mothers was done by Dr. Elizabeth McAnarney et. al. and reported in the article "Interactions of Adolescent Mothers and Their One-Year-Old Children" in *Pediatrics*, Oct. 1986.

pp. 77ff., Rutter's comments in this chapter are from the article "Psychopathology and Development I. Childhood Antecedents of Adult Psychiatric Disorder," in the *Australian and New Zealand Journal of Psychiatry*, 1984.

p. 78, Singer and Wynne's findings and their quote are reported in the article "Family Studies of Schizophrenia," by Joan Liem in *Schizophrenia 1980*.

p. 78, Goldstein's comments were obtained in a telephone interview and reported in the article "Schizophrenia, myths envelop complex illness," by Barbuto and Doris in *The Journal Courier*, Sept. 16, 1985.

p. 78, Lidz's comments were obtained by telephone for a *Journal Courier* newspaper article by Barbuto and Doris, "Schizophrenia, Myths envelop complex illness."

p. 78, Puig-Antioch's comments in this chapter are from an Upjohn Science Information press release, "Can Mental Illness be Prevented?"

p. 79-80, Zigler's comments are from a personal interview and from the article "On being a Parent" by Zigler and Cascione in *Child Socialization and Personality Development.*

p. 80, Patterson's comments were from a personal conversation.

p. 80, Spock's comments were made at a conference at the Yale School of Medicine and reported in the article "Dr. Spock: Society is 'sick,'" by Barbuto in the *New Haven Register,* Oct. 4, 1985.

p. 81, The quotes from the Ann Landers' column are taken from the column "Exceptional Children Need Time to Grow" that ran in the *New Haven Register,* April 11, 1986.

CHAPTER EIGHT

pp. 83-84, Zigler and Casione's comments are from their article "On Being a Parent."

p. 84, Information on the anorexia study by Margo Maine came from a press release from Newington Children's Hospital, Newington, CT.

p. 84, The characteristics of good fathers and the report of the study showing attentive fathers had children who did better in school are summarized from the article "What It Takes to Be a Good Father," by Stanley Englebardt in *Families* magazine, 1982. I was unable to locate the publisher.

CHAPTER NINE

pp. 85-86, Brazelton's suggestions for working parents are from an article entitled "Working Parents" in *Newsweek,* Feb. 13, 1989.

pp. 86-87, Family meetings, how to conduct them and their value are mentioned in a number of sources, including *Developing Capable Young People,* by Glenn and Warner and *Positive Discipline* by Nelsen.

ANGER

p. 89, The quote by Sproul is from *Your Child Step by Step Toward Maturity.*

pp. 91-92, Woolston's comments are from a personal interview.

p. 93, The Teachers' Center at Fairfield University is no longer in existence. The bulletin was written by Dixler et al. for the Title XX Early Childhood Program.

pp. 93-94, Cline's comments are from his book *Parent Education Text.*

BAD DREAMS

p. 96, The comments by Ferber are from his book *Solve Your Child's Sleep Problems.*

BEDWETTING

p. 98, Brazelton's findings on toilet training are mentioned in his book *Toddlers and Parents.*

p. 98-99, The comments by Cline are from his book *Understanding and Treating the Difficult Child.*

p. 100, Ames's comments are from her "Parents Ask" column "Mother seeks help for young son who wets the bed every night," in the *New Haven Register,* June 13, 1987.

p. 100, Salk's observation is from *The Complete Dr. Salk: An A to Z Guide to Raising Your Child^.*

pp. 100-101, Kaplan's comments are from Kochakian's April 25, 1989 column "New method effective for bedwetters," in *The Hartford Courant.*

BITING

p. 102, Stone's comments on biting are found in *A Guide to Discipline,* p. 21.

CONFLICT

pp. 110-111, The passage from Gordon's *P.E.T. Parent Effectiveness Training* is found on pp. 213-214.

CRYING

p. 112, Information on Barr and Hunziker's study is from a news release from the American Academy of Pediatrics. For further information see the May, 1986, issue of *Pediatrics*.

pp. 112-113, For Kochakian's article on Sammons, see "Raising a baby need not be a total scream" in *The Hartford Courant*, Feb. 28, 1989.

p. 113, Forsyth's findings were reported in the article "Parents' anxiety can trigger baby's colic" by Barbuto in a March 18, 1987 article in the *Journal Courier*.

p. 114, The Rock-a-Bye Toys Co. is located in Pompano Beach, Fla. The "Baby Go to Sleep" tape is produced by Audiotherapy Innovations, Colorado Springs, Col. Both are available in stores. Information on Dr. Eller and the companies was obtained from a *Hartford Courant* article, "For colic, time is a cure but cuddling helps" by Ena Nauton, Knight-Ridder newspapers, Jan. 17, 1989, and from Rock-a-Bye Toys.

p. 119, Brazelton's comment is from his book *Toddlers and Parents*, p. 98.

DANGEROUS BEHAVIOR

p. 121, Brenner's six safety rules are summarized from her book *Love and Discipline*, p. 95.

DISOBEYING

p. 126, Cline's comments on avoiding battles over eating and toilet training are from his book *Parent Education Text*, p. 124.

p. 128, Dr. Woolston's comments are from a personal interview.

p. 129, White's observations are from the NIMH pamphlet "Developing a Sense of Competence in Your Children," by Yahraes.

p. 130, Cline's comment on the frequency of "No" situations is from his book *Parent Education Text*, p. 133.

DISRESPECT

p. 132, Salk's comment is from *The Complete Dr. Salk, An A to Z Guide to Raising Your Child.*

EATING PROBLEMS

p. 134, Brazelton's suggestions are from an article by him in *Newsweek* entitled "Working Parents," Feb. 13, 1989.

p. 137, Cline's comment on children who gorge on food are from his book *Understanding and Treating the Severely Disturbed Child.*

FAILURE

pp. 138-139, Rowland's comments in this section are from "Dear Parent, Keep a Level Head," Bulletin 15 of the *Pierre the Pelican* series for new parents published by Family Publications Center, New Orleans, LA.

FEARS

pp. 139ff, Solnit's comments in this section are from a personal interview.

p. 139, Rowland's comments here are from "Suddenly More Mature," Bulletin 23 of the *Pierre the Pelican* series.

pp. 141-142, Rowland's suggestions are from "For Parents and Grandparents," Bulletin 10 of the *Pierre the Pelican* series.

FIGHTING

p. 146, the statistics cited by Nelsen are found in her book *Positive Discipline*, p. 143.

pp. 146-147, Ames's suggestions on preventing fights among siblings are from her book *Questions Parents Ask*.

HARASSMENT BY OTHER CHILDREN

pp. 149-150, Comments by Sexson are from an August, 1986, press release from Emory University, "Geeks, Dorks and Dummies: Misfit Children that Parents Can Help."

HITTING

p. 152, for information on the former Fairfield University Teachers Center bulletin, see Dixler et. al. in bibliography.

pp. 152-153, Stone's comments on handling hitting by children are from *A Guide to Discipline*, p. 20.

HYPERACTIVITY

pp. 154-155, Information from the National Association for the Education of Young Children is from its publication by Stone, *A Guide to Discipline*, p. 18.

p. 155, Brazelton's comments in this section are from his book *Toddlers and Parents*.

KICKING

p. 158, the quoted "I" message is from Gordon, *P.E.T. Parent Effectiveness Training*, p. 118.

LACK OF COMMUNICATION

pp. 159-160, The comments by Wetstone, Faber and Mazlish are from *Hartford Courant* Family Affairs columnist Mary Jo Kochakian's column, "Third degree about school is a bad idea," Oct. 18, 1988.

pp. 160-161, Glenn and Nelson's statistics are from their book *Raising Children for Success*.

LYING

pp. 161-162, Comments by Rowland are from "Parents Are Gaining in Confidence," Bulletin 19 of the *Pierre the Pelican* newsletter series for new parents.

MISBEHAVIOR

p. 164, Gordon's discussion of "I" messages is from *P.E.T. Parent Effectiveness Training*, pp. 115ff.

pp. 164-167, Nelsen's views on the causes of misbehavior and ways of winning cooperation in this chapter are from her book *Positive Discipline*.

A NEW BABY

p. 168, Dr. Brazelton's comments are from his article "Working Parents" in *Newsweek*.

NOISINESS

pp. 169-170, Stone's suggestions come from her booklet *A Guide to Discipline* published by the National Association for the Education of Young Children.

OBSTINACY

p. 171, Ames' comments are from her column "Mulish behavior common in 3-year-olds," which ran in the *New Haven Register* in 1985, and from her book *Questions Parents Ask*.

THREATS TO RUN AWAY

p. 177, Brenner's comments and the quotes are from her book *Love and Discipline*, pp. 67-68.

SCHOOL PROBLEMS

p. 178, Smethurst's comments are from a news release from Emory University, "Don't Pressure Preschoolers to Read, Says Emory Specialist."

pp. 182, Zanga's comments are from "School phobia: Finding cause key to getting child back in school" in "Young Health," Fall, 1987, published by the American Academy of Pediatrics.

SEX QUESTIONS

pp. 184-185, Some of the general information in this chapter comes from "Honest Questions and Honest Answers", Bulletin 20 of the *Pierre the Pelican* new parent bulletin series by Rowland.

p. 185, Salk's comments are from his book *The Complete Dr. Salk, An A to Z Guide to Raising Your Child.*

SHYNESS

p. 188, The comments and quote by Salk are from *The Complete Dr. Salk, An A to Z Guide to Raising Your Child*, p. 217.

SIBLING RIVALRY

pp. 189-190, Rowland's comments are from "Honest Questions and Answers," Bulletin 20 of the *Pierre the Pelican* new parent bulletins series.

pp. 190-191, Oberfeld's observations and the quotes are taken from an article "Children need help coping with sibling rivalry," by the New York University Medical Center, which ran in the *New Haven Register,* Aug. 11, 1987.

p. 191, Rosemond's advice is from his Parent and Child column in the *Hartford Courant*, entitled "Child's roughness with little brother results from conflict," March 5, 1989.

SLEEP PROBLEMS

p. 193, 198, Information from Cuthbertson and Schevill was reported in a "Parents Ask" column by Dr. Louise Bates Ames entitled "Wakefulness common among children" that ran in the *New Haven Register*, Oct. 6, 1985.

p. 193, Brazelton's comment is from "Working Parents," an article he wrote in *Newsweek.*

p. 194, Ferber's suggestions are from his book *Solve Your Child's Sleep Problems.*

p. 195-196, Sproul's comments are from her book *Your Child Step by Step Toward Maturity.*

p. 196, Nelsen's recommendations are from her book *Positive Discipline.*

SPOILED CHILDREN

p. 200, McIntosh's comments are from an article "Spoiled Child Syndrome Isn't Properly Understood" in an American Academy of Pediatrics newsletter and from an article by him in *Pediatrics* magazine, Jan., 1989.

STEALING

pp. 202-203, Cline's session with Ed is taken from his book *Understanding and Treating the Difficult Child*, pp. 129-133.

TELEVISION

p. 205, The statistics on the amount of time children spend watching television each day are from Peggy Charren, founder of Action for Children's Television, who gave the statistics at a conference on Television and Children at the Yale School of Medicine Oct. 3, 1985.

p. 206, Brenner's anecdote comes from her book *Love and Discipline*.

TEMPER TANTRUMS

p. 207, Rowland's comments are from "Even a Baby Needs the Friendship of Other Children," Bulletin 11 of the *Pierre the Pelican* new parent bulletin series.

p. 209, Evidence that some pediatricians have suggested splashing cold water in the face of a child having a tantrum, and parents' reports of success with this method, came from a Dear Abby column by Abigail Van Buren, "Water puts damper on tot's tantrums," Universal Press Syndicate, which ran in the *Record-Journal*, Dec. 26, 1989. My father, a physician who cared for many children, also advised it.

THUMBSUCKING

p. 211, The American Academy of Pediatrics' comments on thumb sucking are from a news release, "A quick cure for thumb sucking," July 5, 1986.

p. 211, Information from Gott comes from his column "Our Health," Aug. 18, 1987, in the *New Haven Register*.

p. 211, Ames' comments are from her column "Pay as little attention to thumb sucking as possible," in the *New Haven Register*, Sept. 20, 1987.

p. 211, Salk's comments are from his book *The Complete Dr. Salk, An A to Z Guide to Raising your Child.*

TOILET TRAINING

pp. 212ff., Rowland's observation and general information on toilet training in this section comes from "Your Baby's First Birthday has Come and Gone," Bulletin 12 of the *Pierre the Pelican* new parents' bulletins by Rowland.

p. 212, Spock's warning against being half-hearted about toilet training comes from his book *Raising Children in a Difficult Time.*

pp. 212, 214, The quote by Brazelton and explanation of his method of toilet training come from his book *Toddlers and Parents*, p. 143.

WHINING

p. 216, Ames' suggestions on handling whining are from her book *Questions Parents Ask.*

CONCLUSION

p. 217, Cline's comments are from his book *Parent Education Text.*, p. 110.

pp. 217, 218, Raspberry's comments and quotes are from the article "A course in parenting would greatly help couples," in the *New Haven Register,* March 18, 1985.

p. 217, The information from the National Network of Runaway and Youth Services was found in an article" I Want to Die so I Won't Hurt No More," by Rader in *Parade* magazine, Aug. 18, 1985.

Bibliography

The American Academy of Pediatrics. "Carrying your baby more may lessen crying." News Release. Elk Grove Village, IL: May 5, 1986.

The American Academy of Pediatrics. "How your child (and you) can sleep more soundly" and "Television and children, a positive relationship." *Young Health*. Elk Grove Village, IL: Spring, 1985.

The American Academy of Pediatrics. "Pediatrics in the future: the child of the 21st Century." News Release. Elk Grove Village, IL: July 8, 1989.

The American Academy of Pediatrics. "A quick cure for thumb-sucking." News Release. Elk Grove Village, IL: July 5, 1986.

The American Academy of Pediatrics. "School Phobia: Finding cause key to getting child back in school." *Young Health*. Elk Grove Village, IL: Fall, 1987.

The American Academy of Pediatrics. "Spoiled child syndrome isn't properly understood." Region 1 PNQ Winter Newsletter. 1988-89.

The American Academy of Pediatrics. "When Parents Get Divorced, Children React in Various Ways." News Release. Elk Grove Village, IL: July 8, 1978.

American Family Physician. "Parental Arguing." Oct., 1985, 283-284.

American Hospital Association, *American Hospital Association News*. "Institute of Medicine Report: Mental disorders afflict 12% of U.S. children." Vol. 25, No. 26, June 26, 1989.

American Psychiatric Association. "Psychiatric Briefs." News Release. Washington, D.C.: June 30, 1987.

American Psychiatric Association. "Teacher Evaluations of Preschoolers a Tip-off for Depression Symptoms." News Release 86-21. Washington, D.C.: Sept. 1, 1986.

Ames, Louise Bates. "Child whines all day long." "Parents Ask" Column. *New Haven Register*. New Haven, CT: July 13, 1986.

Ames, Louise Bates. "Heredity, environment influence the child." "Parents Ask" Column. *New Haven Register*. New Haven, CT: (no date).

Ames, Louise Bates. "Mother seeks help for young son who wets the bed every night." "Parents Ask" Column. *New Haven Register*. New Haven, CT: June 13, 1987.

Ames, Louise Bates. "Mother, 6-year-old fight all day." "Parents Ask" Column. *New Haven Register*. New Haven, CT: Aug. 31, 1986.

Ames, Louise Bates. "Mulish behavior common in 3-year-olds." "Parents Ask" Column. *New Haven Register*. New Haven, CT: 1985.

Ames, Louise Bates. "Parent example cited in child bullying." "Parents Ask" Column. *New Haven Register*. New Haven, CT: July 14, 1985.

Ames, Louise Bates. "Pay as little attention as possible to thumb sucking." "Parents Ask" Column. The *New Haven Register*. New Haven, CT: Sept. 20, 1987.

Ames, Louise Bates. "Phrase criticism correctly." "Parents Ask" Column. *New Haven Register*. New Haven, CT: Dec. 29, 1985.

Ames, Louise Bates. *Questions Parents Ask*. Clarkson N. Potter, Inc. Publishers, New York: 1988.

Ames, Louise Bates. "Tot turns Mom into Nighttime Slave." "Parents Ask" Column. *New Haven Register*. New Haven, CT: Dec. 14, 1986.

Ames, Louise Bates. "Treat anger toward child creatively." "Parents Ask" Column. *New Haven Register*. New Haven, CT: June 23, 1985.

Ames, Louise Bates. "Wakefulness common among children." "Parents Ask" Column. *New Haven Register*. New Haven, CT: Oct. 6, 1985.

Ames, Louise Bates. "Youngsters can learn to share--sometimes." "Parents Ask" Column. *New Haven Register*. New Haven, CT: April, 1985.

Anisman, Hymie. "Vulnerability to Depression: Contribution of Stress." *Frontiers of Clinical Neuroscience*, Vol. 1, Williams and Wilkins, NY: 1984.

Associated Press. "School bullies fail to make grade in life, study shows." *New Haven Register*. New Haven, CT: Feb. 24, 1987.

Babbington, Paul. "Three Cognitive Theories of Depression." *Psychological Medicine*, Vol 15. Great Britain: 1985, pp. 759-769.

Barbuto, Joan. "Doctor claims emotional abuse damaging to children." *New Haven Register*. New Haven, CT: March 29, 1985.

Barbuto, Joan. "Little boy, family find solutions at Yale clinic." *New Haven Register*. New Haven, CT: July 14, 1986.

Barbuto, Joan. "Dr. Spock: society is sick." *New Haven Register*. New Haven, CT: Oct. 4, 1985.

Barbuto, Joan. "Parents' anxiety can trigger baby's colic." *The Journal Courier*. New Haven, CT: March 18, 1987.

Barbuto, Joan. "Sad words make sad people, Yale study shows". *New Haven Register*. New Haven, CT: April 5, 1987.

Barbuto, Joan. "Yale unit helping young psychiatric patients." *New Haven Register*. New Haven, CT: July 14, 1986.

Barbuto, Joan. "Cure for causes of suicide far from being discovered." *New Haven Register*. New Haven, CT: Oct. 20, 1985.

Barbuto, Joan, and Doris, Tony. "Schizophrenia, myths envelop complex illness," and series on schizophrenia in*The Journal Courier*. New Haven, CT: Sept. 16, 17,18, 1985.

Barbuto, Joan. "Psychiatric study cites main problems in area." *New Haven Register*. New Haven, CT: Oct. 3, 1984.

Brazelton, T. Berry. "Issues for Working Parents." *The Parental Leave Crisis*. ed. Zigler, E. and Frank, M. Yale University Press. New Haven, CT: 1989.

Brazelton, T. Berry. "Working Parents." *Newsweek*: Feb. 13, 1989, pp. 66-69.

Brazelton, T. Berry. *Toddlers and Parents*. Doubleday Dell Publishing Group. New York: 1989.

Better Homes and Gardens Column. "Prepare tot for the arrival of the second child." *New Haven Register*. New Haven, CT: Jan., 1987.

Brenner, Barbara. *Love and Discipline*. The Bank Street College of Education Child Development Series. Ballantine Books. New York: c. 1983.

Brook, J. S.; Brook, D.; Whiteman, M.; Gordon, A. "Depressive Mood in Male College Students--Father-Son Interactional Patterns." *Archives of General Psychiatry*, June, 1983.

Carlson, Allan C. "Study finds religion could stem teen suicide." *New Haven Register*. New Haven, CT: Jan. 29, 1986.

Chollar, Susan. "We Reap What We Sow." *Psychology Today*, Dec. 1987, p. 12.

Cline, Foster, *Parent Education Text*, from the series "What Shall We Do With This Kid," available through Evergreen Consultants, P.O.Box 2380, Evergreen, Colorado 80439: c.1982.

Cline, Foster, *Understanding and Treating the Difficult Child*, available through Evergreen Consultants, P.O Box 2380, Evergreen, Colorado 80439: c. 1979.

Cline, Foster, *Understanding and Treating the Severely Disturbed Child*, available through Evergreen Consultants, P.O Box 2380, Evergreen, Colorado 80439: c. 1979.

Coleman, Brenda C. "Survey finds child abuse killed 1,200 in '88 alone." *The Record Journal*. Associated Press story, Meriden, CT: March 31, 1989.

Dixler, Debby; Robas, Gena; Goldstein, Ellen; Siegel, Alice; Klock, Liz. "Building Trust and Guiding Behavior." Teachers' Center at Fairfield University, Title XX Early Childhood Program, Fairfield, CT: c. 1979.

Dubow, Eric F., Huesmann, L. Rowell, Eron, Leonard D. "Childhood Correlates of Adult Ego Development." *Child Development.* Vol. 58, No. 3, June, 1987, 859-869.

Egland, Janice A. and Sussex, James N. "Suicide and Family Loading for Affective Disorders." *Journal of the American Medical Association,* Vol. 257, No. 7, Aug. 16, 1985.

Emory University. "Don't Pressure Preschoolers to Read, Says Emory Specialist." Press Release. Atlanta, GA: August, 1986.

Emory University. "Geeks, Dorks and Dummies: Misfit Children That Parents Can Help." Press Release. Atlanta, GA: August, 1986.

Emory University. "Babies Cry Less If They're Carried More." Press Release. Atlanta, GA: Jan, 1986.

Englebert, Stanley L. "What It Takes To Be a Good Father." *Families* magazine, Feb., 1982.

Faber, Adele and Mazlish, Elaine. *How to Talk So Kids Will Listen and Listen So Kids Will Talk.* Avon Books, New York: c. 1980.

Falloon, Ian R.H. "Family Management in the Prevention of Morbidity of Schizophrenia." *Archives of General Psychiatry,* 42 (9), Sept., 1985, 887-896.

Family Counseling of Greater New Haven, Inc. "Children need to learn sharing, caring." "What's Your Problem" Column. *New Haven Register.* New Haven, CT: Nov. 3, 1985.

Ferber, Richard. *Solve Your Child's Sleep Problems.* Simon & Schuster, New York, 1985.

Finholm, Valerie. "Courses help parents cope." *The Hartford Courant.* Hartford, CT: April, 1989.

Frankenberg, W.K., Denver II revision, Denver Developmental Screening Test, *Pediatrics,* Jan. 1992. vol. 89, p. 91.

Frankin, Jon. "Criminality is Linked to Brain Chemistry Imbalances." in *The Mind Fixers,* supplement to *The Evening Sun.* Baltimore, MD: July 30, 1984.

Glenn, H. Stephen and Warner, Joel W. *Developing Capable Young People.* Humansphere, Inc. Hurst, TX: 1985.

Glenn, H. Stephen, and Nelsen, Jane. *Raising Children for Success.* Sunrise Press. Fair Oaks, CA: c. 1987.

Gold, Mark S. *The Good News About Depression.* Villard Books. New York: 1987.

Gordon, Thomas. *P.E.T. Parent Effectiveness Training.* The American Library. New York: c. 1975.

Gott, Peter. "Our Health." *New Haven Register.* New Haven, CT: Aug. 18, 1987.

Hart, Stuart H. and Brassard, Marla R. "A Major Threat to Children's Mental Health--Psychological Maltreatment." *American Psychologist,* Vol. 2, No. 2, Feb., 1987, 160-165.

The Hartford Courant. "Mentally Ill Children Neglected". Hartford, CT: June 8, 1989.

Henley, Arthur. *Phobias.* Carol Publishing Group, a Lyle Stuart Book. New York: c. 1987.

Hoehn-Saric, Rudolf, and McLeod, Daniel R. "Generalized Anxiety Disorder." Symposium on Anxiety Disorders in *Psychiatric Clinics of North America.* Vol. 8. No. 1, March, 1985.

Holmes, S.J. and Robins, L.N. "The Influences of Childhood Disciplinary Experience on the Development of Alcoholism and Depression." *Child Psychology and Psychiatry,* 28, No. 3, 1987, 399-415.

Huesmann, L. Rowells; Eron, Leonard; and Yarmel, Patty Warnick. "Intellectual Functioning and Aggression." *Journal of Personality and Social Psychology,* Vol 52, No. 1, Jan. 1987, 232-240.

Hunziker, Urs, and Barr, Ronald. "Increased Carrying Reduces Infant Crying." *Pediatrics,* May, 1986.

Jacoby, Susan. "Emotional Abuse: The Invisible Plague". *Readers Digest,* New York: Feb., 1985, condensed from *Glamour* magazine, Oct, 1984.

Journal of the American Medical Association. "Early Parental Separation and Adult Depression." Dec. 27, 1985, Vol 254, No. 24.

Journalists' Medical Digest of the Nation Women's Health Awareness Forum "Parental Arguing." Rosslyn, VA: Dec. 1985, Vol 2, No.10.

Journalists' Medical Digest of the National Women's Health Awareness Forum. Vol, 3, No. 6, Rosslyn, VA: Sept., 1986.

The Journal Courier. "Diet linked to dad." New Haven, CT: Jan., 1986.

The Journal Courier. "Former altar boy charged in stabbing death of mom." New Haven, CT: Feb. 26, 1986.

The Journal Courier. "Kids' Stress." New Haven, CT: March 3, 1986.

Kandel, D.B. et al. "Adult Sequelae of Adolescent Depressive Symptoms." *Archives of General Psychiatry*, 43 (3), March, 1986, 255-262.

Kashani, J H., Carlson, G.A., Beck, N.C. Hoeper, E.W., Reed, J.C. "Depression, Depressive Symptoms, and Depressed Mood Among a Community Sample of Adolescents." *American Journal of Psychiatry*, 144 (7) July, 1987, 931-934.

Kashani, Javad H. M.D. "Depression and Depressive Symptoms in Preschool Children from the General Population." *American Journal of Psychiatry*, 142:9, Sept., 1986, 1138-1143.

Kashani, J.H., Carlson, G.A. "Seriously Depressed Preschoolers." *American Journal of Psychiatry*, 144 (3), March, 1987, 398-350.

Kochakian, Mary Jo. "New method effective for bed-wetters." "Family affairs" column. *The Hartford Courant*. Hartford, CT: April 25, 1989.

Kochakian, Mary Jo. "Raising a baby need not be a total scream." "Family affairs" column. *The Hartford Courant*. Hartford. CT: Feb. 28, 1989.

Kochakian, Mary Jo. "Spousal abuse also affects youngsters." "Family affairs" column. *The Hartford Courant*. Hartford, CT: May 16, 1989.

Kochakian, Mary Jo. "Third degree about school is a bad idea." "Family affairs" column. *The Hartford Courant*. Hartford, CT: Oct. 18,1988.

Kutner, Lawrence. "Parent and Child." *The New York Times*. New York: Aug. 18, 1988.

Ladoca Publishing Foundation. Denver Developmental Screening Test. Larendon Hall and Residential Training Center, Denver, CO.

Landers, Ann. "Alternatives to Child Abuse Listed." *New Haven Register*. New Haven, CT: Oct. 13, 1985.

Landers, Ann. "Depressed woman cries out for help." *New Haven Register*. New Haven, CT: Sept. 20, 1985.

Landers, Ann. "Exceptional Children Need Time to Grow." *New Haven Register*. New Haven, CT: April 11, 1986.

Landers, Ann. "Leaving a Child for a Minute May Be Too Long." *New Haven Register*. New Haven, CT: April 26, 1986.

Lansky, Vicki. *Best Practical Parenting Tips*. Meadowbrook Press. Deephaven, MN: 1980.

Lauerman, Connie. "The Kid Won't Stop Crying? Try Massage, Some Say." *Chicago Tribune*, reprinted in the *New Haven Register*. New Haven, CT: April, 1985.

Lewis, Claude. "We Can't Be Brothers' Keeper, but Must Be Brothers' Brother." Knight Ridder Service. *The Journal Courier*. Oct. 14, 1986.

Lewis, D. L.; Pincus, J.; M.D. Feldman, M.; Jackson, L.; Bard, B. "Psychiatric, Neurological, & Psychoeducational Characteristics of 15 Death Row Inmates in the U.S." *American Journal of Psychiatry*, July, 1986, 838-845.

Lewis, D.; Moy, E.; Jackson, L.D.; Aaronson, R.; Restifo, N.; Serra, S.; Simos, A. "Biopsychosocial Characteristics of Children Who Later Murder: A Prospective Study." *American Journal of Psychiatry*, October, 1985.

Lewis, D.O.; Shanok, S.S.; Pincus, J.H., Glaser, G. Violent Juvenile Delinquents: "Psychiatric, Neurological, Psychological and Abuse Factors." *Journal of the American Academy of Child Psychiatry*, 18, Spring, 1979, 307-319.

Lewis, D.O; Shanok, S.S.; Balla, D.A. "Perinatal Difficulties, Head and Face Trauma, and Child Abuse in the Medical Histories of Seriously Delinquent Children." *American Journal of Psychiatry*, 136 (4A) April, 1979, 419-423.

Liem, Joan Huser. "Family Studies of Schizophrenia: An Update and Commentary." *Schizophrenia*, 1980. National Institute of Mental Health, 82-105.

Livingston, Richard; Nugent, Helen; Rader, Lloyd; Smith, G. Richard. "Family Histories of Depressed and Severely Anxious Children." *American Journal of Psychiatry*, 142:12, Dec. 1985, 1497-1499.

Lowery, Father Daniel L. "A Time for Affirmation." *Advent and You*, Dec. 7, 1986, Liguori Publications, Liguori, MO.

McAnarney, Elizabeth R., et al. "Interactions of Adolescent Mothers and Their One-Year-Old Children." *Pediatrics*, 78:4, Oct. 1986, 585-590.

McIntosh, Bruce J. "Spoiled Child Syndrome." *Pediatrics*, Jan. 1989.

Magid, Ken and McKelvey, Carole A. *High Risk: Children without a Conscience.* Bantam Books, NY: 1988 by arrangement with M & M Publishing. Golden, CO: c. 1987.

Mann, J. John, et al. "Increased Serotonin and Beta-Adrenergic Receptor Binding in the Frontal Cortices of Suicide Victims." *Archives of General Psychiatry*, 43, Oct. 1986, 954-959.

Meany, M.J.; Aitken, D.H.; Ven Berkel, C.; Bhatnagar, S.; Sapolsky, R.M. "Effect of Neonatal Handling on Age-Related Impairments Associated with the Hippocampus." *Science*, Vol. 239, Feb. 1988.

Ment, Laura R; Duncan, Charles C.; Rowe, Daniel S. "Central Nervous System Manifestations of Abuse." *Connecticut Medicine*, June, 1982.

Merikangas, James R. "The Neurology of Violence." *Brain Behavior Relationships*. Lexington Books, D.C. Heath and Co. Lexington, MA: c. 1981.

Nauton, Ena. "For colic, time is a cure, but cuddling helps." "Family affairs" column. *The Hartford Courant*. Hartford, CT: Jan. 17, 1989.

National Institute of Mental Health. "Depressive Disorders: Causes and Treatment." DHHS Publication (ADM)83-1081, Rockville, MD: 1983.

National Institute of Mental Health. "Plain Talk about Raising Children." DHHS Publication ADM81-875, 1979 (adapted from article by Dr. Charles E. Schaeter. "Children Today." Nov. Dec., 1978).

National Institute of Mental Health. "Plain Talk about Dealing with the Angry Child." DHHS Publication (ADM)80-781, Rockville, MD: 1980.

National Institute of Mental Health. "Useful Information on Suicide." DHHS Publication (ADM)86-1489, Rockville, MD: 1980.

Nelsen, Jane. *Positive Discipline.* Adlerian Counseling Center, Fair Oaks, CA: c. 1981.

Neurosciences Information Center. "Evidence of a biological basis for mental illness hard to refute." The Upjohn Co. Press Release. New York: Jan. 1987.

New York University Medical Center. "Children need help coping with sibling rivalry." *New Haven Register*, New Haven, CT: Aug. 17, 1987.

New Haven Register. "Self Esteem Key to Kids' Well-Being." United Press International. Date not known.

Newington Children's Hospital. "Dad's Attitude Affects Daughter's Eating." News Release. Newington, CT: Jan., 1986.

Newsweek Magazine. "Depression." May 4, 1989, 48-54.

Noyes, Russell, Jr.; Crowe, R.R.; Harris, E.L.; Hamara, B.J.; McChesney, C.M.; Chaudhry, D.R. "Relationship Between Panic Disorder and Agoraphobia. A Family Study." *Archives of General Psychiatry*, 43(3), March, 1986, 227-232.

Offer, Daniel. "In Defense of Adolescents." *Journal of the American Medical Association*, 257 (24), June 26, 1987, 3407-3408.

Papadatos, C.D. "Speech before International Congress of Pediatrics." American Academy of Pediatrics Press Release, July 8, 1985.

Parents Anonymous of Connecticut, "Checkpoints" Newsletter, Vol. 1, No. 1, Hartford, CT: 1984.

Proctor, Pam. "Dr. Karl Menninger Pleads: Stop Beating Your Kids." *Parade* magazine, New York: Oct. 9, 1977.

Puig-Antich, Joaquim. "Can Mental Illness Be Prevented?" Upjohn Science Information Center Press Release, Manning, Selvage & Lee. New York: Feb. 1987.

Rader, Dotson. "I Want to Die So I Won't Hurt No More." *Parade* magazine. New York: Aug. 18, 1985.

Raspberry, William. "A Course in Parenting Would Greatly Help Couples." *New Haven Register*. New Haven, CT: March 18, 1985.

The Record Journal. "Teasing is natural but hurtful for children." Meriden, CT: Sept. 20, 1988.

Reed, Mary S. "Stress Invades a Child's World". *Journal-Courier*, New Haven, CT: March 3, 1986.

Rodnick, Eliot H.; Goldstein, Michael J.; Doane, Jeri A.; Lewis Julia M. "Association between parent-child transactions and risk for schizophrenia: Implications for early intervention." *Preventive Intervention in Schizophrenia*. The National Institute of Mental Health, Michael J. Goldstein, editor. Rockville, MD: 1982.

Rosemond, John. "Child's roughness with little brother results from conflict." "Parent & Child" column. *The Hartford Courant*. Hartford, CT: March 5, 1989.

Rosemond, John. "Household duties teach children responsibility." "Parent & Child" column. *The Hartford Courant*. Hartford, CT.

Rowland, Loyd. *Pierre the Pelican* bulletins for new parents, numbers 1-24, Family Publications Center. New Orleans, LA: c. 1976.

Roy, A. "Early Parental Separation and Adult Depression." *The Archives of General Psychiatry*, Vol. 42, No. 10, Oct. 1985, 987-991.

Rutter, Michael. "Psychopathology and Development: Childhood antecedents of adult psychiatric disorder." *Australian and New Zealand Journal of Psychiatry,* 1984 Vol. 18, 225-234.

Rutter, Michael. "Prevention of Children's Psychosocial Disorders: Myth and Substance." *Pediatrics*, New York: Vol. 70, No. 6, Dec. 1982.

Ryan, Michael. "We All Have a Place We Feel Locked Out Of." *Parade* magazine. New York: April 6, 1986.

Salk, Lee. "A Letter from Dr. Lee Salk" (newsletter). Aug. 1982, Vol. 1, No. 6, 4-6.

Salk, Lee. *The Complete Dr. Salk, An A to Z Guide to Raising Your Child*. The New Amersterdam Library. New York: c.1983.

Sammons, William A.H. *The Self-Calmed Baby*. Little, Brown. New York: 1989.

Sargent, Marilyn and Swearingen, Joyce. "Depressive Disorders: Causes and Treatment. National Institute of Mental Health." Department of Health and Human Services Publication No. (ADM) 83-1081. Rockville, MD: 1981.

Self Magazine. Press Release on article on Barbara Long and what counts most to kids. April, 1986.

Shulins, Nancy. "Violent children spawn research into why kids kill." Associated Press. *New Haven Register*. New Haven, CT: June 29, 1986.

Sifford, Darrell. "Tell Kids They're Loved While There's Time." Knight Ridder Service. *The Journal Courier*. June 4, 1986.

Smith, Martha N. "Children need lessons about honor and morals." "Learning Together" column. *New Haven Register*. New Haven, CT: July 15, 1984.

Smith, Martha N. "Mom Wrestles with Violence." "Learning Together" column, *New Haven Register*. New Haven, CT: March 23, 1986.

Smith, Martha N. "No Need to Equate Rewards with Bribes." "Learning Together" column, *New Haven Register*. New Haven, CT: Oct. 20, 1985.

Smith, Martha N. "The socially and emotionally maladjusted child." "Learning Together" column, *New Haven Register*. New Haven, CT: Feb. 1, 1987.

Spitz, Rene A. "Hospitalism: An Inquiry into the Genesis of Psychiatric Conditions in Early Childhood." *Psychoanalytic Study of the Child*. International Universities Press, 1945; article reprinted in *The Competent Infant*, ed. L. Joseph Stone, Henrietta Smith, Lois Murphy. Basic Books; New York: 1973, 775-785.

Spock, Benjamin. *Raising Children in a Difficult Time*. Pocket Books. New York: c. 1985.

Spock, Benjamin. *Dr. Spock on Parenting*. Simon and Shuster. New York: c. 1988.

Sproul, Dorothy Noyes. *Your Child Step By Step Toward Maturity*. Doubleday and Co. Inc. Garden City, NY: 1963.

Stein, Rob. "Chaotic families linked to teen obesity." United Press International. *New Haven Register*. New Haven, CT: Oct. 16, 1987.

Stone, Jeannette Galambos. *A Guide to Discipline*, Revised Edition. National Association for the Education of Young Children. Washington, DC: 1978.

The Stork Club. Information Booklet on Child Discipline Policy and Philosophy. The Stork Club Child Care and Development Centers. Meriden, CT (no date given).

Thomas, Alexander, and Chess, Stella. "Genesis and Evolution of Behavioral Disorders: from Infancy to Early Life." *American Journal of Psychiatry*, 141:1, Jan. 1984.

Toufexis, Anastasia, and Harbison, Georgia. "The Lasting Wounds of Divorce." *Time* magazine, New York: Feb. 6, 1989, 61.

Time magazine. "The Thermostat Stuck at Hot." New York: Dec. 24, 1984, 62.

Ubell, Earl. "Is That Child Bad--or Depressed?" *Parade* magazine, Nov. 2, 1986, 10.

United Press International. "Age determines how kids handle parents divorce." *New Haven Register*. New Haven, CT: March 12, 1987.

United Press International. "Many Latchkey Teens Found to Be Depressed." *New Haven Register*. New Haven, CT: Aug., 1986.

The Upjohn Co. "CNS News Tips." Kalamazoo, MI: Jan., 1987.

Van Buren, Abigal. "Water puts damper on tots' tantrums." "Dear Abby" column. Universal Press Syndicate, *The Record-Journal*. Meriden CT: Dec. 26, 1989.

Wallerstein, J. and Blakeslee, Sandra. Second Chances. Ticknor and Fields. New York: 1989.

Webster's New International Dictionary, Second Edition, unabridged. G. & C. Merriam, H.O. Houghton & Co. & The Priceside Press, Cambridge, MA: c. 1950.

Wessel, Morris. "Corporal Punishment Never the Solution." *The Hartford Courant*. Hartford, CT: March 25, 1980.

Wessel, Morris. "The Pediatrician and Corporal Punishment." *Pediatrics*, Vol. 66, No. 4, Oct., 1980. 639-641.

Yahraes, Herbert. "Causes, Detection and Treatment of Childhood Depression." National Institute of Mental Health. DHEW Publication (ADM)78-612, Rockville, MD: 1978.

Yahraes, Herbert. "Childhood Environment and Mental Health: A Conversation with Dr. Jerome Kagan." National Institute of Mental Health. Rockville, MD Dept. of Health, Education and Welfare Publication No. ADM 78-611, 1978.

Yahraes, Herbert. "Developing a Sense of Competence in Young Children." The National Institute of Mental Health. Rockville, MD DHEW Publication ADM78-643, 1978.

Yahraes, Herbert. "Styles in Temperament and Their Effect on Behavior." The National Institute of Mental Health. Rockville, MD Department of Health, Education and Welfare Publication ADM78-462, 1977.

Yahraes, Herbert. "Why Young People Become Antisocial." National Institute of Mental Health Science Reports. DHEW Publication (ADM)78-642, Rockville, MD 1978.

Yale University. "Witnessing Family Violence May Threaten Children's Social and Emotional Development." News Release. New Haven, CT: Feb. 10, 1987.

Zigler, E. and Cascione, R. "On Being a Parent," in Zigler, E. Lamb, M. *Child Socialization and Personality Development*, 2nd edition. New York: Oxford University Press, 1982.

Nursery school directors consulted: Janet Verney, Children's Discovery Center, Branford, CT; Dolores Andreucci, Cradles to Crayons Day Care Center, Guilford, CT.; Rosalyn Small, West Hills Day Care Center, New Haven, CT.; Sue Marcio, R&K Tiny Tots Nursery School, Hamden, CT; Louise Miller, Spring Glen Church School, Hamden, CT.; Maureen Myers, New School for Young Children, Hamden, CT; teachers at The Stork Club Child Care and Development Centers based in Meriden, CT.; Susan Hunter, Masonic Home and Hospital Child Development Center, Wallingford, CT; Josee Bancroft.

Personal or telephone interviews with: Dr. Morris Wessel; Dr. Selby Jacobs; Dr. Melvin Lewis; Dr. H.Stephen Glenn; Dr. Albert Solnit; Dr. Edward Zigler, Dr. Earl Patterson; Dr. Michael J. Goldstein; Dr. Robert LaCamera; Dr. Joseph Woolston; Dr. Scott Woods, Dr. Bruce Wexler, Dr. Dorothy Noyes Sproul and Dr. Donald Grinder.

OTHER FINE BOOKS FROM R&E ! ! !

THE ABCs OF PARENTING: Keep Your Kids in Touch and Out of Trouble by Joan Barbuto. Raising children in our society is more difficult than ever before. This book gives parents the practical tools they need to raise responsible, capable and well-adjusted children. It teaches parents the 20 rules of discipline they must know and apply and how to avoid the types of discipline that are ineffective and psychologically damaging.

$14.95   ISBN 1-56875-062-5
Soft Cover   Order #062-5

WHAT IS HAPPENING TO OUR CHILDREN: How to Raise them Right by Mardel Gustafson. Here is a book that will help parents to restore some old-fashioned values in our children. It is time, the author believes, for women to return to the most important job of all—raising their children. Only in this way will the strength of the family be restored. With this stronger parental influence, children can be taught the values that will make them responsible citizens and have the strength to stay off of drugs and alcohol. Written by a former teacher and Sunday school instructor.

$7.95   ISBN 1-56875-044-7   Order #044-7

SURVIVING SUMMERS WITH KIDS: Fun Filled Activities for All by Rita B. Herron. It comes every year, inexorably like death and taxes, the dreaded summer break. When schools close, parents are at the mercy of their unoccupied and restless children. This light-hearted, easy-to-read book is filled with anecdotes and tips for surviving summer vacations with your psyche intact. Written by a teacher and mother.

$9.95   ISBN 1-56875-052-8
Soft Cover   Order #052-8

TAKING CHARGE: A Parent and Teacher Guide to Loving Discipline by Jo Anne Nordling. At last, here is a book that shows both parents and teachers everything they need to know to discipline children effectively and fairly.

This easy-to-understand action guide will show you how to handle the most critical disciplinary issues in teaching and raising children.

$11.95   ISBN 0-88247-906-7
Trade Paper   Order #9906-7

TALKING JUSTICE: 602 Ways to Build & Promote Racial Harmony by Tamera Trotter & Jocelyn Allen. It is said that a journey of a thousand miles begins with a single step. This important new book is a map to the small steps that each of us can take on the path to ending prejudice and hatred. We can use these methods to bridge the gap that exists between us and members of other races. With each small, tenuous action we take, we are that much closer to understanding each other. This simple yet profound guide is ideal for teachers, clergy and individuals who want to end the hatred and venture into a strange, but beautiful new land of harmony and cooperation.

$6.95   ISBN 0-88247-982-2
Soft Cover   Order #982-2

- -

YOUR ORDER				Please rush me the following books. I want to save by order-ing three books and receive FREE shipping charges. Orders under 3 books please include $2.50 shipping. CA residents add 8.25% tax.
ORDER #	QTY	UNIT PRICE	TOTAL PRICE	

SHIP TO:

(Please Print) Name: _____

Organization:_____

Address: _____

City/State/Zip: _____

PAYMENT METHOD

☐ Enclosed check or money order

☐ MasterCard   Card Expires _____   Signature _____

☐ Visa | | | | | | | | | | | | | | | | | |

Bob Reed • R & E Publishers • P.O. Box 2008 • Saratoga, CA 95070 • (408) 866-6303

OTHER FINE BOOKS FROM R&E ! ! !

THE ABCs OF PARENTING: Keep Your Kids in Touch and Out of Trouble by Joan Barbuto. Raising children in our society is more difficult than ever before. This book gives parents the practical tools they need to raise responsible, capable and well-adjusted children. It teaches parents the 20 rules of discipline they must know and apply and how to avoid the types of discipline that are ineffective and psychologically damaging.

$14.95	ISBN 1-56875-062-5
Soft Cover	Order #062-5

WHAT IS HAPPENING TO OUR CHILDREN: How to Raise them Right by Mardel Gustafson. Here is a book that will help parents to restore some old-fashioned values in our children. It is time, the author believes, for women to return to the most important job of all—raising their children. Only in this way will the strength of the family be restored. With this stronger parental influence, children can be taught the values that will make them responsible citizens and have the strength to stay off of drugs and alcohol. Written by a former teacher and Sunday school instructor.

$7.95	ISBN 1-56875-044-7	Order #044-7

SURVIVING SUMMERS WITH KIDS: Fun Filled Activities for All by Rita B. Herron. It comes every year, inexorably like death and taxes, the dreaded summer break. When schools close, parents are at the mercy of their unoccupied and restless children. This light-hearted, easy-to-read book is filled with anecdotes and tips for surviving summer vacations with your psyche intact. Written by a teacher and mother.

$9.95	ISBN 1-56875-052-8
Soft Cover	Order #052-8

TAKING CHARGE: A Parent and Teacher Guide to Loving Discipline by Jo Anne Nordling. At last, here is a book that shows both parents and teachers everything they need to know to discipline children effectively and fairly.

This easy-to-understand action guide will show you how to handle the most critical disciplinary issues in teaching and raising children.

$11.95	ISBN 0-88247-906-7
Trade Paper	Order #9906-7

TALKING JUSTICE: 602 Ways to Build & Promote Racial Harmony by Tamera Trotter & Jocelyn Allen. It is said that a journey of a thousand miles begins with a single step. This important new book is a map to the small steps that each of us can take on the path to ending prejudice and hatred. We can use these methods to bridge the gap that exists between us and members of other races. With each small, tenuous action we take, we are that much closer to understanding each other. This simple yet profound guide is ideal for teachers, clergy and individuals who want to end the hatred and venture into a strange, but beautiful new land of harmony and cooperation.

$6.95	ISBN 0-88247-982-2
Soft Cover	Order #982-2